business
abroad

business abroad

Lawrence E. Koslow, Ph.D., J.D.

Gulf Publishing Company
Houston, London, Paris, Zurich, Tokyo

For Teresa, with love

business abroad

Gulf Publishing Company
Book Division
P.O. Box 2608 □ Houston, Texas 77252-2608

10 9 8 7 6 5 4 3 2 1

Library of Congress Cataloging-in-Publication Data
Koslow, Lawrence E.
    Business abroad / Lawrence E. Koslow.
        p.   cm.
    Includes bibliographical references and index.
    ISBN 0-88415-414-9
    1. International business enterprises—Management.
2. Strategic alliances (Management) 3. Export marketing—
Management. I. Title.
    HD62.4.K675   1996
    658′.049—dc20   95-42265
                                                          CIP

CONTENTS

Part Two
Building a Global Business Without Leaving Home 48

ACKNOWLEDGMENTS

Writing a book while working full-time is, at best, a difficult task but was made a labor of love by the cooperation of many colleagues and friends. I wish to thank Arthur Sumner, who provided great encouragement for me to undertake this effort, and my colleagues at Fredrikson & Byron, P.A., and particularly Corinna Vecsey, Marilynn Hallen, and Gloria Jean Glasbrenner, for providing time and understanding to complete it.

I would also like to thank Tim Calk of Gulf Publishing for his patience; and special thanks to Kathy Munro who worked diligently in preparing the manuscript, while providing encouragement and valuable editorial comment. Valuable assistance was also provided by Basil Janavaras of the University of St. Thomas. Julie Causey of K.M.P.G. Peat Marwick, LLP offered some special perspectives on the manuscript.

Special thanks also go to my many business students who, over the years, allowed me to test my thoughts and ideas on active and creative minds.

The greatest sacrifice, however, was made by my family—my daughters Larissa and Melinda who put up with their father during this exciting but sometimes exasperating period; and to my wife, Teresa, whose contributions were so valuable that this book would have been impossible without her.

Lawrence E. Koslow, Ph.D., J.D.
Minneapolis, Minnesota

FOREWORD

Many companies have stepped up their efforts to be present in foreign markets. The business decision to enter international markets should not be taken lightly and requires considerable analysis within an organized framework. Dr. Lawrence E. Koslow's *Business Abroad: 10 Proven Methods for Building a Global Business* offers a step-by-step approach for entering and excelling in the international business arena.

From the initial stages of helping to determine whether going international is right for a company to the specific aspects of dealing with import/exports, distribution, licensing, franchising, joint ventures, and subsidiary creation, this useful book presents proven, practical methods for accessing and capitalizing upon the growing world market.

Business Abroad is useful on two levels. For those who are new to international business, it offers a straightforward plan of action for starting and conducting overseas business. For the seasoned professional, the insights provided by the author, with his 20+ years of international experience, are very much worth the valuable time it takes to read this volume. A special feature of the book is its final chapter, which describes six evolving international trends. Knowledge of these trends will help the reader comprehend the changing global environment in which business decisions will be made.

I could never understand why business schools insist on teaching from a disciplinary focus when, in the real world, few projects fall within a single discipline. International business transactions do not fall neatly into marketing, management, or operations, but clearly require knowledge of all of the disciplines. *Business Abroad* has finally broken the disciplinary mold and provides us with the first truly useable work for making intelligent choices about which transactions to undertake and how to use the transactional approach to accomplish your business goals.

Almost all of us are now involved in international business to some extent, so it is nice to finally have a practical guide to the subject.

> *Dr. Homayoun Firouztash*
> Group Vice-President
> Global Sales and Customer Service
> Consumer Products Division, AT&T
> Parsippany, New Jersey

PREFACE

This book had its origins in the search for a good textbook to use for a practical course on international business. As a sometimes professor, but mainly a lawyer-businessperson, I found that international business books gave very little attention to how business was actually conducted and devoted their efforts either to one discipline (e.g., marketing or operations), or were general books on international business filled with massive sections on international politics and economics which, while interesting reading, did not tell you how to appoint a distributor, for example.

The more I searched, and the more I complained, the more I heard: "If you cannot find what you want, then write it yourself." I finally decided to take that advice and the result is a unique approach to the understanding of international business transactions that is based on the following factors:

▶**Transactional Approach:** Building on the interdisciplinary character of international business, this book explores the various components from a *transactional* approach. This is distinct from the *functional* approach to the understanding of international business where each function—marketing and sales, operations, finance, law, human resources, and manufacturing—are treated as separate components. While useful as an educational tool, and in providing expertise in given areas, the functional approach is of limited utility in examining specific types of business transactions.

For example, while the appointment of an international distributor may fall within the purview of the marketing and sales department, a viable transaction cannot be completed without input from operations, finance, and legal. Establishing a subsidiary abroad would require input from virtually all functional organizations. Knowledge of how all functions work together to complete a transaction is therefore essential to a complete understanding of international business.

▶**Practical Analysis:** The information provided in this book can be put to immediate use. Each business must determine which international business transactions are suitable to its products, services, financial abilities, and corporate cultures. For example, in the area of international licensing, some businesses will not license technology because of their concern over the security of their intellectual property, while others will have licensing as their primary strategy, to take advantage of their research and development expenditures and the limited up-front costs of international licensing. While some businesses desire to enter into equity joint ventures and strategic alliances to improve their market, knowledge, economies of scale, and lessen their operating costs, other companies have a very good reason to retain independent control over all aspects of their business.

▶**Chapters Stand Alone:** Each chapter of this book is designed to stand alone by containing the necessary material to understand the theme, or to provide the elements needed to complete a particular type of international business transaction (Technology Transfer). You can read each of the chapters in any order, although the book does follow a logical pattern.

After an initial analysis of reasons why businesses internationalize their operations, this book explores the readiness of companies to enter the international marketplace. Later chapters investigate, in more detail, the ten key international business transactions and provide tactics for success. The Ten Methods are divided into two parts. The first part, "Building a Global Business Without Leaving Home" covers international sourcing, representing foreign products in your domestic market, and exporting from the home country. "Taking Your Business Abroad" covers international agents and distributors, international franchising, technology licensing, international alliances, and establishing direct operations abroad. The final chapter describes evolving international trends and their potential meaning to the international business community.

Part One

ARE YOU READY FOR GLOBAL EXPANSION?

Because you are reading this book, you probably have some interest in entering into the global marketplace, or expanding your current international markets. Before that interest can be pursued, you need to consider your readiness for global expansion. This is not an easy task and I do not offer all of the answers, but the first three chapters of this book should be helpful in determining whether you are ready to enter into or expand your international business.

Chapter 1 explores what "going international" means, and offers twenty-five reasons why businesses choose to go international. Some of these reasons are very obvious, while others may surprise you. In some cases, (e.g., "your current customers have gone overseas") one reason may be enough; while some companies will look at myriad reasons before deciding to expand globally. Chapter 1 also offers some analysis on "What Is Going Global?" which includes a discussion on how to go global without leaving your home country.

If enough of these reasons apply to you, it is then time to look at potential roadblocks that could keep your business solely within the domestic marketplace. Chapter 2 explores such roadblocks as internal resource constraints, inexperience constraints, limited international opportunities, dispersion of corporate focus, and trade restrictions that may keep your products out of the global marketplace.

1

If these roadblocks do not apply, or can be overcome, you will then want to explore how to plan for international operations and negotiations. Chapter 3 offers insights on how to identify global employees; how to develop international business plans; and how to prepare for international negotiations.

If, after reading these three chapters, you decide that international business falls into the "not at this time" category, then your time will have been well spent simply in knowing that you are not ready. However, if the first three chapters do not discourage you (and most of you should not be discouraged), then we invite you to explore which of the *Ten Proven Methods* best meet your needs.

Chapter 1

TWENTY FIVE REASONS TO GO INTERNATIONAL

INTRODUCTION: IT'S AN INTERNATIONAL WORLD

As we enter the 21st century, more and more companies will have to choose whether they are willing (or able) to continue doing business only in their domestic markets, or whether they will be required to move in a significant way into the international marketplace. Most companies will have to increase their presence in foreign markets. The manner of entering these markets will be as varied as the companies involved. They will run the gamut of sourcing from international markets for sale in the home market to the establishing of complete manufacturing subsidiaries abroad. The business decision to go international is not an easy one, but one thing is clear, this decision should be based on facts and knowledge as opposed to fear and hesitation.

This book demystifies some of the idiosyncrasies of international business transactions by providing anyone dealing with and in foreign countries a succinct and clear roadmap for doing business. Additionally, it offers a convenient way to review the basic elements of transactional commerce, to explore emerging market trends. Finally, it offers ideas about how businesses can increase their effectiveness in overseas markets.

This is not a textbook analysis of specific technical international issues, but rather an overview for conducting specific international business transactions. The book blends theory, practice, and international savvy to describe the *art* of international business. It gives you the information to ask the right questions, and then discusses some of the proven techniques for success.

First, however, it might be useful to reflect for a moment on just how international this world has already become. The following brief discussion in "A Day in the Life of the American Consumer" no longer fits just our American audience but now reflects the life of consumers throughout the world. Consider where we are, and then consider where we are all likely to be heading.

A DAY IN THE LIFE OF AN AMERICAN CONSUMER[1]

Your alarm clock (made in China) rings at 6:30 A.M. You hop into your Ford truck (assembled in Mexico). On your way to work, if you stop at Burger King for coffee, a percentage of the cost, via a franchise fee, goes to a British company. You arrive at your job with Firestone (a Japanese company), and turn on your Apple P.C. Although Apple is a U.S. company, the system was most likely assembled in Singapore or Ireland, with components supplied from many manufacturers from around the world. If you are part of upper management, there is a chance that you are wearing Brooks Brothers clothing (Canadian owned). Your Texas Instruments calculator was assembled in Taiwan, the Alcatel Friden postage meter was made in England, the Minolta copier was made in Japan, the automatic pencil sharpener was made in the PRC, and your Nokia cellular phone was made in Finland.

At lunchtime, if you are shopping for colored pencils or crayons from Binney and Smith, the Crayola brand, for your grandchildren, these may have been made in Brazil. You may also look at Lego blocks (Denmark). After work, you stop for a glass of Corona Beer (Mexico) or Inglenook wine (British owned), and some shopping for a Gucci (Italian) belt or Pierre Cardin (France) scarf.

When you arrive home, you prepare a meal of Orange Roughy (New Zealand) and Pillsbury frozen peas (British owned and grown in Mexico), white Mouton Cadet wine (France) and Colombian coffee. The General Electric microwave used was manufactured in Korea. You look at your Citizen (Japan) or Rado (Swiss) watch and discover it is time for your favorite television show, Masterpiece Theatre (British), which you watch on your Japanese television. Before bed, you turn on your C.D. player and listen to the latest release from CBS Records (the player is manufactured in Japan or Korea and CBS Records is Japanese owned), and have a cup of hot Carnation cocoa (Swiss-owned).

Finally, you settle into bed with a good book from MacMillan Publishing (British owned) and a blanket you purchased at Jordan Marsh (Canadian). While you sleep, a police car patrols the area in a Chrysler car, also assembled in Mexico, with the officers wearing Smith and Wesson guns (British owned).

So goes the day in the life of a typical American consumer.[2]

WHAT IS GOING INTERNATIONAL?

With many consumers and companies at least indirectly involved in international trade, one may ask, "What does it mean to go international?" A company begins the internationalization process by first becoming aware of the influences of international activities on its present and future business. This occurs by viewing the world around it, and includes an analysis of the make-up of its products and services, an understanding of its capabilities, an analysis of its existing marketplace, a view of where its industry is going, and finally, an understanding of what the competitors are doing, or are likely to do, in the near future. The next step in the process would be to begin to consider what steps the company must take in what other countries to bring it into the global marketplace.

INTERNAL INTERNATIONALIZATION

From a practical point of view, a company can become involved in international business without ever exporting from its home market. Think, for example, of the large grocery chains and mass retailers who sell (at least until recently, for most), entirely in one country, but purchase products from all over the globe. This has been described as internal internationalization. Some of the opportunities to be involved in international business for the domestic markets are as follows:

Source or Obtain Foreign Components or Labor

To stay competitive in the domestic market, many companies are buying components from abroad, or assembling components or complete products using less expensive, or more efficient, labor available in foreign countries. IBM, for example, sources component parts such as memories and screen monitors from various Asian countries, which are then imported for final assembly in the United States. Costa Rica, Honduras, and the Caribbean have become assembly points for clothing in which material from the Untied States is sent for sewing and then returned for sale in the United States market. Volvo now does some of their final assembly in Belgium, and many U.S. and Japanese automobile manufacturers use a similar system to reduce the cost of their completed units.

Represent a Foreign Business or Sell Imported Products in the Domestic Market

Remembering the previous "A Day in the Life of an American Consumer," consider that the sale of all those products is almost always accomplished by a domestic company that carries the line(s) of the importer.

Contract for the Local Assembly/Manufacture of Foreign Parts

The United States plant of Honda Motor Company manufactures automobiles that are exported back to Japan for sale in the Japanese domestic market.

License Foreign Technologies

Germany, Japan, and more recently, Russia, have become additional sources of technology for the United States market. The Ford Motor Company licenses engineering technology used to build the Ford Festiva from Mazda of Japan. Likewise, General Motors licenses its Pontiac LeMans technology from its German subsidiary, who originally designed the German Opel from which the LeMans is designed. Companies from all over the world are now seriously considering, or have already acquired, Russian technologies in the areas of ferrous and non-ferrous metallurgy, certain areas of chemistry and chemicals, instrument building and farm machinery, and some medical advances.

Provide Services to Foreign Firms

Accounting and law firms have built a substantial business in providing services to foreign companies in the various countries where they are located. Insurance companies, real estate companies, freight and shipping companies are all examples of firms that have services required by foreign companies in domestic markets.

Seek Foreign Equity and/or Financing

Foreign financial firms are sometimes more willing to provide credit than their domestic counterparts and, at times, on better terms. Additionally, companies will often go abroad to raise equity capital by selling part of their equity offerings outside the United States.

Participating in any of these activities will clearly bring a company into the global marketplace and require it to begin to think like an international company. However, because it is still operating in the domestic market, it is spared some of the complexities of external internationalization.

EXTERNAL INTERNATIONALIZATION

Once you begin to market your products and services abroad, you now have to consider a wholly different set of variables. Can your products and services be exported? What changes must be made to the products to conform to international standards? Are there any barriers to entry in the countries in which you wish to market? What is your competitive position? Should you attempt to sell through your own sales force or should you appoint intermediaries? With these (and many other potential questions) dealt with, there are many ways in which to address the international marketplace.

Sell Products Abroad from the Domestic Base

Many companies advertise in foreign markets, use local or foreign trade shows, or use catalogs to sell their products into foreign markets. These methods do not require any foreign presence or local distributors to sell the products. For example, Land's End has sold its casual clothes very successfully using catalog sales in Japan. The U.S. Department of Commerce (DOC), and its equivalent in other countries, helps sponsor foreign buying missions to the United States where foreign buyers come to purchase various types of products. The DOC also has services to show U.S. products at trade shows abroad and forward any leads to the U.S. company.

Sell To or Through Trading Companies

Trading companies will buy your products at home in order to resell them in foreign markets. This is a very common way of doing business in Japan and Europe and is becoming more common in the United States. This type of transaction is similar to selling to a wholesaler in your domestic market. Again, it does not involve a foreign presence of your company.

Use Agents or Co-Marketers

Agents are normally appointed to market products abroad. They work on commissions by finding your company customers. The sale is made between your company and the customer. Co-marketing is similar to an agency approach except that a co-marketer shows your products, along with its own, to foreign prospects. Both of these approaches are used to minimize the costs associated with entering a foreign market.

Use Foreign Distributors as Your Marketing Channels

In this approach, the company sells its products (passes title) to the foreign distributor, which then determines the final price to the customer. Distributors normally hold inventory and have the sole contact with the prospect, or customer, in all aspects of the sale, and any post-sale activity.

Licensing and Franchising Intellectual Property and/or Know-How

A franchise is a typical type of a know-how licensing arrangement common in the fast-food and printing businesses. However, almost any type of product or service can be licensed in the global marketplace. This licensing process can provide upfront payments as well as ongoing payment to the license holder.

Using Strategic Alliances, Consortia, or Equity Joint Ventures

This type of arrangement involves forming a group to pursue one or more international business opportunities. The group may be a legal entity (equity joint venture); may be formed for a specific purpose, such as marketing or manufacturing (strategic alliance); or may be a loosely formed group to pursue a certain business opportunity (consortium).

Start a Marketing or Manufacturing Subsidiary

As international business increases in a specific foreign country or region, a local subsidiary may be needed to sell, support, assemble, or manufacture to meet local needs and requirements. Most large companies have marketing and/or manufacturing operations in many foreign countries. At this point, you have made the decision to be physically present in the country, with an operation that is normally owned by the parent corporation, or one of its first-tier subsidiaries.

TWENTY-FIVE REASONS TO GO INTERNATIONAL

Deciding to enter the international marketplace, or to expand operations abroad, is not easy. Some companies are pulled into the international marketplace by promises of larger revenues and profits, while others are pushed into the global arena because their competitors are forcing them to do so. For most companies, the decision is based on a variety of reasons. This section presents twenty-five of the common reasons why companies decide to go international.

REASON 1
THE DOMESTIC MARKET IS EITHER SATURATED
OR HAS LOW GROWTH POTENTIAL

Most small companies will generally avoid the international marketplace as long as they have sufficient opportunities in their domestic market. This has been the case, particularly for United States companies, because of the large internal market. According to the U.S. Department of Commerce, only one in five American businesses are involved in international trading. Less than 1% of American companies account for over 70% of all manufactured goods that are exported.[3] The decision to go into the global marketplace is often made when companies find their domestic markets saturated or with low growth potential. This has long been true for companies with mature products but in recent years has been applied more frequently, even with newer or high-tech products and services.

As discussed in Reason 10, companies may find that certain products or product lines may be in the declining stages within the domestic market while the same products may still yield high growth opportunities if taken into the international market. Finally, companies may find it more prof-

itable to go abroad than to take the actions necessary to increase their
market share in the home market, such as significantly increasing their
marketing expenditures to capture only a point or two of market share.

REASON 2
FOREIGN COMPETITORS THREATEN DOMESTIC MARKETSHARE

In this case, you may still have a growing, or high potential, domestic
market for your products, but now find that your foreign competitors
have moved to challenge your existing marketshare. The strategy here is
to counter an aggressive move with an aggressive move. If your industry
is becoming global, you may then respond by finding new markets
through entering the global marketplace or by designing your products to
fit the global market in order to increase your competitive position.

REASON 3
FORCE FOREIGN COMPETITORS TO USE LIMITED RESOURCES ABROAD
WHICH COULD HAVE BEEN USED AGAINST YOU AT HOME

The situation posed here reminds one of the board game Risk™,
where a common gambit is to move some of your pieces into attack position in an opponent's territory after the opponent has moved its pieces to
attack your territory. This can be done at various levels. A company may
invest aggressively in the home or other critical markets of a competitor
to provide a defense against competition in the domestic market. Kodak,
it is said, adopted this strategy by opening a manufacturing plant in Japan
shortly after Fuji began construction of its first manufacturing facility in
the United States. A lower cost alternative, which is often equally successful, would be to appoint a well-healed distributor in the competitor's
home country to carry stocks of your product and to aggressively market
for your mutual behalf.

REASON 4
BEAT COMPETITORS TO NEW MARKETS

Besides the advantage of being the first company in a new market,
governments may react very favorably with such incentives as tax holidays and reduction in import duties and other trade barriers to the first
foreign company with a product or service of significant interest to their
country. However, such benefits are normally dependent on making a

reasonable investment (in cash, products, and/or technology), or in finding a local company to handle your products that has significant influence with the government.

Once you have established your foothold, your competitors may be placed at a significant disadvantage because the government is not likely to grant them the same favorable terms. Additionally, certain markets with a small demand for a product may only provide sufficient revenues for a single company; so being first is critical to obtaining a competitive edge.

REASON 5
RESPOND TO COMPETITORS' FOOTHOLDS IN NEW MARKETS

This is the reactive alternative to Reason 4, where your competitor has already retained a foothold. This reactive position will usually require a company to "up the ante," which usually means responding to your competitor with a higher level of in-country commitment to make up for the late entry into the market. A "higher level of in-country commitment" means to develop some set of marketing and product strategies to exceed the efforts of the competitor. Usually, this extra level of commitment has a higher cost so that the late entrant to the market faces a significant competitive disadvantage.

REASON 6
YOUR CURRENT CUSTOMERS HAVE GONE OVERSEAS

Equipment suppliers and professional service companies, among others, often follow their customers overseas. If your company is a supplier to a multinational corporation in your domestic market, and the multinational expands into other territories, you may also need to expand or take the risk that a competitor will become the supplier for the multinational.

Japanese suppliers have long understood and practiced this strategy. The Japanese-brand automobiles, built today in the United States, are often supplied by other Japanese equipment suppliers from their plants that are sometimes located very close to the U.S. factories.

Professional service organizations, such as accounting and law firms, also tend to follow their customers abroad or risk losing key business to local suppliers. Recently, a prominent Mexican law firm opened an office in New York City to meet the needs of its Mexican clients in the United States.

REASON 7
CREATE INCREMENTAL PROFITS FROM INCREASED PRODUCTION

If a manufacturing operation of a certain product, or product line, has excess capacity and relatively fixed capital equipment and technology costs, then economies of scale created may exceed the additional costs of marketing the product abroad. This would result in incremental profits for the company.

REASON 8
DIVERSIFY YOUR CUSTOMER BASE

A company may wish to diversify its customer base by creating and increasing its foreign market outlets. If the domestic customer base is composed of a few large customers, the successful expansion into the international marketplace should lead to a larger customer base with less dependency on individual customers.

REASON 9
GEOGRAPHIC EXPANSION OF YOUR CURRENT LINES TO AVOID, OR LESSEN, PRODUCT DIVERSIFICATION IN THE HOME MARKET

Many companies find it more cost effective to expand the territory for its current products, or product lines, than to expand their product lines. When a company has a competitive edge in a specific market niche, it is usually less expensive to expand into selected areas in the international marketplace than to introduce new products.

REASON 10
EXPAND PRODUCT LIFE CYCLE: INTERNATIONAL HARVESTING

The goal here is to take advantage of the fact that what is a mature product in the domestic market may be a state-of-the-art in other markets. The Japanese have developed a wireless remote-tape player where the tape player does not need any connection between the tape player and the ear set of the listener. This technology has been available in Japan since 1989, but has not yet been introduced into the United States and European marketplaces.

The former Control Data Corporation found the market for Cybernet™ Data Services declining in the United States in the early 1980s because of the declining prices and increased power of PCs and small mainframe computers, and the wider availability of software programs which run on the smaller machines. Yet, because of "market reserve" policies in places like Brazil, which kept computer equipment prices high, the market for data services remained solid throughout the mid-1980s.

REASON 11
PRESERVE YOUR DOMESTIC WORKFORCE

Exports create jobs. The United States Department of Commerce estimates that 15,000 new jobs are created for every $1 billion in new exports.[3] Exporting part of your manufacturing abroad to create products for the domestic and international marketplace also creates jobs in the home market—that are high paying and offer interesting work.

The Japanese have long learned this lesson. Japan, like most post-industrial societies, has allowed much of its shipbuilding and steel industries to move to countries with lower wages and greater natural resources. Even in key industries, however, the Japanese have learned that it is sometimes better to allow for some production abroad to increase overall global revenues. The automobile industry is a case in point. In this industry, Japanese auto manufacturers have learned to keep their engineering, product development, and early advanced manufacturing functions for their products in the home country in order to keep their domestic workforce employed in higher quality, well-paid jobs. The trick is to prepare the workforce for this new global world, something the Japanese quietly did while America talked about it.

REASON 12
TAKE ADVANTAGE OF LOWER MANUFACTURING AND LABOR COSTS

If one looks at clothing labels, you will see that many of the products are assembled in Asia or Latin American countries, often from components provided from the home country. These clothing manufacturers are taking advantage of inexpensive labor and other costs in these countries. The offshore production in a maquiladora, or in a free trade zone, offers low cost labor and other government incentives to promote local operations. Mexico's maquiladoras, for example, are now set up to do everything from counting manufacturers' coupons to assembling high-tech components for reexport to the United States and Japan. Guatemala has also set up a maquiladora program that has, among its largest users, Korean companies seeking to lower costs for the global marketplace.

REASON 13
TAKE ADVANTAGE OF FOREIGN TECHNOLOGIES AND MANAGEMENT KNOW-HOW

Science and technology are international. Today, by cross-licensing and other means, companies are sharing technologies through strategic alliances and equity joint ventures. The General Motors and Toyota joint venture for the manufacture of Saturn sub-compacts in California is a good example of this type of arrangement. General Motors is heavily involved in product design. The production system uses Japanese design and parts to assemble the automobile in a GM plant. The plant uses American employees who implement Japanese manufacturing concepts such as "just in time" inventory control and the team assembly system.

REASON 14
FLATTEN OUT SEASONAL FLUCTUATIONS

Developing a significant export business can be very helpful for companies whose business fluctuates on a seasonal basis. In the southern hemisphere, people in Australia, Argentina, and South Africa are going to the beach, cutting lawns, and playing golf in January. A northern hemisphere manufacturer of seasonal products can have brisk sales in these countries during periods of low domestic demand. Likewise, in July, a U.S. or European manufacturer of winter ski clothing and ski equipment might enjoy brisk sales to ski areas of Argentina and Chile.

Additionally, because export sales often have longer lead times, manufacturers of virtually any type of products may be able to keep their factories humming during slack production periods.

REASON 15
ASSURE YOUR PRODUCTS ARE DISTRIBUTED AND/OR SERVICED PROPERLY

Your company may be selling internationally and not know it. Anyone who has spent time in the Miami financial district or shopping centers knows that this southern Florida city is truly the capital of Latin America. Tourists from all over the region come there to make purchases of United

States goods. In recent years, Buffalo, New York, has played the same role for Canada, and the major cities on the U.S. and Canadian Pacific coast are obtaining more Asian business.

Before you know it, requests for more products and services are coming from these areas. This is of immediate concern for companies who want to assure that their products are used and serviced properly. At that point, you may wish to appoint distributors to stock your products or at least provide some service capability.

REASON 16
REPLACE INDIRECT CHANNELS WITH DIRECT CHANNELS

Companies who are selling their products through export trading companies may, at some time, decide to replace these companies with distributors. By the same token, companies that use distributors may wish to establish their own local stock and sales force to have more control of marketing and increase profits that have been lessened because of distributor margins.

REASON 17
RESPOND TO REQUESTS FROM ABROAD

Foreign visitors to your domestic markets may learn of, or use, your products. Domestic catalogs and other marketing devices often find their way to places you would never expect. Trade shows often result in foreign inquiries. In my business, which is assisting small and growing companies entering the international marketplace, I find that the largest single reason why small domestic companies contact me is that they have received unsolicited inquiries from abroad.

REASON 18
TAKING ADVANTAGE OF GOVERNMENT PROGRAMS AND INCENTIVES

Every government in the world has some program(s) to encourage exports and seek foreign investment. The United States, for example, has income tax incentives for exporters (Foreign Sales Corporations) and mechanisms to assist in financing exports (Ex-Im Bank). Additionally, the U.S. Department of Commerce has many free and inexpensive programs for export. Besides the U.S. federal government, most states have developed trade offices to offer many of the same services. The state of

Minnesota has an excellent program to provide financing for small exporters, which work closely with the federal programs.

In the battle to obtain foreign investments, the incentives offered by various governments are even more numerous. Almost all countries have programs that allow people to immigrate to manage their investment. Some countries—Canada, Ireland, Belgium, and Luxembourg are examples—offer such incentives as free factory space, tax holidays, and subsidized labor in exchange for commitments to establish manufacturing or assembly plants on their soil. Mexico is willing to allow foreign companies to dispense with some of the complicated legalities of operating in that country for those who choose to establish export-oriented maquiladoras.

REASON 19
ACQUIRE PRODUCTS FOR THE HOME MARKET

A company can become international, even if it does not export, if it decides to handle foreign product lines. Taking on foreign products is usually the result of the fact that the product is not available in the home market (e.g., VCRs in the United States or automobiles in Finland), because a demand for products has resulted from foreign travels (e.g., French wine or Mexican beer), or because foreign suppliers have found a better way to produce a product than domestic suppliers (e.g., toothpaste pumps from Germany).

REASON 20
GUARANTEED SOURCES OF RAW MATERIAL

Companies may source, or manufacture, abroad because certain raw materials are unavailable, or in short supply, in domestic markets. The United States now restricts the export of petroleum and red cedar shingles. The U.S., Japan, and European countries are now largely dependent on certain developing nations for supplies of aluminum, chromium, and nickel. Japan is almost totally dependent upon foreign oil and its government has worked with local industries to assure sources of that commodity.

REASON 21
TAKE ADVANTAGE OF BUSINESS CYCLES

As the world economy becomes more complex, global business cycles are being replaced by regional cycles. The entire 1980s found Japan, the

Asian "tigers," and most of Europe booming while the United States and Latin America, in particular, were witnessing slow growth. By the end of the decade, and well into the 1990s, the tables reversed. A global company is now better prepared to take advantage of regional cycles with the ability to concentrate manufacture in weak currency countries and to seek financing where capital is available.

REASON 22
PRESTIGE AND GROWTH PRESSURES

Adding the word "international" to a company's title is now a symbol of prestige throughout the world. As a company goes international, it usually finds more positive interest from stockbrokers and other financial advisors, many of whom cannot believe that a company can be a major player in its industry without having significant international operations.

Additionally, the desire for growth normally sought by a company's stakeholders (e.g., employees, owners/investors, suppliers and communities where it is located) often pushes a company to enter into, or expand within the international market.

REASON 23
TO INCREASE THE VALUE OF YOUR BUSINESS

The old adage that the whole is worth more than the sum of its parts may be applied here. An international company has the ability to take advantage of tax and monetary planning, international business cycles, and access to global finance, just to name a few. All of these tend to increase a company's goodwill and may increase demand for its equity placement or its value as an acquisition candidate.

A word of caution, however, is necessary. A company that does not approach the international marketplace in an organized manner may find that its value is decreased, especially if it is a smaller company about to be acquired by a larger company. Corporate examiners (due diligence teams) may recommend a lower price, or no sale, if a company has several poor international operations or distributors, simply because of the difficulty of ending their relationships when a deeper pocket is involved.

REASON 24
ATTRACT AND RETAIN BETTER EMPLOYEES

International companies can attract and retain better people because they offer greater opportunities and perceived stability. This is true in the home country as well as in the foreign subsidiaries and affiliates. The chance to broaden your cultural, intellectual, and business horizons is an attraction that cannot be matched even by the best domestically-oriented companies. Just look at the lists of the best places to work and you will find that the overwhelming majority are companies with significant international operations.

REASON 25
BECAUSE IT'S FUN!

Ask the person who travels for both tourism and business, and he or she will tell you that the most lasting relationships will come as the result of business. Few, if any, lasting relationships will come from tourism, but lifelong friendships are developed from continuing business contacts. These contacts have resulted in family exchanges, investment possibilities, and more meaningful and inexpensive vacations and retirements. Once people begin to travel internationally, they find it difficult to stop. If one talks to almost anyone who deals in international business, and travels extensively outside their country, one will find that the vast majority of these people enjoy the international workplace, and have fun doing business with foreigners.

Do any of these reasons apply to your company? If so, in Chapter 2, we are ready to look at whether your business can overcome the common roadblocks to going international.

REFERENCES

1. Hymowitz, Carol, "Day in the Life of Tomorrow's Manager," *Wall Street Journal,* March 20, 1989, p. 1; for a futuristic overview of the year 2010.
2. For a Trivial Pursuit™ version of identifying product nationality, see "Made in the U.S.A.?," *Profiles,* January, 1995, p. 22.
3. Axtell, R. E. (ed.), *Do's and Taboos of International Trade: A Small Business Primer,* New York: John Wiley & Sons, 1991.

Chapter 2

ROADBLOCKS TO GOING INTERNATIONAL

INTRODUCTION

In Chapter 1, we explored twenty-five reasons why a company would choose to enter into the international marketplace. Most companies will eventually decide to take that step, but going international is not for all companies. This brief chapter explores five basic reasons why a company will choose *not* to go international, or at least delay that decision until conditions change. These five reasons are: internal resource constraints; inexperience constraints; limited international opportunities; dispersion of corporate focus; and trade restrictions that make international business difficult, or impossible.

INTERNAL RESOURCE CONSTRAINTS

Even if a company has excellent products with solid international prospects, it must first consider whether it has the internal resources necessary to undertake a meaningful international campaign. As you will see later in this book, the level of internal resources needed will be largely dependent upon the approach and/or strategy taken to enter the international marketplace. While operating through export trading companies, agents or distributors will take less effort and resources than establishing equity joint ventures or direct operations; any approach or strategy selected will require some level of commitment of internal resources.

FINANCIAL RESOURCES

A company must first examine its **financial resources.** It must consider whether it has the funds available for *market exploration* (whether done by the company or through consultants) to determine the viability of international sales. Even if this is completed with the assistance of government agencies (for example, the U.S. Department of Commerce), the costs can be considerable. One manner of reducing this cost is by simply responding to requests from abroad. For example, a potential distributor could solicit representation by providing the company with its analysis of the potential market for the company's products in its requested territory.

The company must also consider whether it has the financial wherewithal to *modify its products for international markets.* Modification may be necessary for the products to function or to meet local or international standards. United States products with a U.L. approval may not meet the German V.D.E. standards. Additionally, more and more customers are demanding that products shipped to them meet the global ISO 9000 standards. Even if all these standards are met, international sales may require different packaging and the preparation of instructions in a number of languages.

Even the selection of a relatively simple international strategy may require considerable *operations expenses.* As we will explore later, doing business abroad requires trained personnel with a knowledge of foreign trade procedures and financing. The upfront costs of training and/or adding personnel, coupled with the establishment of an export department, may prevent some companies from entering the international marketplace.

Finally, a company must consider *the costs of hiring outside professionals* to prepare it for international operations. International business requires more sophisticated accountants and other financial professionals. Your existing sales agreements should be reviewed and "internationalized" by competent international legal counsel. Generally, these professionals are more difficult to find and more expensive than their domestic counterparts.

HUMAN RESOURCES

Even if a company is willing to devote some financial resources to its international efforts, it may not have the person-power available for running and supporting international activity. In these days of tight human resources budgets, it is essential to ask whether it is possible to stretch the existing staff to undertake the new responsibilities. Additionally, a company should be prepared for the unexpected. For example, if a company decides to license its technology, it may find considerable demand placed on its R&D staff until the technology is up and running. Even if the company is paid for such service, these payments may not be worth pulling a key person(s) off of important R&D projects to meet the needs of the licensee.

PRODUCTION

It must be determined whether your company has the production capabilities to meet demands from the international marketplace. While this, at first, sounds like a nice problem, you do not want to put yourself in the position of not meeting the needs of your loyal domestic customers in order to meet demands of new customers abroad.

DEVELOPMENT

If your development (R&D) department is now heavily involved in creating new products and/or significantly modifying existing ones, you must determine whether it is possible, and a valuable use of time and resources, to involve your development personnel in the design or customization of products to meet international requirements.

INEXPERIENCE CONSTRAINTS

Most companies enter the international market on a "trial-and-error" basis with emphasis being placed on those strategies where the company feels it has, or can acquire efficiently, the needed international experience. Nevertheless, a company, as a threshold, needs to examine whether it has the basic experience level to enter into any type of international activities. A certain level of experience is needed in the following areas:

PAYMENTS AND COLLECTIONS

It is very risky to provide credit to overseas customers without some proper experience in dealing with them. Companies doing international business need to know about site drafts and the various types of letters of credit. Additionally, you may not be able to rely on the methods of enforcing collections that are available in the home country. Chapter 3 contains some additional information on this subject.

SHIPPING AND DOCUMENTATION

Shipping in and out of countries can be a nightmare without a proper understanding of the international shipping terms (INCOTERMS). The United States and some other countries still require export licenses and many countries have complex import licensing requirements. While shipping and freight forwarders are helpful, they do represent an additional cost and can be very expensive if your staff does not know how to use them properly.

NEGOTIATING INTERNATIONAL BUSINESS TRANSACTIONS

Negotiating such transactions are extremely personal and time consuming, and require people with relevant experience if they are to be properly completed. This goes also for managing relationships which are already under contract. (See Chapter 3.)

MAINTAINING LEGAL PROTECTION

Setting up a distribution network in a number of countries may require you to register your tradenames and trademarks in those countries. Besides being complex and somewhat expensive, it requires someone to look after these registrations and their renewals. Additionally, some companies will decide not to enter international markets out of fear of losing their proprietary secrets. This is especially true in certain Asian counties where newly introduced foreign products are freely copied and new "local" versions arise to compete.

LIMITED INTERNATIONAL OPPORTUNITIES

Later in this Chapter, we will discuss some of the trade barriers and restrictions that make doing international business difficult or impossible. This section discusses the question of limited international opportunities from a company's internal perspective.

IS THERE A MARKET FOR THE PRODUCTS?

As someone who has been involved in international business for 25 years, I find it difficult to name a single product or service that cannot be sold across borders in one way or another. (See example of licensing brick technology on p. 146) Yet, it is clear that in the case of some products such a sale might fall into the "too hard" category. Some products and services just do not transfer well because they are culturally indigenous or over-engineered. If you have such a product, you are generally better off trying to increase your marketshare in your home market.

IS THE PRODUCT COST COMPETITIVE? CAN IT BE MADE COST-COMPETITIVE?

Experienced global companies that have both domestic and international price lists normally charge 15% to 25% more for products going abroad. This is true, even if the customer is going to directly pay the shipping costs and import duties. Simply stated, it costs more to sell abroad. Consider long distance calls, design and packaging costs for international versions, export documentation services, costs for financial and legal services, and the cost of additional time associated with foreign sales. If your product or services is not able to bear those costs and remain competitive, then you have to consider foreign production with its high initial costs and increased intellectual property risks. Overall, the product may simply not be price-competitive.

DOES YOUR PRODUCT MEET THE QUALITY OR PERCEIVED QUALITY STANDARDS OF THE INTERNATIONAL MARKETPLACE?

For selling in highly sophisticated markets, you must examine whether the products are perceived as state-of-the-art, particularly if another nationality is perceived as making the best product in your particular product line. In developing markets, on the other hand, you may face the problem of products being overengineered and too high quality to be "appropriate" in the local marketplace (e.g. large U.S. automobiles in developing nations).

DISPERSION OF CORPORATE FOCUS

Deciding to "go international" is as important as deciding to enter new domestic markets, to offer new products, or to change the corporate focus. Ultimately, it must be looked at in terms of the priorities of the company. Companies normally enter the international marketplace in "fits" and "starts," often created by external criteria. *This is not the way to do it!* Going international nine times out of ten is the right decision, but it must be planned carefully, with the other priorities of the company considered. The strategy of "First we take Chicago, and then we take Sao Paulo" may be the correct one. However, if you have taken Chicago, or find you are unable to do so, you may then decide to take Sao Paulo. Only do not wait too long or you will to find your competitors already entrenched.

TRADE RESTRICTIONS

One final area that must be considered before making the decision of whether to go international are the barriers to trade. That is, those barriers imposed by governments, non-governmental agencies, and others on the international flow of goods and services. Before discussing these barriers or restrictions individually, I would like to begin with a number of general statements about trade restrictions:

- While tariff and nontariff barriers seem to be declining on the national level with the development of the World Trade Organization (WTO), and as more countries move to more open economies, there is still significant pressure towards forms of protectionism on the regional level (European Economic Community and the North American Free Trade Agreement), and through buyer and seller controls (OPEC or the Multifibre Agreements). The movement towards intense nationalism in some areas of the world may also increase protectionism. This is discussed in more detail in the final chapter.

- As a general rule, nations in the intermediate stages of development (India, Brazil) are more likely to impose trade barriers than developed nations, or those just at the initial stages of economic development.

- Nondemocratic nations are more likely to open their economies than democratic nations, where the general population has a greater say in protecting its vested interests. The situation regarding trade barriers remains unclear in areas undergoing rapid political changes such as those of the former Soviet Union, Eastern Europe, and Southern Africa.

- As a general rule, the more unique a product is, the less chance it has to be subjected to significant trade barriers.

PRICE-CONTROLLING TECHNIQUES: TARIFFS AND SUBSIDIES

Tariffs have a public purpose of raising government revenues, protecting local industry, and improving the balance of trade through the creation of local production or the reduction of imports. Some products are particularly sensitive to high tariffs. These include agricultural products and textiles. Additionally, a country may impose high tariffs when it decides to develop a local industry. Brazil, in the 1970s and 1980s, decided that it was going to develop a sophisticated local computer industry. It tried to accomplish this by setting very high tariffs (in some cases around 200%) on some products and forbidding the importation of other products (e.g., personal computers).

Subsidies are the support given to local industry by governments to allow local products to compete effectively with imports or to make the products more competitive in the global marketplace. This might include cash payments, tax breaks, or low-interest loans. In recent years, the United States has protested such policies in France, Brazil, and Korea.

QUANTITY LIMITING TECHNIQUES: QUOTAS AND EMBARGOES

Quotas are limitations, sometimes voluntary, on the amounts of products or services that can be imported. They may also apply on the limits to which foreign investment can enter certain industries. The United States has for a long time placed quotas on the importation of sugar, usually allowing larger quotas to countries which are friendly to U.S. foreign policy interests.

An **embargo** is a policy that sets a limit of zero imports. In the past decade, the United States, primarily for political reasons, had or continues to impose embargoes on the PRC, Cuba, Libya, Iraq, and Iran.

OTHER NON-TARIFF BARRIERS

Non-tariff barriers are all forms of discrimination against imports except for import duties. We have already discussed some non-tariff barriers (subsidies, quotas, and embargoes). Other non-tariff barriers include: voluntary export restraints, required countertrade or coproduction, complicated customs and administrative procedures, quality and other standards, and local rules and regulations.

- **Voluntary export restraints** (VERs) are quotas imposed not by the importing country but by the exporting country. The classic examples of VERs are those imposed by the Japanese in regard to the United States. In one case, Japan agreed to limit its export of automobiles to the United States to 1.65 million units per year. While this number was generally adhered to, the Japanese actually increased their revenues by exporting more expensive models. Additionally, Japanese automobile manufacturers were able to maximize profits by decreasing supply in such a manner to increase demand. Many Americans remember the mid-1980s when U.S. models were heavily discounted while Japanese models (such as Toyotas and Mazdas) had an "ADP" on their window stickers. If you took the time to ask what "ADP" was, the salesperson would tell you "additional dealer's profit." In 1986, and again in 1991, Japan and the United States entered into semiconductor accords whose purpose was to increase American marketshare in Japan. These accords have met with marginal success.

- **Required countertrade or co-production** is the process in which goods are exchanged in whole or part for other goods. There are many examples of this; the most interesting one was the sale of U.S. computers for Romanian railroad cars, which were eventually sold to Brazil. A more sophisticated version of countertrade is government-required policies of co-production. Under this policy, a country agrees to allow a certain amount of finished, or nearly finished, product to enter the country in exchange for the importing company agreeing to allow some degree of technology transfer and final assembly in the country of import. This policy of co-production is very popular in countries like Spain.

- Examples of complicated **customs and administrative procedures** include limiting the number of points of entry, changing classification of products, requiring an import license, and limiting imports to particular times of the year. Countries that are particularly good at (or guilty of) such procedures are France, Italy, Canada, and Japan.

- **Quality requirements**, while often justified, are still another example of non-tariff barriers. The French imposed standards on meat importation based on the use of feed and hormones. Denmark will not allow soft drinks to be imported unless they are in reusable bottles. Germany will not allow the import of beer if it contains corn or rice. Japan severely restricts the importation of rice on the basis of its texture and stickiness.

■ Finally, even if national regulations do not limit imports, it is sometimes necessary to look at **local requirements**. When one U.S. toy retailer was trying to open its first high-volume, discount store in Japan, it was faced with local regulations that required all existing merchants in the same field to approve new stores. Additionally, the toy retailer was also up against locally imposed space restrictions that limited the concept of a high-volume discount store.

FINANCIAL LIMITATIONS

Even if a country seems to have an open importation policy, it can effectively limit importations by restricting the movement of money. In this manner, importers will be discouraged because of the uncertainty of being paid in a timely fashion for their goods. Such financial limitations are normally imposed through various exchange controls. The two most common are: (1) the need to apply to a certain bank to obtain foreign currency; and (2) the requirement to convert local currency to foreign currency at government-imposed exchange rates that are less favorable to those that exist on the open market. During the international monetary debt crisis of the 1980s, many countries imposed exchange controls such as Brazil, Poland, and Venezuela. Even Mexico was forced to impose such controls for a brief period during 1982.

CONCLUSION: ARE YOU READY?

In this brief chapter, we had tried to explore the key roadblocks to taking your company into the international marketplace. Particularly in the early stages, going international requires a lot of effort and a considerable investment of time and capital. Immediate returns on investment may not be forthcoming as the decision to enter international markets may require a long-term effort and some changes of your company's approaches and mindsets.

Virtually all exporters agree that the decision to go international must include the development of a carefully conceived strategic plan. This is covered in the next chapter.

ESTABLISHING YOUR INTERNATIONAL PLAN

INTRODUCTION

Once you have decided that the roadblocks to going international can be overcome, it is now time to develop and establish your international plan. This chapter is designed to provide the reader with a step-by-step analysis for creating such a plan. We begin with an analysis of how a company can create cultural awareness, and use this awareness to develop employees who can operate internationally.

The bulk of the chapter explores eight key areas that must be covered in developing your international plan. This includes everything from goal definition to how you fit your international plan into the overall company plans. A section on the key issues associated with international negotiations is also included.

This chapter provides you with the basics to establish a snapshot of where you are, and a plan of where you might want to be. Subsequent chapters discuss how to best implement the plan(s) created.

CULTURAL AWARENESS

Becoming an international company requires the development of a strong sense of cultural awareness—on the individual and company levels.

This cultural awareness should go beyond factual cultural knowledge and comparisons to include the development of global employees who have the ability to interpret cultural differences. That is, they develop the ability to understand and appreciate the nuances of different cultural traits and patterns, and be able to apply what they have learned to business and social contexts.

In this section, we will review the personality characteristics needed for employees involved in international projects, and discuss how these characteristics can be developed. Before doing so, however, we need a working definition of what we mean by global employees. Global employees are those individuals who either work in another country (expatriates), *or* who work in the country of their nationality and/or citizenship, but who have significant business dealings with other countries.

People throughout the world use culture as a problem-solving tool to cope in their particular environment. It is difficult to generalize about business customs and practices throughout the world, but it is safe to generalize that those who can learn to be culturally sensitive will make the best global employees.

Table 3-1
Personality Traits of a Successful Global Employee

• Acculturation	• Adaptability	• World Culture
• Country Knowledge	• Culturally Sensitive	• Cosmopolitan
• Emotional Stability	• Empathy	• Curiosity
• Experience Collector	• Fair/Sense of Justice	• Entrepreneur
• Risk Taker	• Good Guest	• Flexible
• Integration	• Intuitive	• Humility
• Listener	• Informal Management	• Language Ability
• People Person	Style	• Negotiation Skills
• Resourceful	• Positive Regard for	• Product Knowledge
• Technical	Others	• Sense of Humor
Competence	• Respectful/Commands	• Tolerant
• Work Culture	Respect	
Adaptable	• Tempo Adjustments	

Choosing people for global business should begin with an analysis of whether the person has a substantial number of the traits cited in Table 3-1. These fall into four general categories:

Flexibility and Adaptability. Individuals chosen to work on international projects must be able to adapt to different work styles and sense of time. This is not the province of the 8-hours-a-day, 40-hours-a-week, person. However, people with continuing responsibilities (such as young children) should not be excluded if they have other traits, because of the availability of home computers, fax machines, and other forms of modern technology.

Interpersonal Skills. International work is better suited to friendly, outgoing people who have broad-based knowledge and can converse well on several levels. I was having great difficulty in dealing with a Venezuelan engineer until I asked him how the music of his country compared with Mexican and Brazilian music. He immediately invited me to his house where we spent a good part of the evening listening to the local music. We have been friends since.

Entrepreneurial Skills. People involved in international business are going to be in positions where they may have to make decisions without backup from the home office. Individuals who are not self-assured, or who require that all bases be covered, may not be suitable for the international division.

Technical competence. For flexible entrepreneurs with good interpersonal skills to be effective, they must know the business of the company. This is necessary, not only to allow for flexible decision-making, but also to assure that they command respect from the vendors and/or customers. There are two ways to approach this combination. The first would be to identify people with technical competence within your existing organization who possess many of the personality traits previously described. These people can then be "seasoned" for international assignments. The other would be to find individuals who possess the personality characteristics and have been trained in the general concepts of international management. These individuals can then be trained in the products and/or technologies. People in the second category are particularly helpful in companies dominated by the technically-oriented leadership, that may not themselves possess the appropriate number of the personality traits, or in companies that are just beginning their international operations.

Once your company has found people with the appropriate personality traits and technical knowledge and competence, it should then begin to look for ways in which it can increase their cultural awareness. By far the best technique to increase cultural awareness and international business acumen is by undertaking international travel. It is not recommended that you enter into any international business relationship without visiting the site of your potential business partner or customer. International travel broadens your experiences and gives you the opportunity to test your abilities in the real world.

Second-best to international travel, or residence, is to have your people network with those who have recently had that experience. One company I represent was just beginning its expansion into Latin America. They hired a person with strong product experience and the appropriate personality traits. However, he lacked the contact base necessary to speed up the move. I introduced him to another individual from a complementary company, who had just spent the last two years in the region. Both parties benefited. The person new to the operations gained immediate insight and invaluable contacts. The seasoned professional was able to leverage the complementary product to offer his distributors a broader base of products, which increased the sales of both companies.

Another excellent way to increase cultural awareness is to learn a foreign language. True knowledge of a language requires an understanding of the culture behind it. A deep understanding of more than one culture likely means that the person is capable of relating to many cultures. People ask me what language should they study. My answer (unless a specific language is likely to be a requirement of the job) is to study the language that best reflects your travel and cultural interests. Being an international person does not require knowledge of all languages and cultures, but a sensitivity to cultures, which allows the individual the ability to interpret cultural differences. My languages are Spanish and Portuguese, yet I was recently able to function well in German-speaking Switzerland where the parties recognized that although we were speaking English, they were sitting across from a trilingual American.

Recently, a whole industry has developed in cross-cultural communications training. Such training is helpful for all employees who deal abroad, and essential for expatriates. It comes in two general forms. The first type is an analysis of comparative cultures ("Do's and Taboos").[1]

This type is fine, and useful, if you know you are dealing with a particular geographic area. However, it is not as effective in teaching the interpretive skills. The second type is more macro in character and is designed to create interpretive skills. The attempt is to look at behavioral norms and try to bring cultural awareness to various divisions of a global company. The approach ranges from challenging people by putting them on the defensive ("whack on the head")[2] to a more reasonable academic approach tied to the key elements of international business.[3]

Cross-cultural training is normally included in various academic programs in international business. Such programs range from technical training in customs and/or export administration to a bachelor's degree in business with languages and study abroad requirements to a number of very fine master's of international management programs, which go beyond simply internationalizing the M.B.A. to include intercultural communications, business languages, and international political economy studies.

Such programs are highly recommended for employees with strong product skills who need international seasoning, and as sources of employees for companies with a heavy technical bent and/or those just beginning their international operations.

Finally, companies should not neglect the potential and real international skills that exist among their "ethnic" employees. Countries like the United States, Australia, Canada, Great Britain, Brazil, France, and India have diverse populations with a multitude of cultural experiences. Companies in the United States have found Polish-Americans useful in opening markets in Poland, while Latino-Americans often do well in assignments south of the border. These assets should not be overlooked.

Once you have inventoried your cultural capabilities and have at least thought about how you would prepare people for cultural awareness, you are now ready to begin to develop your international plan.

DEVELOPING YOUR INTERNATIONAL PLAN

Most companies do not begin their international business with the development of an international plan. More likely they will begin with an export sale that resulted from an unsolicited order, or by sourcing an odd component or product. This often results in a patch quilt of international activities without consideration of how to maximize the resources devoted to the international efforts. In fact, the company may not even be aware which resources are being devoted to international business, or to the fact that it is doing international business. For example, could it be that your Miami distributor is doing so well because it is selling to customers who take the product into Latin America?

Developing an international plan can assist your company in:

■ Goal definition
■ Territory evaluation and selection
■ Obtaining upper management commitment
■ Selection of the proper business channels
■ Completing its legal and financial homework
■ Finding partners
■ Assuring the internal preparedness of the company
■ Fitting your international plan into your overall company plans

GOAL DEFINITION

International goals can be as different as "Where do we source products?" to "Should we establish manufacturing in France to accompany our marketing subsidiary?" These goals can be concrete (e.g., U.S. $100 million in sales by the year 2000), or qualitative (e.g., estimate the Indonesian market for our products), but they should be as clear as possible. Clarity, to start, is important because it also should be recognized that goals in the international marketplace will take longer to develop and are more likely to be subjected to reassessment and change. Therefore, while short-term goals should be established, longer-term goals (3 years or more) should be as specifically stated as possible. Examples of such goals might be:

■ International sales as a percentage of total sales
■ Unit and revenue sales by territory
■ Market share of territory
■ Customer base by territory
■ Product mix by territory
■ Distribution channels by territory
■ Maintenance/service channels by territory
■ International training budget
■ International advertising budget
■ Literature requirements
■ Legal concerns:
  (a) Development of agreements

(b) Protection of intellectual property

(c) Effective termination provisions

■ Financial concerns:

(a) Accounts receivable aging

(b) Develop alternative collection formats

(c) Limitation, or elimination, of currency exposure

TERRITORY EVALUATION AND SELECTION

Territory evaluation and selection is concerned with "Where to buy?" "Where and what to produce?" and "Where to sell?" Where to buy deals with the purchase of components and/or finished products and may have nothing to do with where you sell, especially if your product is sourced in low-income countries and sold in the "developed" world. Where to produce may be tied to where you sell. For example, you may choose to produce in Ireland or Portugal to be able to sell "European products" in the EEC. European and Japanese companies are now "producing" in Mexico to meet NAFTA rules of origin guidelines, which will allow for duty-free sale to the United States and Canada.

In regard to marketing and sales, you need to consider whether you will develop your international plan on the basis of regional groups or individual countries. The regional approach might have you develop a plan for Europe, Asia, or Latin America, while a country plan would have you target key national markets like France, Japan, and Mexico. Smaller companies should probably begin with targeting key countries before trying to develop elaborate regional plans.

Another consideration is which countries to target. United States companies almost always start with Canada because of language, cultural, and market similarities, and then move to Great Britain, Mexico, and Australia. However, companies may begin with countries where their products are in demand (Saudi Arabia or Venezuela for petroleum production equipment), or where there is a strong ethnic tie. One client insisted on beginning its international business in the Czech Republic because it was the country of his ancestors.

Finally, a company developing its international plan should try to seek a balance between the risk of overlooking opportunities vs. the possibility of exhausting valuable resources in examining too many opportunities. This, to a certain extent, depends on the type of international business selected. Using agents and/or distributors would probably allow the company to concentrate on more markets than would the decision to establish marketing subsidiaries with their own direct sales force.

Overall, the following variables should be considered in territory evaluation and selection:

Market Size. While the key variable, it is important also to view market size in relation to the company's products. It should also be considered, especially in the area of consumer products, that Brazil, China, India, Indonesia, and Mexico may have more consumers in the middle and upper class than do the medium-sized countries of Europe.

Competitive Risk. Large market size may look less impressive if your competitors already have a good head-start in the territory. This may require using more assets to reach the marketshare, which may be accessed far more readily in a territory where the competitors have a weaker position. Ease of market access and the ability to retain and grow market position must be considered.

Territorial Fit in Relation to the Company's Capabilities and Policies. This covers the following subcategories:

- Geography: Ability to get products to the geography and distribute within the geography.
- Language: Ease of translation, importance of the native language(s) to the citizens.
- Market similarities: Open or closed economies; methods of advertising and promotion; degree of development of marketing and distribution channels.
- Internal costs and red tape: The cost of services and materials needed to sell the product, complexity of license and other government regulations.
- Availability of people: Either an educated workforce for the subsidiary, or the availability of business partners as agents, distributors, licensees, or joint venture partners.

Monetary Risk. This basically can take two forms:
- Risk exposure from a currency which is fluctuating greatly in relation to the home currency.
- Government restrictions on repatriation of sales proceeds, profits, royalties, and/or investment.

Political Risk. Government stability and the ability to rely on government promises from one regime to another; the possibility of terrorism, riots, or strikes that could stop business and perhaps even destroy assets.

OBTAINING UPPER MANAGEMENT COMMITMENT TO THE INTERNATIONAL PLAN

In almost every case, upper management is always willing to give at least lip service to taking their companies "international." The problem is many in upper management do not understand what international really is, or what is necessary to build an international business. In many countries, the United States being perhaps the best example, top management is still oriented towards quarterly results and are not willing to give international projects and sales the time and resources necessary to develop. It cannot be stressed enough that upper management understand the objectives, costs, problems, and rewards of international business. Without that understanding and support, even the best international plans are doomed to failure.

COMPLETION OF LEGAL AND FINANCIAL HOMEWORK

As a practitioner who works frequently with companies just entering the international marketplace, I am usually asked three questions by knowledgeable businesspersons. These are:

- How do we get paid?
- How do we protect our intellectual property?
- What happens if disputes arise?

While these are not the only legal and financial issues a company must be aware of, these are, by far, the most important.

Obtaining Payment

Table 3-2 describes the various methods of payment, along with the advantages and disadvantages of each form. Each company should determine the level of risk it is willing to take, and what forms of international payment systems it is willing to accept. In determining what type of international payment system the company should adopt, the following general principles should be considered:

Table 3-2
Basic Forms of International Commercial Payment
from the Seller's Perspective

Payment Type	Advantages	Disadvantages
Cash before or upon Shipment	Normally cash deposit or direct wire transfer. No risk to seller. No bank charges other than wire transfer costs.	Buyer's reluctance, or inability, to make payment before or upon shipment.
Letters of Credit (drawn between buyer's and seller's bank)		
Irrevocable, Confirmed L.C.'s	Little risk to Seller. Buyer's risk somewhat reduced because L.C. normally requires the showing of certain shipping documents.	Buyer reluctant to make payment at shipment. Additional costs of L.C.s.
Bills of Exchange (drawn between buyer's and seller's bank)		
• Upon site (site draft) payment upon view of documents	Favors Seller, because it requires acceptance and payment on site of documents, often before delivery.	Goods must leave seller's control before payment is received.
• Payment upon arrival of goods	Although risk is increased, it may increase seller's volume.	Favors buyer, because payment is not made until goods arrive.
• Payment at fixed payment date	Superior to open account because it gives seller a document it can discount, and offers proof of acceptance, which is strong evidence in the event of litigation.	Favors buyer, because it is like open account.
Open Account Net 30 or net 60	Once buyers have been qualified, this approach offers the greatest amount of sales opportunity.	No risk to buyer; seller at a great legal and financial disadvantage if payment is not made.

(continued on next page)

Table 3-2 (continued)
Basic Forms of International Commercial Payment
from the Seller's Perspective

Payment Type	Advantages	Disadvantages
Forfeiting Seller sells long-term accounts to a bank or financial institution.	Excellent to limit risk on major transactions where payment will be delayed for some time.	Requires large transactions with a creditworthy customer. Expensive and difficult to arrange.
Countertrade Take goods for goods; popular in Eastern Europe and the former Soviet Union	Allows sales to be made that are otherwise impossible.	May obtain products which are difficult to sell. Costs can be prohibitive.

- Availability of risk capital of the seller.
- Credit worthiness of the buyer.
- Degree of profit margin in the goods.
- Industry standards.
- Use of goods—if for manufacture, different and longer payment scheme may be needed than finished products for direct sale.
- Government policies regarding foreign exchange, which may make it difficult to collect in hard currencies, even if the buyer is willing to pay its accounts.

Companies beginning a relationship with a buyer who is relatively unknown will normally begin with cash before delivery, or letters of credit. They then may move to allow a small amount on open account with restricted credit until that amount is paid, and after the relationship is fully established, move to a revolving line of credit or complete open account.

Protecting Intellectual Property

Despite the existence of several international treaties and conventions (International Convention for the Protection of Industrial Property, or the Paris Convention; the Patent Cooperation Treaty; and the Universal Copyright Convention), holders of intellectual property rights still must rely on national laws and regulations to protect their intellectual property. This requires country-by-country registration, which is both time-consuming and expensive.

On the practical level, this is one area in which smaller companies are at a considerable disadvantage over their larger counterparts. Consider, for example, a relatively common and simple situation of a small company with three trademarks and the desire to appoint agents and/or distributors in twenty countries. Sixty trademark registrations (3 × 20) would likely cost between US $60,000 and US $75,000, forcing the company to make a considerable upfront investment before it can even offer products for sale. This situation becomes even more complex and expensive when litigation is involved. However, there are some ways to protect intellectual property at reasonable expense and effort:

- Only register those trademarks that you know you are going to use, because such registration is subject to use requirements.
- Limit your international focus to include only those countries where you have a likelihood of doing a reasonable amount of business. Do not respond positively to the unsolicited letter from Bolivia if you do not see possibilities in that country.
- In the areas of technology transfer and licensing, consider the major non-legal ways of protecting your intellectual property (e.g., hold something back that you must sell to create a finished product), or put safeguards in your software, and other information.
- Rely as much on partnership selection as you do on establishing legal protection. The best protection for intellectual property is to be dealing with honest and trustworthy people.
- Consider sharing legal costs. Require, or request, your foreign partner to pay some of the costs of local registration in their country. However, make sure that all registrations are in the name of your company.

Dispute Resolution

Disputes arising from companies of different nationalities are always more complicated than domestic disputes. Bringing legal disputes before local courts is fraught with all kinds of dangers, including likely bias by the court towards the local party. Additionally, the costs of service of process, depositions, and translations can make it too expensive to litigate, except when very large amounts are involved. Even winning does not assure you will be able to collect, and even if you do collect, to convert your recovery to the currency of your choice.

Therefore, it is essential that each legal agreement contain provisions of conciliation short of arbitration, using an internationally-recognized form of arbitration. The form and type of these provisions should be determined by your attorney, but there are several international conventions that offer a broad variety of dispute resolution mechanisms.

FINDING PARTNERS

A substantial part of this book deals with finding, and qualifying, international partners. At this point, it is only necessary to say that partner selection should be part of your company's international strategic plan.

INTERNAL PREPAREDNESS

International business cannot be conducted in a vacuum. At some point, nearly every part of the company will be involved in the transaction. Using a relatively simple sales transaction—exporting a product—Table 3-3 illustrates the transaction cannot be made solely by your marketing or sales department, but requires coordination of many departments of the company.

Table 3-3
Company Functions Involved in Export Sales

Scope	Department(s)
Is product available for export?	Marketing /Manufacturing
Does product meet foreign requirements?	Engineering/Quality Control
Needed modifications	Engineering
Can product be supported technically?	Marketing Services/Engineering
Can product be exported?	Legal
Cost of exporting product	Materials/Customer Services
Order Invoicing	Customer Services/MIS
Sales support literature	Marketing Services
Foreign currency issues	Finance/Treasury
Warranty terms and conditions	Quality Control/Accounting/Legal
Customer credit-worthiness?	Finance
Export sales terms and conditions	Finance/Accounting/Legal
Agreements	Legal/Marketing

FITTING THE INTERNATIONAL PLAN INTO THE COMPANY

As Table 3-3 illustrates, the decision to take a company across borders should be one in which all major elements of the company are informed and, if possible, involved. Additionally, this involvement is essential to determine how the international plan will fit into the overall plan. A company cannot simply look to international sales as another revenue generator, unless it has assessed whether they may set off other forces that could negatively impact the company, or send it down roads it does not want, or is unprepared, to travel. There are many ways to enter the global marketplace and, as you will see, some involve limited risk. Whichever way is chosen, however, should not be commenced until the impact on the entire company is understood and accounted for.

PREPARING FOR INTERNATIONAL NEGOTIATIONS

With the right people, and an international plan in place, it is now time to consider how to prepare for the negotiations that are sure to come as the company moves abroad. In no area is an understanding of culture, and the ability to undertake cross-cultural communications, as important as it is in negotiations between individuals and companies of different nationalities. Table 3-4 lists seventeen key variables that enter into international negotiations.

It is important, before entering into an international negotiation, to consider what the other party may value in its own *leadership,* and in the leadership of others. North Americans tend to value technical competence in their leadership, while Latin Americans and people from the Middle East may look more to personal qualities and social position. In other cultures (Japan immediately comes to mind), seniority plays a major role in leadership selection. There is no correct way to value leadership skills, but you should consider what the people on the other side of the table may value, and how it might impact the negotiation process.

Although this may be obvious, many negotiations fail because one or both parties do not understand the *goals* of their negotiation opposites. The classic example of this is the representative of the U.S. company who is trying to make a quarterly sales quota, and faces a customer in the Middle East who is trying to build a long-term relationship. This is why I previously stressed the need for companies that are tied to short-term cycles to obtain an upper management understanding of the international plan.

Table 3–4
Key Variables of the International Negotiation process[4]

Variable	Comment
1. Negotiation leadership	Technical competence, professionalism or seniority?
2. Negotiation goal(s)	The sale, or a long-term relationship?
3. Negotiation attitude	Adversarial or friendly
4. Negotiation outcome	Win/Win or Win/Lose
5. Negotiation style	Informal/Formal
6. Communication	Direct/Indirect
7. Language/Interpreters	One language of negotiation/Use of interpreters
8. Time sensitivity	High/Low
9. Emotional level	High/Low
10. Form of agreement	Generic/Specific
11. Use of prepared agreements	Advisable/Not advisable
12. Role of the Government	Active/Ghost/Passive
13. Renegotiation	Likely/Unlikely
14. Team organization	One spokesperson/Group consensus
15. Process for reaching agreement	Top-Down or Bottom-Up
16. Risk-taking	High/Low
17. Procedure for ending negotiation	Direct/Indirect

Another consideration of the negotiation process is the *attitude* of the parties towards the negotiation. This is often tied to the perceived outcome of the process. If there is one almost universal proposition in international negotiations, it is that the parties cannot take an aggressive/adversarial approach. Individuals and companies who operate with a win/lose attitude are unlikely to be successful outside of their own culture. I have witnessed some "wins" by parties using this approach (they were the only game in town), but, in every case, the "other side" found a way to get even in some future dealing.

Companies should be aware of negotiation *styles* in different cultures. North Americans are generally used to more informal negotiations. Latin Americans and Japanese, however, sometimes prefer a more formal style of negotiation in which extensive notes are taken and both parties are asked to certify their accuracy at the end of each day. Generally, negotiations with government agencies tend to be more formal than negotiations with the private sector.

The style of *communications* should also be considered. North Americans and some Northern Europeans tend to adapt very direct forms of communication with the negotiations actually taking place at the negotiation table. Other cultures prefer more indirect forms of communication. Japanese will shake their heads up and down to say "Yes, I understand," but not necessarily "Yes, I agree." In Latin America, a large meal away from the negotiation table may be where the actual deal is made, while the formal negotiations are used to work out the details.

Jeswald Sulacuse[4] suggests that the major *language* of international negotiations is broken English. If at all possible, it is best that the parties agree to conduct all negotiations in one language. If this is not possible, it is better that each party have their own interpreters. If that is not possible, it is best that the interpreter not represent either party and be paid equally by both. Interpreters should be briefed beforehand on the subject of the negotiations.

Nothing can be more frustrating in negotiations than when the parties do not understand each other's *sense of time*. North Americans prefer to act fast, and are often imbued with a "time is money" attitude. This approach leads to considerable frustration when the other party does not look at time in the same manner. This is especially true when that party is looking towards establishing a long-term relationship and wants to spend the time to get to know the other party better. Both place a high value on time, but tend to look at it differently. To the extent possible, do not leave home for an international negotiation unless you have a sense of how long it will take, and what you can expect on each trip.

Different cultures have different levels of publicly-expressed *emotion*, and this may impact the success or failure of the negotiations. Understand the role that shows of emotionalism (or lack thereof), plays in the negotiations, and attempt to determine what are the acceptable subjects to show emotion and which are not acceptable. Most of all, recognize that a stone face does not mean you have lost the deal, and an expression of gratitude for your presentation and products does not mean you will make the sale.

A company I represent recently closed a nearly U.S. $20 million sale to a major Japanese university. After considerable negotiations, the university agreed to accept a three-page legal agreement. They wanted the offered 80-page agreement to be reduced to a one-page terms of sale. This reflects how the *form of agreement* may differ from culture to culture. The university wanted merely to know what was being delivered, when, and at what cost. It was assumed that the seller would provide all appropriate service and warranties, as it had been investigated thoroughly and found to be an outstanding company. If the seller did not do so, it would lose both face and future business. In the Middle East, it is often assumed that the parties will negotiate a very simple agreement, not because they have the same expectations as the Japanese, but more likely because they fully expect conditions to change and that the project will constantly be under negotiation.

A corollary to the issue of the form of agreement is whether to use a *prepared legal agreement* as the basis of the negotiation. There are only two reasons I can think of to do so:

- It is the only agreement you will use. In this case, the legal department's tail may be wagging the business dog.
- It will be used to structure the discussions. In this case, an outline of issues may be more appropriate.

North American companies, particularly large ones, are guilty of such an approach. Do not use prepared legal agreements in the opening phase of negotiations unless they are the only terms you will accept.

In many countries, *the government* may choose to be involved in the negotiations. I have been involved in a few cases where they actually wanted to sit at the table. More likely, they will be involved as a "ghost" in the negotiations because of registration and approval criteria that will be imposed once the deal is made. The local party may attempt to use government regulations to improve its negotiating position. Worse yet is to come in with your prepared legal agreement, have the local party accept it, and then have it unilaterally negotiated by an agency of the government that will probably take a tougher position than the one you could have negotiated. Before leaving home, try to understand what government involvement might be.

Negotiators should always plan for *renegotiation*. Few complex international transactions will not be subject to renegotiation. As a general rule, it is always better not to go all the way to the bottom line because more may be requested after everything is "finalized."

Different negotiating styles often lead to different conceptions of *team organization*. Japanese tend to lean towards larger teams, but with one individual as the key spokesperson. The Chinese also tend towards large teams, but with each individual able to negotiate on his/her particular area of concern. Latin Americans prefer breaking larger teams into groups (legal, technical, business), and meeting in general session from time-to-time.

The process for reaching agreement (making decisions) differs greatly by culture. North Americans, Mexicans, and the French tend to make decisions from the top down while the Japanese work, at least publicly, from a bottom-up consensus. My experience in negotiating with the Japanese is that it is better to work out a general agreement at the outset because the Japanese will agree to sensible changes after the contract is signed.

North Americans and some Northern Europeans are great public *risk-takers*. In most other cultures, the attempt will be to limit public risks although considerable risks may be taken in a private context. If you sense the other party perceives itself in a risk situation, perhaps it is best to recommend a private discussion between the two chief negotiators.

Finally, it might be useful to know when the other side has decided to *end the negotiation process*. This may come directly by notice at the end of a meeting, but more likely is to be conveyed indirectly by unreturned phone calls, or by failure to set up additional meetings when requested. In any case, it is always recommended to end negotiations on the most sociable basis possible to preserve the possibility of receiving business in the future.

NEGOTIATING TIPS

Before leaving this section, I would like to offer a selection of negotiating tips that I have learned over the years. These are:

- Always try to put yourself in the other person's shoes. What do they really want? What must they really have? What may they offer in return? When in doubt, always attempt to look at the longer-range implications of your actions.
- Understand the cultures, or situations, in which you must negotiate. In these situations, do not go in with your fixed contracts and do not accept their first offer, even if it is acceptable to your company.
- Understand the organization you are negotiating with. Where are the real decision-makers? What is their negotiation style and method of closing?
- Negotiations are not confined only to big deals, or major parts of deals. In some cultures, everything is negotiated.

- Do not use a "closer." North American negotiation teams are famous for bringing in a "closer" as negotiations wind towards their final conclusion. This is usually a top vice president or division head brought in at the last minute to "close" the deal. More often than not, the other team is insulted by such a technique, and questions the long-term nature of the relationship. This approach does not work!

- If possible, avoid "Deals Teams." These are common in large North American companies where a group associated with "International Business Development" goes around the world making "deals." The problem with these teams is that they rarely represent the actual division and/or subsidiary of the company that must perform the agreement. There should be at least one person at the negotiations who is identified and, in fact, will be the person who will be continually responsible for the project under negotiation.

- Do not be in a hurry. If possible, make concessions near the end of the negotiations. Attempt to learn *all* of the major demands and requests of the other party before beginning to make concessions.

- Consider the negotiations that must be made within your company. Try to complete those before leaving home.

- If possible, avoid setting time limits. If the other party knows you are leaving at 5:00 pm on Friday, they will probably force you to conclude the negotiations at around that time.

- Be prepared to walk away. No deal is better than a bad deal. However, the key to walking away is to do so with dignity being preserved by both sides so that business can be conducted between the parties in the future.

CONCLUSION

Chapters 2 and 3 of this book ask "Are you ready?" If you have determined that your company can overcome the roadblocks to going international, you have established a plausible international plan, and have made a commitment to obtain and/or train the people you need, then it is time to take the plunge. The next ten chapters address the proven methods for building a global business. It is now appropriate to examine those methods.

REFERENCES

1. Axtell, R. E. (ed.), *Do's and Taboos Around the World: Guide to International Behavior*, New York: John Wiley & Sons, 1990.
2. Von Oech, Roger, *A Whack on the Side of the Head,* Rev. ed., New York: Warner Books, 1990.
3. Harris, P. and Moran R., *Managing Cultural Differences,* 4th ed., Houston: Gulf Publishing Company, 1996.
4. Sulacuse, Jeswald W., *Making Global Deals*, Boston: Houghton Mifflin Co., 1991, see pp. 58–70. Table 3-4 was partially based on the contents of those pages.

BUILDING A GLOBAL BUSINESS WITHOUT LEAVING HOME

Going international can be accomplished by several methods, one of which is being an importer of goods, services, or capital (defined here as "internal internationalization"). In fact, if you examined the number of companies that only import, you would probably find, particularly in the United States, that they exceed the companies that both import and export. *A company that only imports is also an international company,* so importers must be concerned about cultural differences, too. They need to be just as savvy in negotiating across borders and, like exporters, may be involved in adapting products for local markets. Finally, importers also need to develop the personnel and management tools necessary to undertake international trade and finance.

Importers, however, are often on their own. While the governments may have programs to help exporters, few offer assistance to importers. The United States, for example, has the Export-Import Bank (Ex-Im Bank), but no one can remember when that Bank has last financed an import transaction. Often, service providers (e.g., international consultants, accountants, and lawyers), are oriented towards helping their clients overseas and not towards assisting their clients in the home market. Additionally, importing often creates a message to the public of the home country that is not as positive as exporting. Concern over foreign trade deficits, unemployment, and loss of control of a country's land and natural resources (patrimony) makes it sometimes necessary to undertake importing activities in a less public manner.

The next three chapters (Chapters 4–6) explore the following aspects of internal internationalization:

- Sourcing foreign components and labor.
- Representing a foreign business or selling foreign products into the domestic market: agents and distributors, licensing foreign technology, including franchising.
- Providing services to foreign individuals and companies in your home market.

Following these three chapters is a chapter on Exporting from the Home Country (Chapter 7). This chapter explores how some companies have been able to build considerable international business without establishing any significant overseas operations or commitments. Taken together, these four chapters give the reader a good idea of how to build a global business without leaving the home market.

Chapter 4

METHOD 1:
INTERNATIONAL SOURCING

INTRODUCTION

To remain competitive in the home and global markets, many companies are now choosing to acquire some of their products, parts, and/or components from abroad. Even companies that produce a large portion of their products within their own facilities are now finding, for many reasons, it is better to begin to use suppliers, both domestic and foreign, to reduce the costs and labor commitments and to protect the interests of their shareholders.

For many, international sourcing creates an image of a heartless company moving its high-paying jobs to developing countries where inexpensive labor, toiling long hours, allows the company to increase its profits. When a recession hits the home country, or when the developing country workers increase their demands, the company merely pulls out and moves to a more friendly environment.

While there are examples of this scenario, especially in the less technologically oriented businesses, in general, most international sourcing is undertaken between the existing developed (OECD) nations. Table 4-1 illustrates this for the U.S. electronics industry.

Table 4-1
Top Ten U.S. Electronics Trading Partners[1]

Total Value of Imports to U.S. (US $ billions)	
Japan	$30.6
Singapore	6.8
Taiwan	6.2
South Korea	5.5
Mexico	5.3
Canada	5.3
Malaysia	3.2
Germany	2.5
Hong Kong	2.0
U.K.	1.9

Table 4-1 indicates that four of the OECD (advanced) nations, including Japan, are among the top ten importers to the U.S.A. Japan alone contributes 44%, and the total of the top four OECD nations (Japan, Canada, Germany, and the U.K.) accounted for over 58% of the top ten. While there is some shift away from the OECD nations, this shift is not towards Vietnam or Bangladesh, but towards Mexico and the Asian "Tigers" already on the list.

In fact, there is solid evidence to show that variants such as the strength of the United States dollar has very little to do with international sourcing. In the early 1980s, when the dollar was strong, it was logical to assume that U.S. manufacturers would move operations abroad to take advantage of lower labor costs. However, after 1985, when the dollar began to weaken, offshore sourcing continued to increase. Between 1985 and 1989, U.S. imports from offshore sourcing increased 147% despite a general rise of imports of only 27%.[2]

How can this be explained? The answer indicates the increasing complexities associated with international sourcing. In today's world, many of the large companies are participating in two general trends: the separation of R&D from procurement, and increased sourcing of R&D, components, and products from within global corporate systems.[2]

Traditional companies undertake research and development in the home country, and on the results of that effort, may move to procure components and products from abroad. As companies globalize, they recognize the possibility, and sometimes necessity, to "source" R&D from wherever it is most suitable. The global company then may procure R&D in one country, source components and products in another, market and sell in still another, and take its general strategy from the home country, which may not be involved in any of the other above-mentioned areas.

To accomplish this strategy, it is usually necessary, for the purposes of control and security, to source R&D, components, and products from within its own corporate system. Therefore, it will move to create a series of subsidiaries and affiliates to supply the items it had previously sourced from unrelated parties.

However, companies of all sizes can participate in the advantages of international sourcing. This chapter first explores the advantages and disadvantages of international sourcing from a small, or middle-sized, company's point of view. It then looks at contract manufacturing and one of its most popular variants, the maquiladora. International sourcing is often the first global move for the domestic business and is well worth considering.

ADVANTAGES AND DISADVANTAGES OF INTERNATIONAL SOURCING

When a company is considering replacing domestic suppliers, or subsidiaries with foreign suppliers or subsidiaries, or moving from domestic production to foreign production, it will do so for the following reasons:

- *Price.* Can a company reduce costs by moving production to countries where labor and/or production costs are lower?
- *Quality.* Can quality be improved or retained in a lower price environment, or can quality be significantly increased with no, or only slight, price increases?
- *Unavailability of domestic products or lack of consistency of local production.*
- *Faster delivery.* U.S. companies on or near the Canadian and Mexican borders sometimes find faster turnaround from companies in Northern Mexico and/or Canada than from companies in the United States. In fact, many large Japanese companies established final-assembly operations in Tijuana, Mexico to be close to their customers in California.
- *Better technology* or technical services such as just-in-time inventory management.

■ *Competition.* Source abroad as a vehicle to keep the prices of domestic suppliers low and to assure continuity of supply.

However, international sourcing also has its share of problems. Some of these are:

■ *Difficulties in evaluating and selecting foreign suppliers.* Sourcing abroad requires additional resources to locate and qualify foreign suppliers. Buyer's agents must sometimes be sought. Once selected, the management process can be considerably more difficult.

■ *Quality.* More efforts must be made to assure quality control and to limit the percentage of rejects.

■ *Delivery time.* The potential importer must consider the additional variables that could extend delivery times. Even the best production and inventory management techniques can be defeated by customs problems.

■ *Political and labor problems.* These are less under control of the importer.

■ *Currency fluctuations and payment problems.* This has become a considerable problem for U.S. companies sourcing from Japan and Germany.

■ *Paperwork and extra documentation costs.*

■ *Marking and labeling issues* to assure proper entry into the home market.

CONTRACT MANUFACTURING

To attempt to have the best of both worlds, more and more companies are adopting an import strategy which uses *contract manufacturing abroad.* Instead of simply ordering products as needed, the company enters into a contract with the foreign supplier, which fixes production amounts and delivery times and allows the supplier to maintain hands-on management of the production process. This gives the importer a greater assurance of supply and quality control while capitalizing on lower wage rates and still limiting the company's commitment to the manufacturer and the country of manufacture. This program can be used either to acquire a lower-cost source of components or for a production base for final assembly of products.

Contract manufacturing is often advantageous to the foreign manufacturer because it guarantees revenues and allows the manufacturer to provide steady employment. It has, in fact, become a major industry in some countries as discussed below in the analysis of Mexico's maquiladora program. However, before entering into contract manufacture, the importer must consider some of its *disadvantages*. These include:

1. Because the contract manufacturer expects a reasonable profit for its efforts, this may reduce the overall profits of the importer. Importers must carefully examine the savings to be acquired from contract manufacturing and be sure to consider such factors as duties and the potential expatriate costs required for personnel sent to manage the production process.

2. One manner to reduce costs, and perhaps to acquire some know-how from the contract manufacturer, is to allow for an *exchange of certain intellectual property*. However, if not controlled properly, this could result in a contract manufacturer being able to compete with the importer after the end of the contract manufacture arrangement.

3. Normally, a contract manufacture arrangement will not work unless the importer is willing to agree to accept a certain volume of product from the contract manufacturer. This is known as *off-take*. Agreeing to off-take certain volumes should be beneficial to both parties. However, intervening conditions can often result in problems for both the importer and contract manufacturer when:

   ■ The importer overestimates the needed off-take and is forced to take product into inventory it does not need or cannot sell.

   ■ The importer goes out of that business or sells that product line to another company before the end of the contractual period.

4. In general, some other potential problems with contract manufacturing are:

   ■ Requires complex, expensive legal documents.

   ■ May need to be altered quickly to meet changing business conditions.

   ■ May limit future management and investment decisions.

   ■ Limits the number of personnel available for use in other operations of the importer.

   ■ Creates business and political problems for such importer stakeholders as employees, other suppliers and the communities in which the existing manufacturing operations are located.

MAQUILADORAS

One of the most popular forms of contract manufacturing in recent years has been the maquiladora. The maquiladora is normally associated with Mexico but is found in different forms in other countries. Korean manufacturers, for example, favor Guatemala for their maquila programs. A maquiladora is a production facility that manufactures, processes, or assembles raw materials or components imported in-bond and duty free for eventual reexport. The Mexican program, for example, is of particular interest to U.S. manufacturers as, under the U.S. Tariff Act of 1930, the duties are applied only to the "value-added" in Mexico. If a U.S. manufacturer sends $0.80 worth of components to a Mexican maquila, which then adds $0.20 in value, the duty is only applied to the $0.20 added. With the passage of NAFTA, this duty (already low in most cases) is considerably lessened or eliminated, and Mexico will phase out this aspect of the program over the next few years.

Maquiladora "production sharing" allows U.S. companies to combine their technology and content with low-cost labor and sometimes new materials. In the process, the foreign manufacturer maintains control of their business operations, their proprietary and patent rights, and their manufacturing business in the home country. The Mexican program has expanded dramatically in the last decade from 600 such plants in 1983 to nearly 2,000 in 1993. Over 500,000 Mexicans are employed and maquiladora operations have become Mexico's third largest source of foreign exchange after petroleum and tourism. The Japanese have also found the maquiladora program attractive. By the end of 1991, twenty-seven Japanese firms had established maquiladora operations on the Baja California/California border.

There are three types of Mexican maquiladora operations. The first two are similar to what you might find elsewhere. The first is straight contract manufacture, where you contract with a local operation to produce finished goods. The second is to establish a wholly-owned operation controlled by the foreign company, which functions as a Mexican corporation for all legal, fiscal, and labor purposes.

The third program, called the *shelter program,* is a unique way of establishing Mexican production. In this case, the importer contracts with a shelter plan operator who provides, for an agreed price:

- The direct labor workforce, which are employees of the shelter plan operator.
- A fully-equipped production plant, which often is configured to the importers specifications.
- Building maintenance and insurance.
- Utilities, including telephone lines.
- Janitorial services and supplies.
- Assistance in hiring the indirect Mexican workers.
- Personnel, accounting, and payroll administration.
- Interface with Mexican government officials.
- All the necessary Mexican permits.
- U.S. and Mexican customs documentation services.
- Staging warehouse space in the United States.

Therefore, under the typical shelter plan operations, the foreign company only provides:

- Raw materials and components.
- Production equipment.
- On-site plant management, if necessary.
- Technology, as required.

Rates charged to companies depend upon the number of employees, size of the plant, and additional services provided. For example, a full-service shelter operation in Cuidad Juarez in the early 1990s (across from El Paso, Texas), was around $5.00 per hour per employee with 25 employees operating in a 20,000-square-foot building, or $3.00 per hour per employee for 200 employees in a 100,000-square-foot building.

One of the disadvantages of maquiladoras was the limitation on the sale of the production in Mexico. With the passage of NAFTA, Mexico amended its maquiladora restrictions to allow sale of maquila off-take in Mexico at 55% of production for 1994 and increasing 5% per year until the year 2000. In 2001, there will be no limitation whatsoever. Additionally, the program has been severely criticized because of the lack of environmental protection and the social problems caused by the population growth it helped initiate in Northern Mexico. There are provisions in the NAFTA Agreement to address all of these problems, although the results remain to be seen. The lowering of tariff barriers will reduce the need for value-added importation and will probably encourage some growth in all forms of contract manufacture in Mexico. These operations can now be established in any area of Mexico and this, coupled with the increasing ability to sell off-take in Mexico, will encourage even more development of contract manufacture throughout Mexico. Finally, the two NAFTA Side Agreements on the Environment and Labor will at least begin to address the environmental and social problems related to maquiladoras.

Acquiring R&D, components, and products from abroad can help even a domestic company be competitive in its home market, and be able to compete globally. We will now move, in Chapter 5, to cover the marketing of foreign products in home markets.

REFERENCES

1. *Global Trade*, April, 1992, p. 42.
2. Kotabe and Swan, "Offshore Sourcing: Reaction, Maturation, and Consolidation of U.S. Multinationals," *Journal of International Business Studies*, 1st Qtr., 1994, p. 116.

Chapter 5

METHOD 2: REPRESENTING FOREIGN PRODUCTS IN YOUR HOME MARKET

INTRODUCTION

Almost all large grocery chains and department stores must be global companies because they acquire rights to market and sell the products of many countries. This is equally true for the Japanese car dealer in Uruguay and the holder of a McDonald's franchise in France. These companies require many of the international skills defined in Chapter 3. They must choose employees and agents with global savvy. They will be involved in negotiations across borders. They will have to adjust to currency and global financial changes, and they will carry the international name and prestige of the company they represent.

Chapters 8 through 10 cover the issues associated with the appointment of agents, distributors, licensing, and franchising abroad. They look at these global methods from the point of view of the seller, licensor, and franchisor. This chapter looks at these topics from the other point of view, that is from the perspective of being an agent, distributor, licensee, or franchisee. Taken together, this chapter, along with Chapters 8 through 10, will give you a clear roadmap to each of these key proven methods.

AGENTS

These are independent companies (and sometimes individuals) who represent foreign exporters and take orders on the exporter's behalf. Agents normally work on a commission basis and are paid when the exporter makes a direct sale to the customer. They do not take title to, or possession of, the goods they represent. *The prices to be charged are agreed to between the exporter and the customer.* Normally, agents do not stock products, nor do they provide pre- and post-sales support to the customer.

Companies will normally appoint foreign agents if they are not ready to establish their own operations but wish to deal directly with distinct individual customers, or to seek customers on a Request for Proposal (RFP) or project basis. The skill requirements for agents are normally personal contacts and some industry experience. Technical skills will not be sought except in particular cases.

The biggest single area of disputes involving agents, both during and after the relationship, is over commissions and the commission structure. The following issues are typical:

- *When commissions will be paid.* Consider whether you will need a nonrefundable up-front payment, particularly if up-front expenses may be high and/or the possibility of success may be limited. Additionally, it needs to be determined whether your commissions are due upon completion of the sale and/or whether your responsibilities will be tied to collections.

- *Methods of resolving disputed commissions.* Disputed commissions arise when there is more than one agent involved, when the principal feels that it has "handled" the sale, or when the relationship between the principal and agent has ended before the work is completed and/or the customer has made all payments.

- *How long will commissions apply?* About five years ago, I was involved with a local agent who signed a one-year agreement with a foreign principal. The principal needed the agent primarily to make some critical introductions. These introductions were made, a small sale was accomplished, and the commission paid to the agent. The agreement expired shortly thereafter and about three months later the same customer placed a very large order with the principal.

The agent was told by the principal that he would not receive a commission because the agreement had expired. In some countries, this would be true, in others it would depend on the circumstances. Table 5-1 cites some characteristics that an agent should seek of a principal before committing to a long-term relationship.

■ *Effects of price reductions on commission structure/additional commissions for orders sold at high prices.* Agent commissions are often set with the assumption of a sales price to the customer within a certain range. Disputes arise when customer negotiations result in considerable price reductions. Often the agent is then requested to decrease his/her commission to make the sale and/or to increase the principal's margin. The flip side of this is the "blue bird" sale, where the product is offered at, say, 100 with full expectation that it will sell for 90, but the customer either pays list or selects several high-priced options. In these cases, the issue is whether the agent is entitled to a bonus for the higher price obtained.

■ *Whether the agent will obtain commissions on products or services sold directly by the principal in the agent's territory* (that is, without the agent's involvement). To avoid such problems, it is necessary to define these commission issues as clearly as possible in a definitive legal agreement, and to understand the legal rights you might have upon termination or expiration of the relationship. Chapter 8 discusses termination issues.

Table 5-1
Principal's Profile

1. International reputation as a fair and honest business operation.
2. International experience and knowledge, especially in working with agents.
3. Have a clear understanding of how the agency relationship works, and that it truly needs agents.
4. Willing to sign an agreement that clearly specifies territory, commission structure, and payment.
5. Willing to give exclusivity in certain markets, or in regard to certain customers.
6. Willing to provide training and marketing materials.
7. Offer clear guidelines on the agent's discretionary authority, if any.
8. Willing to take sufficient time to develop the local market.

DISTRIBUTORS

These are independent companies that purchase products (take title) from the exporters for resale to their customers who may be end-users of the product or other intermediaries who then sell to end-users. While sometimes it is necessary to make alterations to the product, distributors normally sell exactly what they purchase. They will assume the risks of buying and stocking the products in the local market and normally will also provide product support and other after-market services. Distributors establish and maintain their own contacts with the customers *including setting the prices they will charge to those customers.* They are also normally responsible for local advertising and promotion.

Before becoming a distributor of a foreign company, it might first be appropriate to develop an importer's profile, that is, a profile of an ideal business partner. Table 5-2 cites the characteristics of the ideal importer. You may consider prioritizing these general characteristics to establish your own profile.

Table 5-2
Importer's Profile

1. International reputation as a fair and honest business operation.
2. International experience and knowledge.
3. Reputation for quality products and services.
4. Have, or be developing, a distributor relations function in its corporate or regional headquarters.
5. Willing to designate a contact person or function who is responsible for dealing with your operations.
6. Committed to using marketeers in your territory for sometime in the future.
7. Willing to offer a balanced and realistic legal agreement.
8. Willing to provide sufficient marketing materials.
9. Willing to offer training on a regular basis.
10. Recognition of the unique characteristics of your marketplace (e.g., U.S. marking and labeling requirements).
11. Willing to provide you with sufficient territory and allow expansion if you are successful.
12. Offer pricing that is realistic and suits the vagaries of your marketplace.

The last two points of Table 5-2, territory and pricing, are of particular importance. Your company should not take a distributor appointment unless you are absolutely sure that you will obtain a reasonable territory. What is a reasonable territory is ultimately a business decision based on a multitude of factors. However, your company should be sure to resolve, beforehand, how many other local competitors the importer will allow into the market, and whether the importer desires to sell direct *or* will refer all contacts in the territory to your company and/or others appointed in the territory.

You should also be sure that the importer's pricing to you is sufficient to provide you with a reasonable rate of return on investment. In the case of distributors, your company will control the prices in the territory, not the importer. It is up to you to determine whether you will be able to price the products (given transportation, finance charges, and import duties), to be competitive in the marketplace. For example, a 25% discount off importer's international list may be sufficient if you can charge a premium in the marketplace, but may not be enough in an extremely competitive environment. Throughout the entire relationship, you will need to work with the importer to achieve the optimal price that provides for competitive flexibility while maintaining a volume of sales.

Before becoming a distributor, it is recommended that you review Chapter 8 which covers, in depth, what companies look for in their distributors. That chapter also has an extensive section on termination issues.

INTERNATIONAL LICENSING

This type of licensing is normally a contractual arrangement in which the *licensor* (granting company) grants access to its technology, patents, trademarks, copyrights, trade secrets, know-how, and other intellectual property to a foreign *licensee* (receiving company) to be used by the licensee in exchange for a fee and/or other considerations. This grant may be in the form of a direct sale of rights or be limited to a certain period of time. International licensing can be tied to sourcing, joint ventures, distributors, and agents, and can be part of intercompany agreements between the parent and subsidiary.

BECOMING A LICENSEE

The decision to license is a complex one. Many licensing relationships do not succeed because the parties fail to understand each other's real

Table 5-3
Licensor's Profile

1. Experience in licensing, particularly international licensing with high quality technology.
2. Fairly-priced services and components.
3. Available and willing to provide continuing assistance, either included as part of the royalties or at reasonable fees.
4. Willing to allow for licensee innovations.
5. Willing to provide updates, enhancements, and new products.
6. Willing to consider granting exclusive rights, or to allow licensee to earn exclusive rights.
7. Willing to allow for increased vertical integration, that is, allowing more of the product to be produced by the licensee as it learns the technology.
8. Willing to consider reasonable territorial expansion.
9. Desire a long-term relationship.
10. Consider your territory a valuable one.
11. Willing to protect the licensee from encroachment from other licensees.
12. Willing to protect the licensee against challenges to the licensor's intellectual property.

agenda. To assist in finding the proper licensor, the licensee might look at the characteristics cited in the licensor profile in Table 5-3.

MAINTAINING THE LICENSE RELATIONSHIP

The twelve points in Table 5-3 are essential in foreign licensor selection, but they will also enter into the maintenance functions between licensor and licensee. From the licensee's perspective, the following points should be kept in mind:

■ *To what degree will the licensor attempt to become involved in the licensee's activities?* If the technology transferred is complicated, the licensee may seek the licensor's assistance early on to understand and implement the technology. At that point, it may be important to assure the availability of foreign technicians. However, if the licensor continues to insist on close monitoring of the licensee's activities, make sure the reason for this is not to learn the local nuances and customer base so that the licensor will be prepared to enter the market directly at some later date.

■ *Apply the fairness principle.* From the licensee's perspective, high royalties and component prices will have to be adjusted downwards if the licensee perceives and can show the licensor that it is not receiving its fair share of the profits. However, licensors will soon lose interest in licensees who are not providing it with sufficient revenues and/or profits to justify the relationship.

■ Include some mechanism for resolving misunderstandings short of the standard legal mechanisms. The licensee should assure that the licensor will assign one individual (normally one of its employees), who will stay with the project throughout completion. This individual should attempt to understand the workings of the licensee and to "represent its views" before the licensor. Additionally, communications should be regularized and problems not allowed to fester.

Chapter 10 should be consulted before entering into a licensing relationship.

FRANCHISING

One third of all retail businesses in the United States are now franchises. While this country is by far the greatest exporter of franchising, the possibility now exists that more and more foreign companies will try this approach in the United States. Some that have already done so are food franchisors—Wimpy's (U.K.) and Wienerwald Germany—and Pronuptia, a French bridal-wear franchisor.[1] Additionally, U.S. franchisors are finding that more and more of their potential franchisees are foreign individuals and companies, some hoping to use the franchise vehicle to achieve a certain immigration status.

A franchise operation is a contractual relationship between the franchisor and franchisee, in which the franchisor offers, or is obligated to maintain, a continuous interest in the business of the franchisee in such areas as know-how and training, wherein the franchisee operates under a common tradename, format or procedure owned or controlled by the franchisor, and in which the franchisee has made, or will make, a substantial capital investment in the business from his own resources.

As with importers and licensors, the potential franchisee should develop a franchisor profile that addresses the characteristics cited in Table 5-4.

Table 5-4
Franchisor's Profile

1. Successful in franchising in its home market and other markets.
2. Good and workable procedures and operations guides.
3. Willing to adjust its upfront and continuing costs to reflect market size and conditions.
4. Viable training programs with sufficient staff to develop them.
5. Products and services that are viable in your market.
6. Availability of products and services at reasonable costs, willing to assist franchisees in obtaining local products, as relevant.
7. Recognizable intellectual property.
8. Desire a long-term relationship.
9. Ability to provide financial assistance or delay payments for problems that are not the fault of the franchisee.
10. Willing to allow some independence in local operations.
11. Desire to expand and willing to include franchisee in that expansion.
12. Advertising techniques and programs that are suitable for your territory.

Anyone who reads the Thursday edition of the *Wall Street Journal* is deluged with franchising opportunities. To take advantage of those opportunities, the franchisee (the company who takes the franchise) should consider the following about their ability to be a franchisee:

■ Business experience, knowledge, and acumen in one area does not necessarily equate to the same in another area. An international banker may not have the acumen to run a restaurant. Likewise, a former executive from a major food corporation may not do well in selling tires and related services.

■ Lack of business experience in the subject matter of the franchise can be overcome if the franchisee is willing to accept advice and guidance from the franchisor. However, if you belong to the "can't teach an old dog new tricks" school, you should refrain from being a franchisee.

■ Many franchises fail because of lack of financial and/or human resources. If the estimate to start a franchise is U.S. $250,000, be willing or able to place an extra U.S. $75,000–$100,000 in reserve. If you will be involved in the direct management of the franchise, consider whether this is really what you want to do with your time. If you will turn the management over to others, be sure to provide for sufficient financial resources to cover these needs and consider that, at times, you may need to manage the managers.

Chapter 9 offers an extensive analysis of international franchising. This chapter considers some of the factors involved in representing foreign *products* in your home market. Chapter 6 discusses similar concerns in the *service* area.

REFERENCE

1. Daniels, John D., and Radebaugh, Lee H., *International Business: Environments and Operations*, (6th ed.), Boston: Addison-Wesley, 1992, p. 552.

Chapter 6

METHOD 3: PROVIDING SERVICES TO FOREIGN COMPANIES IN YOUR DOMESTIC MARKET

INTRODUCTION

It has been estimated that one quarter of all international trade is derived from the sale of services.[1] Most experts would probably agree that services are likely to be the biggest growth area of international trade in the years to come. Just as product companies have followed their customers overseas, so have service companies. Everything from rental car companies to law firms have followed their customers abroad and many have found lucrative markets in creating and filling needs in these new geographies.

This news is very good for the United States of America which, while running chronic trade deficits for the past generation, has been able to achieve substantial surpluses in the service area. As you will see later, much of this has been accomplished in the area of franchising and other forms of technology transfer.

While providing services abroad is exciting and full of challenges, it may not be as exciting or lucrative as assisting foreign individuals and companies in your own domestic market. This is a particularly good strategy for service providers in saturated and/or low growth markets, and for those businesses that may be oriented to service foreign individuals and/or companies because of geographical location or because of ethnic and cultural considerations.

The skills needed for this type of service business are quite similar to those needed in achieving global expansion. Representing a Japanese company in the United States is not so different from representing a United States company in Japan. You still need language and cultural skills, and owners and employees who exhibit many of the international characteristics described at the beginning of Chapter 3.

However, if, as an American service provider, you represent a U.S. company in Japan, you must either establish an expensive local office, or eventually defer to the skills of your Japanese associates to get the job done. "Inward" business can be more lucrative because the fixed costs are already made for the domestic clients, and the company is now the local expert with the knowledge and means to solve the client's business problems.

This chapter is designed for such service providers as accountants, advertising agencies, consultants, data processing services, insurance providers, investment counselors, lawyers, real estate professionals, and tax advisors. In recent years, many of these service professionals have found their markets changing from sellers markets to buyers markets. In this case, the push towards acquiring international clients may be of particular interest as information on this subject is not easy to come by. We will begin with an assessment of resources, move to market identification, briefly discuss how to identify your services and conclude with how to identify and reach international customers.

ASSESS YOUR RESOURCES

You may already have some, or all, of the resources necessary to service the foreign client. Determine whether you have among your existing employees and consultants people with the personality traits of a successful global employee (see Chapter 3). Do you have an employee(s) with ethnic origins and language skills that are critical to serving certain foreign clients? Determine whether the location of your business is convenient to foreign visitors. Is it located near tourist attractions, hotels, restaurants, banks and other places where foreign visitors will feel comfortable. This alone may often be the reason why one local service provider is selected over another.

Assess your facilities. Do you have appropriate communications facilities? Are your phones answered beyond your normal office hours? Can you communicate in other languages? Are your marketing capabilities sufficient to offer a convincing package to potential business clients?

Look at your current customer base to determine what success you may already have. You might already represent foreign individuals and/or companies. If so, determine how these clients came to your business. Try to understand why they selected your company, and find out if they can recommend others.

While servicing international companies in your home market may be more lucrative than following your existing customers overseas, it is not without a price, that price being that it is harder to obtain business with a "market-seeking strategy" than with a "client follower strategy".[2] Most marketeers will tell you that it is easier to try to obtain more business from existing customers than to seek new customers. Here you are seeking customers that may not even fit the profile of your customer base. Later in this chapter, we will identify and discuss some of the ways to reach those customers. Consider, at this point, whether your company has the resources and desire necessary to seek new, and sometimes quite unique, markets. That is, is the additional marketshare worth the effort?

STRESS THE VALUE OF YOUR COUNTRY OR REGION

I spent a lot of time in Uruguay, a small country located between Argentina and Brazil. This country long ago decided to try to become the service provider for the region around it. Sometimes, calling itself "The Switzerland of Latin America," the country promotes itself as a relatively crime-free, banking center location for regional headquarters, and a place to rest and recreate after the rapid pace of São Paulo or Buenos Aires. It is the headquarters of the Latin American Free Trade Organization and of the Mercosur Common Market. Therefore, the local service providers promote themselves as having the international sophistication necessary to meet the needs of a good part of South America.

When a local law firm in Minneapolis/St. Paul first began its campaign to attract foreign business, it saw that the greatest competitors were not other service providers in the region, but those on the coasts of the United States. Europeans and South Americans look to New York and Miami; Asians to Los Angeles, San Francisco, or Seattle. The impression many foreigners have of the United States is that they must work through Washington, D.C. to accomplish their goals. This is not unusual when you consider that in many countries of the world all power, political and economic, emanates from the capital city.

To counter this perception, the firm developed marketing materials that stress the advantages of its local area, which includes a strong work ethic and a lower cost of living than the coastal cities. It packaged that with materials from the state of Minnesota, which also promotes the region. One of the brochures includes the following message:

> As more and more trade with the U.S. extends beyond the East and West coasts, so does the choice of lawyers. _____, a full-service law firm, has many years of experience assisting international business people with broad-based needs in national and international markets . . .
>
> The metropolitan area of Minneapolis and neighboring St. Paul has a 2.5-million population, the largest between Chicago and Seattle. There are more *Fortune 500* companies . . . per capita in the Twin Cities than any city in the U.S. except New York . . . With its central geographical position in North America, Minneapolis has excellent access to Canada and Mexico.[3]

IDENTIFY YOUR MARKETS

At least at the beginning, seeking and serving foreign clients will take a lot of time and energy. The first decision that must be made is whether you are going to make a broadbase attempt at business, or attempt to target a particular niche. The broadbase approach may work if you are a large diverse organization. The best example I can think of would be a full service law firm that contains or develops a business immigration function headed up with an individual(s) with considerable marketing capabilities. This approach could also work with big accounting and consulting firms that have a significant referral network through existing overseas operations.

Selecting a market niche would be more appropriate for smaller organizations or those who provide a smaller range of services. One factor that usually works is to determine whether your organization has an affinity with any area(s) of the world and target those markets. Organizations run by individuals of particular ethnic backgrounds may seek to market to those with similar backgrounds. Finally, those with professional credentials may likewise target those with identical or similar credentials (e.g., American architects marketing to their French counterparts).

Two other considerations merit discussion. In identifying your markets, your organization should determine whether it is a *protected market,* or one that might be subject to foreign competition. The market may be protected because of license requirements or supply and demand. However, even though both may apply (e.g., in the case of lawyers), this may not be enough to stop a foreign firm from operating in your territory with local professionals, especially if large companies from their home country are operating in your domestic market. One of the large Mexican law firms has opened an office in New York for just that reason.

Finally, consider whether there are any *incentives* to foreign individuals or businesses offered in your national or local markets that can be used as a bridge to obtain business. Such incentives may include monetary or tax breaks for establishing local business and job creation, discounted office, warehouse or factory space, local financial and/or loans, and government-provided advice and training. Examples include the immigration policies of the United States, Canada, and Australia, which often award permanent residence to those foreign individuals willing to make substantial direct investments that result in employment of the local population.

IDENTIFY YOUR SERVICES

Actually, this is probably the easiest part of preparing to service international clients. Table 6-1 cites twenty services typically provided to foreign individuals and companies by domestic lawyers. Two things are striking about this list. First, with the possible exception of immigration, these are already performed by a full-service law firm with its existing clients. They will have to be adjusted somewhat to fit foreign clients' needs, but that usually can be accomplished with far less resource commitment than gearing-up to assist domestic clients abroad.

Secondly, the services mentioned in Table 6-1, with limited exceptions, are merely the legal variant of the more general services that can be provided by any number of service providers. You will see in the next

Table 6-1
Services Provided to Foreign Companies by Domestic Lawyers

1. Acquisitions and mergers	10. Franchising
2. Acquisition of real estate	11. Human resources and workplace
3. Appointment of agents and	issues
distributors	12. Immigration
4. Assistance with banks and	13. Incentives to foreign investors
credit facilities	14. Intellectual property
5. Business type selection	15. Licensing
6. Contacts and networks	16. Product sourcing
7. Establishing strategic	17. Resolving disputes
alliances and joint ventures	18. Securities transactions
8. Environmental legal issues	19. Taxation
9. Family legal issues	20. Trusts and estates

section why it is advised to work with other non-competitive service providers to offer the foreign individuals and companies a complete package of services.

IDENTIFY HOW TO REACH INTERNATIONAL CUSTOMERS

By now you should be convinced that opting for a strategy to obtain international customers in your domestic market may be a sensible decision. While preparing your company to deal with foreign individuals and companies may require some additional resource commitment, all of this will come to naught unless you are able to make connections with international customers. This will not come easy, as market-seeking strategies are generally difficult, but the rewards are incredible if you succeed.

In general, there are seven major ways in which to generate an international clientele. The first is *referrals*. We have found that once you have done business with one company from a particular country, that it is likely to refer other companies from the same country. In addition, you could obtain referrals from a domestic company that has international ties. One large local company moved its Latin American headquarters from Miami to the corporate headquarters in Minneapolis. With this knowledge, we approached the company about referring its Latin American suppliers and employees to us when they had local needs. Often these needs had little to do directly with the relationship between the companies, but were subsidiary to that relationship. For example, supplier management often decided to make local investments, acquire property, or need immigration services. Sometimes, the suppliers were from diversified companies and they sought advice on their other businesses.

Next to direct referrals, the best means of obtaining international clients is by *establishing a network of service providers abroad.* Informal arrangement can be made to refer business to each other, or a more formal network may be created, such as *Lex Mundi,* an association of independent law firms, in a consortium to be able to compete with the large international law firms. Similar arrangements have been made with accounting and public relations firms. These consortia are very efficient in allowing smaller and middle-sized businesses to compete with large service providers in acquiring the local business of foreign companies.

The third most effective way is to *work with other local non-competitive service providers* to share leads and customers. This is particularly effective as the foreign client typically needs the services of several providers when establishing and implementing his/her business in your domestic market.

A fourth way to generate international clients is to work closely with *government agencies* to obtain their referrals. Almost every embassy and/or consulate has a list of local references from doctors and dentists to accountants and law firms. If possible, you should try to be on that list. Departments of trade or commerce on the national or provincial level are also good referral sources. World trade centers are another good source.

The fifth way would be to establish contacts with *nongovernment entities with international interests.* This could be local chambers of commerce, friendship associations or organizations devoted to establishing and maintaining international goodwill. In particular, you may wish to network with geographic, cultural and ethnic associations.

As a sixth way, you will want to establish a good relationship with your *local colleges and universities.* As more students study abroad (particularly in the United States), they bring with them the interest of their parents, and often the business organizations of their parents. Many stay, and need immigration assistance, homes, life insurance, wills, etc.

Finally, you may choose to *advertise.* While straight advertising is not my preferred method, selective promotion can be quite effective. Three examples come to mind. Writing an article of general interest in a publication read by foreign individuals; creating newsletters with topics of interest to your targeted market(s); and placing advertisements in publications you know will be read by your targeted audiences. This might include airline magazines and airport publications.

Serving customers from abroad in your home market is one of the most enjoyable and lucrative ways of entering the international marketplace. We will now move to Method 4, which is exporting from the home country.

REFERENCES

1. Cateora, Philip, *International Marketing*, 8th ed. Homewood, Illinois. Irwin, 1994, p. 419.

2. Erramilli, M. Krishna, "Entry Mode Choices in Service Industries," *International Marketing Review*, Vol. 7, No. 5, 1991, p. 28.

3. Fredrikson & Byron, P. A., *American Lawyers With A Global Perspective*, 1995.

Chapter 7

METHOD 4: EXPORTING FROM THE HOME COUNTRY

INTRODUCTION

It is possible to develop a significant export business without ever leaving the home country because of two significant developments. The first is the growth of various types of organizations willing to serve as the international arm of companies that have not yet developed export or international functions. These organizations range from companies that represent foreign entities desiring to purchase your products, to those that manage your exports, to those that will actually purchase the product at your dock for their own account. These types of organizations are discussed in the following section *"Indirect Exporting from the Home Country."*

The second development results from a combination of changing lifestyles, technological innovations, and movement towards more favorable government regulations. The combination of these events now allow companies to sell directly to end-users through catalogs and direct sales forces without the use of local or foreign intermediaries. This is discussed later in this chapter under *"Direct Marketing from the Home Country."*

Exporting from the home country is usually undertaken by smaller companies that are not yet capable or ready to establish an overseas presence. However, it may also be used as part of an international strategy by larger companies that use the indirect or direct methods to test-market new territories, or as a means to consolidate orders from smaller markets.

INDIRECT EXPORTING FROM THE HOME COUNTRY

In recent times, it is possible that your company may have received any one or all of the following visitors:

- A local agent of a foreign company calls on you desiring to purchase your products on behalf of that foreign company.
- A representative of a local company in a related business or industry calls on you to see whether you are willing to use that company's international network to market your products, that is, to piggyback them on the sales of their own products.
- A representative from an export management company calls on you to see if you are willing to use their services to become the international arm of your company. They request a retainer and/or commission on what sales they can arrange.
- A representative from an export trading company approaches you about purchasing products at your dock that they will subsequently export through their own international channels.

Any one of these visits can result in significant business, but they can also create substantial problems. This section explores the benefits and problems of using indirect exporters. We will also identify the types of indirect exporters and how you can best work with, or avoid, them.

WHY AND WHEN TO USE INDIRECT EXPORTERS

Indirect exporters come in an almost infinite variety that includes manufacturer's export agents, export management companies (EMCs), export trading companies (ETCs), cooperative exporters (piggybackers), resident export buyers, and export commission agents. All have one thing in common—they allow you to export your products abroad *without* making a direct effort from your home country, or require you to appoint foreign intermediaries.

Companies will appoint indirect exporters for the following reasons:

- They lack international expertise.
- They are in the very early stages of exporting.

■ They wish to avoid committing funds and/or personnel to all international markets or to unexplored markets.

■ They wish to test-market their products, and allow for their trade names and trademarks to be known, before making a more serious commitment to the international marketplace.

■ They wish to increase cash flows, economies of scale, and capacity through incremental sales.

■ They desire to leverage the distribution networks and contacts of others.

■ They hope to find a means of warehousing their products abroad without additional costs and commitments.

PROBLEMS WITH INDIRECT EXPORTING

Indirect exporting is not without its costs and its problems. The following list describes some of the key ones:

■ Indirect exports will syphon off some of the gross profit margins through commissions and/or lower selling prices to the indirect exporters.

■ Because indirect exporters are putting your products in the hands of others, they will limit your direct contact with the customers. Additionally, customer feedback, if any, will come filtered through the indirect exporters.

■ Companies using indirect exporters will lose virtually all control over pricing. If the products are priced too high by the indirect exporter, your company may also lose significant sales.

■ It will be difficult to provide product support, and the future market can be damaged.

■ The indirect exporters may relabel the products, which will prevent product identification necessary for continued sales.

■ If exclusivity is granted to the indirect exporter, they may tie up the market for some time with little effort being made on behalf of those products.

■ They may prevent you from building up the knowledge base you will need to sell directly at a later time.

■ While they may increase sales overall, there is no guarantee that these sales will be stable.

■ The company may find it difficult to take over the markets of the indirect exporter when the relationship has ended.

TYPES OF INDIRECT EXPORTERS

All indirect exporters are middlemen between the exporter and ultimate user of the product. In some cases, this role is played by arranging the sale between those two parties; in other cases, the indirect exporter actually purchases the product from the exporter for resale abroad. This section offers a brief discussion of some of the most frequently used indirect exporters.

Export Commissioned Agent

These agents are local representatives that arrange purchases on behalf of their foreign principals. The sale is made between the local exporter and foreign customer. The agent takes his/her commission from the foreign customer.

Export Management Companies (EMCs)

EMCs approach companies with the idea of becoming, in effect, their export departments. Most work on a retainer and/or a commission based on the sales they generate. They are paid by the exporter. A few will actually purchase products directly from the exporter for resale to customers abroad. Depending on the financial arrangements, EMCs will perform some or all of the following functions:

Consulting Services. EMCs will often work with the exporter to determine the best foreign market for their products. This may include market analysis and identification, visits abroad to determine the most appropriate methods of distribution, and providing the exporter with assistance in export administration, product quality documentation, and selection and use of freight forwarders, insurance, banking, and translation services.

Advertising and Promotion. EMCs will work with the exporters to prepare sales literature and, at times, advertisements for use in international markets. They may also represent the exporter at international trade shows and exhibits, and may assist the exporter in locating and appointing international agents and distributors.

Agent Services. EMCs will often locate customers and assist the exporter in arranging the sale.

Financial and Legal Services. EMCs may assist the exporter in determining its international pricing, credit, and financial policies. They will assist in locating banks and in working with those banks to establish letters of credit, site drafts, and other financial instruments. Occasionally, EMCs have a legal capability that could be used to assist in the drafting of terms of sale, agreements, advising, and overseas patent and trademark protection, and in some cases, negotiating on behalf of the exporter.

Purchase for Resale. Occasionally, the EMC will actually purchase product from the exporter for resale to its own customers.

As stated previously, EMCs will essentially become the exporter's export department and sometimes its international division. They are quite useful for small companies, or for companies of any size that do not desire to involve their own personnel in international activities. In appointing EMCs, three factors should be kept in mind. The first is the *selection* of the EMC. EMCs range from people operating out of their homes to fairly large full-service companies. It is estimated that there were over 2,000 EMCs in the United States in 1992, with the number growing rapidly from year to year.[1] Some are capable of performing only limited functions (e.g., quality, real estate, or strategic planning); others only work in certain product types or limited geographical areas. The exporter must factor all of this in choosing its EMC(s).

A second area is that of *cost.* If a retainer is required, then a very clear plan of services by the EMC should be sought before they are formally contracted. If the EMC is going to work mostly, or entirely, on commissions, then the exporter defers costs until sales are made, but runs the risk of the EMC losing interest if sales do not come immediately. Additionally, the exporter has to view the costs of the EMC against what it would have to expend to build its own international function or group.

Finally is the issue of *knowledge and control.* Even if the EMC is functioning well in terms of generating sales, it may be doing so in a way in which the exporter is not learning international business. When the exporter decides that its volumes are sufficient to go it alone, it may have to expend substantial amounts to develop its own functions and establish its own international network.

Because the EMCs compensation often is dependent upon sales volumes, the EMC will probably do what is necessary to maximize that volume without considering the strategic plans of the exporter. If volumes are low or slow in coming, it may lose interest and/or merely become an order taker for the exporter. This will make it difficult for the exporter to plan its manufacturing and/or sales schedules.

In choosing an EMC, the exporter should consider the characteristics cited in the EMC profile of Table 7-1.

Table 7-1
Export Management Company Profile

1. Sufficient size and resources to meet the exporter's needs.
2. Willing to share its expertise and to train the exporter in international business as part of its compensation.
3. Priced its services competitively.
4. Will take the time to learn the exporter's business, including a full understanding of the after-sale requirements of the products.
5. Well established in the community and can provide appropriate references.
6. The EMC/Exporter Agreement should clearly explain what the EMC will provide, including a reasonable estimation on the effort to be spent in promoting the products.
7. Willing to begin on a nonexclusive basis and to earn exclusivity upon demonstrated success.
8. Will not alter or relabel the exporter's products without the exporter's written permission.
9. Has experience in advertising and sales promotion.
10. Has the needed language capability.

EXPORT TRADING COMPANIES (ETCS)

ETCs are, in many ways, similar to EMCs, except that they tend to be larger, and provide a wider range of services. The major difference, however, is that the ETC normally takes title to the goods and services, while the EMC normally services as a commissioned agent. The United States, primarily as the result of the Export Trading Company Act of 1982, allowed ETCs to operate without some of the complexities of U.S. antitrust laws. In the U.S., ETCs are usually formed by the following entities:

Large Companies, such as W.R. Grace, Sears, General Motors, Honeywell, and K-Mart, promote the sale of their own products and other companies' products. Some of these companies have not met with success and have ceased operations.

Trade associations, such as the American Film Marketing Association, have created ETC's to promote the exports of their members' products.

Bank holding companies have also formed ETCs.

Many of the ETC's also engage in imports and in the development of *counter-trade*. One of the most aggressive companies in the area of ETC's in the late 1970s and early 1980s was the Control Data Corporation (now split into two companies—Ceridian and Control Data Systems). Control Data was very active in counter-trade in order to sell their computer systems to countries that could not pay in hard currency, but were willing to pay in product or by some other creative means. One of its most creative projects was in the attempted sale of a computer system to The Hermitage Museum in St. Petersburg, Russia (then Leningrad, U.S.S.R.).

CDC was to provide the computer system required by The Hermitage in exchange for CDC obtaining rights to the sale of reproductions of paintings and art objects that would come from an exhibit of part of The Hermitage's collection in North America. A percentage of the profits derived from the sale of these reproductions was to be applied to the purchase of the computer system. The exhibits were arranged, and then cancelled as a result of the embargo placed on the Soviet Union in 1979 after that country sent troops to Afghanistan.

CDC took its unusual trade approach further by developing a division called Worldtech, whose purpose was to arrange technology transfers between licensors and licensees in different countries in exchange for a part of the technology fees. Worldtech used CDC's vast data services capabilities to "match" technology suppliers with technology users. Both the trading company and Worldtech were dismantled as a result of the downsizing of the company that began in the mid-1980s.

The attempts to develop ETCs in the United States, as illustrated by Control Data's experience, have met with limited success. The Japanese, however, have used trading companies with great success for a long period of time. The trading companies, called *sogo shosha*, are normally part of a much larger group centered around a bank or an industrial group. These groups are called *keiretsu*. In the *keiretsu* system, companies usually agree to become shareholders of each other to build stronger business ties. This is the primary reason for the U.S. Export Trading Company Act of 1982, which sought to level the playing field by removing certain antitrust law considerations, which prevented U.S. companies from building *keiretsu*-type relationships.

Japanese trading companies are normally quite large. In recent years these companies comprised six of the ten largest companies in the world in terms of sales (Mitsui, Marubeni, and Mitsubishi were the top three)[2] This size allows the *sogo shosha* to provide extensive market coverage and allows a small company to access nearly the entire world without building a dedicated international function. In addition to their importing and exporting capabilities, Japanese trading companies have recently become involved in the full range of international business transactions, including the production of goods, the development of strategic alliances and equity joint ventures, licensing, and technology transfer. Korea has also developed several trading companies that are part of huge banking and industrial conglomerates called *chaebol*, which are similar to the *sogo shosha*.

A Word of Caution

Serious consideration should be given before using Japanese or Korean trading companies. First, the mere size of these companies may cause the small exporter considerable concern as to the degree of attention that will be paid to its products and to the level of authority within those companies that it will be able to access when the exporter has questions or problems.

Second, once the exporter's products are in the hands of the ETC, it will be very difficult for the exporter to know what has happened to them. Therefore, it is *not* advisable to use ETCs if the products are technologically complex and/or if they require specific types of manufacture and service.

Third, the exporter should consider whether it makes sense to grant ETCs the right to sell to a market that it may desire to serve directly in the years to come. One reason for this is that it will be very difficult for the exporter to establish the market after the ETC relationship expires, or is terminated, because it will lack knowledge of the market and even the existing customers. Still another reason is that the ETC may try to maximize sales throughout the world without paying specific attention to development of a given market. As a result, market coverage may be sporadic and unorganized, which would create a difficult set of circumstances once the market is to be addressed directly by the exporter in an organized fashion.

One possible solution would be for the exporter to identify those markets that it may desire to approach directly in the near future. These markets could be identified with the assistance of an export management company that could then serve as the exporter's agent for customers in that market. If the EMC serves only as an agent, the exporter will know the customers and their needs and will be able to develop relationships with them that can be used when the decision is made to directly approach the market. For markets not identified for direct sales in the future, the exporter could then use the services of an ETC to purchase products from it in the home country for sale into those markets.

OTHER INDIRECT EXPORTERS

Before discussing direct marketing from the home country, it is useful to point out three additional types of indirect exporters:

Comarketing

Comarketers are also known as cooperative or piggyback exporters. They are normally established international or global corporations that sell the products of other companies along with their own. This type of arrangement is common in the computer, industrial machinery, and electrical products industries, and is found to some extent in nearly every industry.

Comarketers use their direct sales forces, agents, and distributors to offer other company's products. Usually, these products are complementary to their specific lines (e.g., a computer manufacturer may offer software packages or computer peripherals). Comarketers can work as an agent for the exporter or they can purchase products for resale.

If handled properly, both parties can greatly benefit. The small exporter will have access to the marketing network of an established international company. The international company will be able to offer a fuller line of products or solutions to its customers and leverage the costs of its international marketing by receiving commissions, or mark-ups, from products provided by the small exporter. Companies just beginning to export should give serious consideration to this alternative, as should larger companies, in areas where they do not have direct sales forces, agents and/or distributors.

Export Merchants

These are companies that purchase the exporter's products solely for resale on their own account. The exporter will not have direct contact with the customers as they would with the export commissioned agent previously mentioned. This type of relationship may be considered for exporters with the following characteristics:

- The sale of raw materials or perishable products.
- The sale of odds and ends, or products that are past their prime or are being discontinued.
- Occasional sale of state-of-the-art products where it is known that such products will go into territories that are not considered prime by the exporter.

Export Residence Buyers

Typically, these are agents or employees of a particular foreign firm. They normally purchase only for particular needs of the company(ies) they represent. Their purpose is to avoid middlemen and to establish direct relationships with suppliers. In the right circumstances, they can be very beneficial to the small exporter because they will purchase F.O.B. home country and take care of all exporting activities.

DIRECT MARKETING FROM THE HOME COUNTRY

As an alternative to indirect exporters, or perhaps in addition to them, exporters may consider developing a domestic function that sells directly to customers in other countries. This is normally accomplished through either catalog sales or through the use of traveling sales forces who are domestic employees of the exporter.

If this is appropriate for your company, it can serve as a meaningful alternative to all types of international business transactions. However, this form of business does require some upfront expenditures and commitment of human resources, normally in the form of the creation of an export function. While the salespersons would be employees of the exporter's product division, or marketing and sales department, the company will perhaps have to dedicate additional resources and personnel in two general areas:

■ Creating international transportation, insurance, documentation, packaging and labeling and perhaps quality functions.

■ Creating knowledge (perhaps in its legal or tax departments) of export and import licensing, intellectual property and tax planning considerations.

WHY AND WHEN TO MARKET DIRECTLY FROM THE HOME COUNTRY

Because of a combination of changing lifestyles, technological innovations, and the movement towards more favorable government regulations, the possibility of selling your products and services directly to the end-user without the use of local intermediaries is one of the most rapidly growing areas of international business. This is particularly true with the growing use of the Internet® and in the area of *catalog sales of consumer products,* but is also important for those industrial products that must be individually designed to meet unique customer specifications. This type of marketing should be considered when:

■ *The consumer desires or requires purchasing the product and services directly from the manufacturer or retailer.* Catalog sales are now an accepted manner of doing business in North America (including Mexico), Western Europe, Australia, New Zealand, and Japan. In fact, the changing lifestyles of those countries have increased the interest. More and more, consumers desire to purchase products and services in the leisure of their homes. The growing gender revolution has increased the number of two-job families. The availability of phones, faxes, computers, improved delivery services and internationally valid credit cards also increase desire and capability. Finally, catalog sales can reach small towns and rural areas that are not served by major retail outlets.

While consumers of industrial products can normally be served by agents and distributors, those customers who require specifically-designed products and/or complex installation and maintenance services, may prefer to deal directly with the manufacturers to reduce the involvement of middlemen who cannot provide those services and to deal direct in order to protect significant investments.

■ *The manufacturer or retailer desires to increase its revenues and profits while perhaps providing its products and services at a lower cost to consumers.* Even with the additional costs associated with catalog sales (credit card charges, freight and packaging), it may be possible to provide the products and services at a lower cost to the consumer. A recent study showed that because of high retail prices in Japan, a U.S.-based mail-order company was able to provide such items as audio equipment, cameras, kitchen appliances, watches and perfumes at 50–80% of the prices charged in Tokyo. Even more interesting is that some of these discounts were applied to products manufactured by Japanese-based companies.

Even with this competitive environment, it is possible for the mail-order house to reduce its own costs by the ability to order in volume, avoiding the costs of the middleman, and developing effective internal controls. In the area of industrial products, costs can be saved and prices reduced through direct interface with the consumer.

■ *The manufacturer or retailer desires to provide better service and to protect its company name and image.* Better service can be provided through enhanced technology. Computers provide better reporting and instant customer access through the Internet®. Customers can, through hotlines, access service personnel, customer retention, and complaint functions. Cable television stations devoted to marketing can provide domestic and international access. All this might be better than a contact point through a local distributor. Additionally, direct sales can avoid fraudulent marketeers who overpromise and underdeliver. Selection of the wrong marketeer could result in lost markets and worse—the negative impact on the retailers company name and image.

CATALOG SALES

Since the founding, about a century ago, of the now defunct Sears Catalog, catalog sales have been a significant part of the United States market. Direct sales are increasing dramatically outside the United States. Sales to consumers through mail, telephone or door-to-door have increased tenfold in Japan between 1980 and 1990 and over 300% in Germany during the same period. Products now sold frequently through direct marketing are books and magazines, home furnishings, clothing, housewares, and cosmetics. Services include financial services, travel and tourist services, and various forms of insurance.

A whole support infrastructure has been developed for those who desire to sell direct. This includes excellent globally-oriented packaging and delivery services, the availability of good customer lists in almost every major city in the world and the telecommunications systems we have already discussed. While not inexpensive, the continued declining costs of these infrastructure services, coupled with the savings made by avoiding indirect exporters, now makes catalog sales a viable alternative for many companies.

TRAVELING SALES FORCES

Companies, particularly in the industrial products area, should consider the use of direct sales forces located in the home countries to develop international business. Where products are expensive and/or where they have to be individually designed for each customer, these sales forces could be far more effective than agents, particularly where the number of sales per year is limited.

Under these circumstances, even a fairly large company may be able to address all of Asia, Europe or Latin America with one, or a few, persons per territory. These positions, even with the cost of travel, can be more cost effective than having to establish an overseas organization or relinquish some of your margins to agents or distributors. Additionally, these jobs become effective training grounds for the development of international expertise and savvy, which would be required when the exporter decides to expand its international operations.

TAX CONSIDERATIONS

Finally, the home country exporter should be concerned as to whether it might be subject to taxation in the foreign jurisdictions. If the sale is made abroad, certain countries may try to tax a portion of the sale, although this will often depend on the volume and regularity of the sales. If the exporter's employees are subject to foreign jurisdiction (as service personnel or as traveling salespersons), the exporter should be aware of the possibility of taxation of the individual. This often depends on the amount of time spent in the country and the immigration status afforded by the country to the employee. Venezuela, for example, taxes individuals visiting that country for commercial purposes. These taxes are based on where the services are performed rather than the place of payment, and the employee may not be able to leave the country until the taxes are paid.

The exporter should also check to see if its home country provides any special tax benefits to exporters. One example of these benefits is the Foreign Sales Corporation or Shared Foreign Sales Corporation in the

United States, which allows exporters considerable tax savings on their qualified foreign trade income.

Many jurisdictions, including the United States, allow companies to credit foreign income tax paid against their domestic income tax liability. Certain carry-forward and carry-back provisions apply. The United States and other countries also allow certain foreign tax credits for their citizens who reside abroad. The area of taxation is very complicated and because of a broad network of tax treaties that could determine the tax benefits and liabilities, the exporter is well advised to check with its tax experts before undertaking indirect or direct exports from their home country.

Having explored the various methods of building a global business without leaving home, we will now move to examine the six key methods of taking your business abroad.

REFERENCES

1. Daniels, John D. and Radebaugh, Lee H. *International Business: Environments and Operations* (6th Ed.), Boston: Addison-Wesley, 1992, p. 525.
2. "The Wall Fell Down, and the Continent Took Off," *Business Week*, July 16, 1990, p. 111.

TAKING YOUR BUSINESS ABROAD

Success in global business begins at home, but will most likely take you to the far corners of the globe. Most companies begin by working with unrelated partners such as agents, distributors, licensees, and franchisees. As business increases in volume and complexity, some companies take the next step of entering into strategic alliances with persons and companies in other countries. This often takes the form of an international equity joint venture in which two or more companies of different nationalities hold equity (normally stock) in the joint company. Finally, many businesses decide it is better to approach certain international markets by "going it alone." They move to create branches and/or wholly owned foreign subsidiaries to manufacture and market their products.

Part III examines the final six methods of taking your business abroad. They are:

- Using overseas agents/sales representatives to establish markets and find customers (Chapter 8).
- Selling your products through distributors who purchase from you at a discount and then sell in their marketplace (Chapter 8).
- Developing a network of franchises to carry your product name and image abroad in a conceptualized format. These franchises may generate product sales and will generate fees and royalties (Chapter 9).

- Licensing technology to assist nonrelated partners to develop your product, or related products, for their marketplace where it is impractical for you to do so. This also generates fees and royalties (Chapter 10).
- Establishing strategic alliances with other companies to jointly bid and market a complete solution, or establishing effective legal entities with ownership of two or more unrelated companies to meet a market need (Chapter 11).
- Creating your own companies abroad when you have reached the economies of scale sufficient to establish a physical presence. As we will see later, this step is often taken as a measure of security and control by the parent company, which does not exist in the other five methods (Chapter 12).
- Understanding and capitalizing on international trends (Chapter 13).

In examining these final six methods, you should consider the tradeoff between *costs* and *control*. Using agents and distributors are, in most cases, the least expensive methods to take your company global, but, as you will see, they place much of the control in the hands of your business partners. Setting up and running wholly-owned subsidiaries gives you complete control but is usually the most expensive method of global expansion. Licensing and strategic alliances fall somewhere in between. All of these methods may take your business where you want it to be; but ultimately your company must decide how much control it desires and is willing to pay to obtain.

Chapter 8

METHOD 5: SELLING THROUGH INTERNATIONAL AGENTS AND DISTRIBUTORS

INTRODUCTION AND DEFINITIONS

Chapter 5 briefly explored the possibility of becoming an agent or distributor of a foreign company in your home market. This chapter explores in much greater depth, the process of setting up international agent and/or distributor networks. Included are the following topics:

- Why and when to use international distributors and agents
- Advantages and disadvantages
- The selection process
- The elements of the legal agreement
- Maintaining and motivating distributors and agents
- Evaluating performance
- Terminating distributors and agents

Agents and distributors, although somewhat distinct methods of building a global business, have many characteristics in common. Therefore, they are discussed together in this chapter. We will begin by repeating the definitions of distributors and agents found in Chapter 5.

Distributors are independent companies that purchase products (take title) from the exporters for resale to their customers who may be end-users of the products or other intermediaries who then sell to end-users. While sometimes it is necessary to make alterations to the products, distributors normally sell exactly what they purchase. They will assume the risks of buying and stocking the products in the local market and normally will also provide product support and other after-market services. Distributors establish and maintain their own contacts with the customers *including setting the prices they will charge to those customers.* They are also normally responsible for local advertising and promotion.

Agents are also independent companies (and sometimes individuals) who represent foreign exporters and take orders on the exporter's behalf. Agents normally work on a commission basis and are paid when the exporter makes a direct sale to the customer. They do not take title to, or possession of, the goods they represent. *The prices to be charged are agreed to between the exporter and the customer.* Normally, agents do not stock products, nor do they provide pre- and post-sales support to the customer.

WHY AND WHEN TO USE INTERNATIONAL DISTRIBUTORS

Distributors are normally used when a company wishes to establish sales of completed products in a foreign market, but the company determines that market size, and other variables preclude its direct involvement in the particular market.

For a company to consider appointing distributors in a particular market or as a general international strategy, it should consider the following *internal company characteristics:*

- The company does not have, or is unwilling to commit, sufficient management or financial resources to establish its own salesforce or marketing subsidiary, but the company is willing to commit those resources necessary to develop a viable distributor relations function, to train distributors, and perhaps to take limited financial risks in the area of currency exposure, collections, and termination payments.
- The company does not have, or is not willing to acquire, the experience level to allow it to establish its own local operations, but it has,

or is willing to acquire, experience necessary to evaluate and select potential distributors, retain and motivate them, and evaluate their performance.
■ The company has developed, or is willing to develop or contract for certain international services such as export administration, international traffic, credit and collections, and legal services.

If its internal characteristics lead towards using distributors, the company must then consider its *product characteristics*. Distributors may not be suitable for products that are perishable. Additionally, products that are project-oriented, high in price, or designed individually for each customer, are not suitable for distributors. While millions of personal computers are sold each year through distributors, it would be very difficult to convince a distributor to stock a multimillion dollar supercomputer that would have to be specifically configured to meet the needs of the customer, and has a selling cycle of two years. However, the right distributor could be used to handle products of a highly technical nature if it has the right service equipment and properly trained sales and service staff.

The products most suitable for distributors are those sold in short sales cycles, have regular customers, require limited maintenance, and are at prices that will convince a distributor to handle a sufficient local stock. The more commodity-oriented the product is, the more likely it will be suitable for international distributors.

Market characteristics also help determine the viability of using distributors. Is the market size sufficient to allow for local stock? What type of entities would be the customers for the products? For example, if the market consists of only large customers or public entities, it may not be suitable for distributors because the customer would most likely prefer to deal directly with the exporter. In that case, a local agent may be more suitable. What is the competitive situation in the selected market? How price and quality-sensitive is the market? Finally, is the market ready for your company's product?

The next area a company would explore is the *availability of quality distributors* in the selected market. Selecting good distributors requires careful consideration and not all markets will have suitable distributors. Normally, a company will look for a distributor in a complementary line of business with an established reputation and with suitable knowledge of market conditions. The distributor must be able to stock—and continue to restock—sufficient inventories, handle installations, and cover warranty and other after-sale functions. Distributors must also have trained staffs or be willing to have their people trained by the exporter. Finally, although it is difficult to enforce requirements that a distributor carry only your line of products, it is possible to require that the distributor *treat your line as its primary line.* One of the biggest problems faced by small and middle-sized companies is the case where the distributor adds your line to competitive lines, overprices your products, and then effectively locks you out of the market in favor of your competitors.

Finally, a company should pay careful attention to *unique legal and financial considerations* in the target market. Many countries have, in place, distributor termination laws (discussed later), which make it very costly to terminate distributors, particularly if you are doing so to appoint another distributor or to replace distributors with your own sales office. Such laws are common in Europe and Latin America. In a few countries (like Chile), because of anti-monopoly laws, it is illegal to appoint exclusive distributors. Additionally, some countries use their tax laws to discourage distributor appointments in favor of agents (India).

Financial considerations may also impact whether or not you use distributors. Countries with soft currencies and/or poor balance of payment conditions may require approval of certain agencies (normally a central bank) before granting foreign exchange payments in hard currency. Payment terms and cycles may be longer, which may require your company to consider whether to offer better, or different, payment terms. Typically, if a company does offer better terms (e.g., 60-day net), they will increase the cost of the products (or lower the discounts) to cover their exposure.

WHY AND WHEN TO USE INTERNATIONAL AGENTS

Agents are normally used when a company wishes to establish sales to distinct individual customers, or to service customers on a request for proposal (RFP) or project basis.

For a company to consider appointing agents in a particular market, or as a general international strategy, it should consider the following *internal company characteristics:*

- The company must be willing to deal directly with the customer. While an agent may be used to find and qualify the customer, and perhaps even to make the deal, the exporter will ultimately have to deal with the customer in terms of providing the products, collections, and in pre- and post-sales services.

- If agents are used in requests for proposal (RFP), or on a private project basis, the company will have to develop the expertise needed to respond to RFPs (e.g., qualification as suppliers; bid, performance, and warranty bonds; technical negotiations).
- On the other hand, agents do not require the level of training and constant motivation as do distributors.

Agents are more useful when the company has certain *product characteristics*. Products, which are designed for projects, are individually configured for each customer, are expensive, difficult to stock or have long sales cycles, seem more suitable for sale through agents.

The most appropriate *market characteristics* for agents are the opportunity for a few, but larger, sales, and marketing to public agencies. One client of mine, a blanket manufacturer, uses agents in most of the world because it perceives two essential markets. The first are the governments, which prefer to purchase direct from the manufacturer; the second are the large retail outlets (department and discount stores), whose economies of scale would price most distributors (with their mark-ups) out of the market.

The availability of quality agents is equally important, but have different characteristics than quality distributors. In the case of agents, product knowledge and training may be less important than personal contacts. Sales to the military are often arranged by retired officers and sales to large companies are arranged by people who belong to the right clubs, sometimes more than the right professional associations.

Appointment of agents has it its own *unique legal and financial considerations*. In addition to the termination laws that may apply also to agents, a company must be concerned, in some countries (including the United States to some extent) about the benefits provided to employees. Special care must be taken to assure that your agent is not considered to be an employee of your company. To prevent this problem, some countries require agents to register with public authorities as commercial agents. Agents may also raise certain ethical issues, and in the case of the United States, may raise concerns under the Foreign Corrupt Practices Act. While agents do not raise collection issues (because you pay them), a company must be sure that they have established appropriate payment terms with the customer.

The previous discussion relates to the specific decision a company will make regarding the viability of using distributors and agents to approach the international market. What follows is a more general discussion on the pros and cons of using distributors and agents in the international marketplace.

ADVANTAGES/DISADVANTAGES OF USING INTERNATIONAL DISTRIBUTORS [1]

Distributors represent a relatively low risk strategy to enter into international markets. Properly selected and motivated distributors provide you with the following **advantages:**

- A good distributor will provide you with *knowledge of the local market,* which includes how to import into that market and how to sell within it.
- Because the distributor buys and sells for its own account, *the exporter does not have to carry local inventories,* nor is it involved in credit and collections with the end-user customer. However, the manufacturers should be very concerned with the payment terms offered to the distributor.
- Distributors allow the exporter *to avoid, or limit, commitments to unexplored markets, or market segments.*
- Distributors allow the opportunity *to test new products, or to harvest old products* .
- With proper training, good distributors will *install, service, and provide direct warranty service* to the end-user customer.
- With a distributor relationship functioning, the exporter should receive *forecasting competitive information, and solid reports on political and economic conditions in the territory.*
- Use of distributors normally *does not subject the exporter to taxation in the country of sale.*
- Distributors can assist the exporter in *advertising the products in a manner that conforms to local laws, industry standards, and local customs.*

Despite the numerous advantages, there are several **disadvantages** that must be considered before appointing distributors:

- Distributors can *lower your overall gross profit and limit your ability to achieve revenues and profits from after-sales services.* To motivate distributors to sell, you must provide them with a discount from your net export prices. If, or when, the amount of this discount exceeds the cost of other forms of international business transactions, then distributors may not be the best format for international sales. Additionally, revenues and profits, which normally may come from after-sales services (e.g., extended warranty contracts or service calls), could be lost because distributors normally assume this function.

■ Distributors *limit your control of distribution resale prices.* Theoretically, distributors can underprice your products or, more likely, price your products so high that marketshare and goodwill are lost in the name of short-term profits.

■ In a similar vein, distributors *limit your communications with the users of your products.* Distributors will not want to provide you with customer lists to avoid you dealing directly with their customers.

■ The last two points may *make it more difficult to obtain direct knowledge of the foreign market and significant developments in that market.*

■ Market opportunities may be missed if the distributor *is spread too thinly or doesn't carry the inventory and support personnel to service the market.*

■ Finally, the relationship may be subject to dealer protection legislation *that makes it difficult and costly to terminate distributors.*

ADVANTAGES/DISADVANTAGES OF USING INTERNATIONAL AGENTS

The major **advantages** associated with using agents are as follows:

■ A properly selected agent can provide you with *key contacts and intelligence* in achieving business in the territory. All the product knowledge in the world, solid local stocks, and a top-notch service organization will not result in much business unless the individual(s) representing your product have the contacts to introduce the customer to your company and its products.

■ Agents require *less training and background* than distributors. Therefore, your initial time and financial commitment is lower and you do not have to invest resources unless you are close to an actual sale.

■ Agents do not purchase for resale, therefore you have *more control over pricing and direct interface with the customer.*

■ The proper agent allows you *to reach markets that cannot be met through distributors.* As previously stated, an agent is a better choice for large, public, or project sales.

■ The use of agents normally *does not subject the exporter to taxation in the country of sale.*

The key **disadvantages** in using agents are:

■ *Poor product knowledge and lack of understanding of your market* could result in poor performance by the agent.

■ Agents are *more difficult to evaluate than distributors.* A distributor normally has stores, employees, and a track record. Agents may be only as good as the most recent government or private company leadership. It is more difficult to evaluate claims of agents, and longer-term relationships are less likely.

■ Once a sale is about to be made, *the company may have to make a larger commitment to the customer.* It will assume collections, installation, maintenance, warranty and other pre- and post-sales activities.

■ The company may *have to provide a local stock of product and spare parts,* and it may have to commit its own sales and technical personnel to the territory or hire local companies to provide those services.

■ Agents may be more difficult to control and may tend *to create additional termination problems* in the areas of labor and commissions. One of the biggest problems associated with agent termination is to determine whether a partial commission may be owed if the business closes shortly after termination.

SELECTING DISTRIBUTORS AND AGENTS

Finding good distributors and agents takes planning and persistence. Time spent up-front getting organized can pay large dividends in the future. This section deals with some time-tested mechanisms for locating, qualifying, and selecting good distributors and agents.

The first item to consider is to *organize your international marketing network.* Begin with the development of a general international business plan and develop from it a series of regional plans. You may find, for example, that North America is best served by your own sales force, Europe by distributors, and Asia and Latin America by agents. To arrive at such a decision, you need to have some estimates of market size and potential and an evaluation of customer types. Some of the medical product companies, for example, find that while distributors may be appropriate in Wisconsin and Texas, agents may be better in Europe where buying decisions tend to be made, in part, by government agencies for their national health services. Within each region, you should identify target countries and decide the best marketing channels to use in the countries selected.

Once you have some idea where you would like to be present, the next step would be to determine what you are looking for in the "ideal" distributor and agent. This could be accomplished by developing Distributor and Agent Profiles, as shown in Tables 8-1 and 8-2. You may consider prioritizing these general characteristics to meet your own profile.

Table 8-1
Distributor's Profile

1. Local reputation as a fair and honest business organization.
2. Assertive sales organization.
3. Financially able to carry adequate stocks and expand to match the growth of your industry.
4. Knowledge of the marketplace; ability to inform you regularly on current market conditions.
5. Handles complementary products, but does not handle products that are directly competitive.
6. Able to forecast market changes.
7. Has well-trained sales and support staff and is willing to seek additional training, where necessary.
8. Willing and able to think longer-term by being competitive whenever economically possible.
9. Advises the exporter on any customer resistance encountered in the marketplace.
10. Sells features and quality in addition to price.
11. Informs exporter of safety requirements, specifications, and the requirements imposed by governments or industry standards.
12. Pays on time.
13. Establishes relationships with other suppliers necessary to offer customers complete solutions.
14. Considers your line of major importance, and devotes primary effort to it.
15. A candidate for future technology transfer and/or an equity joint venture (that is, be able to grow with the exporter).

Table 8-2
Agent's Profile

1. Local reputation as a fair and honest business organization.
2. Registered with the appropriate professional associations and governments as an agent; is incorporated.
3. Does not demand advance commissions.
4. Knowledge of the marketplace and customers it would solicit.
5. Experience in the customer's industries or activities.
6. Able to assist the exporter in qualifying for government projects and other RFPs.
7. Has language translation capabilities which are available to you as part of the agreed-to commission.
8. Able and willing to assist in post-sales problems and opportunities.
9. Able and willing to assist in collections.
10. Does not handle competitive products.
11. Advises exporter on any customer resistance encountered in the marketplace.
12. Sells features and quality in addition to price.
13. Considers your line of major importance and will devote considerable effort to it.
14. A candidate for future technology transfer and/or an equity joint venture.

After you have developed your profile, the next step would be to develop a **Distributor and/or Agent Application.** These applications need not be elaborate, and can be prepared with your word processing and desktop publishing capabilities. The application should be *kept simple.* Clients of mine have used such applications as a result of inquiries they receive from prospective distributors and agents. Once sent out, they find the return of the application to be around 30%. This is good, because it represents one of the best screening processes available to you. Any prospective distributor or agent who do not complete the application are clearly not willing to devote significant efforts to your products.

The Distributor and Agent Applications help you with the selection process in the following ways:

■ It forces the prospective distributor or agent to put its intentions in writing.

■ It helps identify the geographic focus. You would certainly question a distributor who wants all of South America but only has offices in Bogota, Colombia.

■ It provides knowledge of their banking relationships and some credit history. Do not appoint a distributor or agent who will not provide banking references.

■ It helps to identify inventory requirements.

■ It helps to determine business fit.

■ It provides information on support personnel.

■ It helps to determine advertising capabilities.

If at all possible, you should consider developing a **Distributor or Agent Brochure.** I recommend a marketing approach to your legal agreements. This approach combines an export-oriented, user-friendly brochure with a more limited, plain-language legal agreement. The brochure, which is incorporated by reference into your agreement, might include the following points:

■ A cover page with a picture of your corporate headquarters or products, which may be entitled "The XYZ Company and Its Distributors: A Global Discussion of Policy and Procedure."

■ A description of your company.

■ A description of your ideal distributor (agent) requirements, e.g., qualifications.

■ A description of the responsibilities of the exporter and of the distributor (agent) in regard to such items as stocking, sales promotion, and being competitive.

■ A discussion of your company's general policies on such things as minimum billing, profit margins, competitive products, conditions of sale, use of trademarks, and allowable product alterations and modifications. This could be done in a Question and Answer format. For example, your Q and A on minimum billings might read as follows:

Q. Why do we have a policy of minimum billing?

A. Our policy of minimum billing was established to help us pay the cost of the invoicing and clerical work associated with processing each individual order. We encourage our distributors (agents) to place orders of economical size to help us give them better service. For further information on minimum billing, see the applicable Conditions of Sale.

The next step would be to develop your *legal agreements,* which are covered in the section that follows.

After you have completed all of your documentation, you now need to consider *how to locate the best distributors and agents.* What follows is a list, and brief discussion, of the various location sources.

- If you are a U.S.-based company, start with the U.S. Department of Commerce (DOC), which has services such as the *Agent/Distributor Service (ADS),* a personalized overseas search for interested and qualified distributors and agents in a specific country. The DOC also has the *Trade Opportunities Program (TOP),* which provides sales leads, and the *National Trade Data Bank (NTDB),* which provides trade and export promotion data. Other countries have government agencies which provide similar services. Consider also, state or provincial trade offices.
- Contact and use international chambers of commerce. For example, the U.S.-Mexican Chamber of Commerce in Mexico City can provide leads for both U.S. and Mexican companies.
- Check with in-country trade and professional associations.
- Advertise in foreign trade association publications.
- Participate in trade shows.
- Contact companies in related businesses. For example, computer software companies can check with hardware suppliers. Suppliers of equipment to banks and financial institutions can check with other suppliers.
- Check, if possible, with competitors. Sometimes they are willing to tell you who not to choose.
- Check business directories and yellow pages, which are available at most major libraries in your home country.
- Check with international banks, accounting and law firms, and other service providers.
- Develop your own list of personal contacts.

Finally, once you have developed your documentation and have located your potential distributor and agent, be sure to *follow through.* Besides careful evaluation of distributors/agents applications, try, if time and finances allow, to visit each potential distributor or agent before appointment. Nothing is better to qualify distributors and agents than visiting their facilities. If you weigh the cost of such visit against the appointment of a poor representative of your business, it will be clear that this is money and time well spent.

ELEMENTS OF AGREEMENTS

It is now time to get your lawyer involved in the process of assisting you to develop the appropriate legal agreements. In this regard, you can take two general approaches.

The first approach would be to *develop a complex legal instrument that covers every eventuality*. While this approach provides you with the greatest legal protection, it does have several distinct disadvantages. These include:

■ The initial costs in developing the agreement(s).

■ Additional legal costs and time lost in having to negotiate the agreement(s) if the distributor or agent balks at the complex legal document(s).

■ The problem of having the agreement(s) conform to different types of legal systems. In common law systems (U.S., Great Britain, Canada, and Australia) contracts tend to be more detailed because of the greater ability to change relationships by contract. In civil law systems (Western Europe and Latin America) contracts tend to be shorter and less detailed because many of their provisions would be covered in the various codes of the countries. The potential distributor or agent in a civil law systems may then ask why do we need such a detailed agreement when most items are covered in the codes.

If you decide to use this approach (most large companies do), then it is suggested that the agreements be printed (to leave the image that you cannot change a printed form), but that provides for a section where amendments can be added to fit individual legal and commercial issues and concerns.

The second approach would be to *develop a letter agreement,* which is relatively short (3 to 5 pages), but which covers the key legal issues. This is recommended for companies that are at the beginning of the relationship with each distributor or agent. It should be limited to a short time period and not be renewable except by another signed agreement. After the initial period, the company may then choose to move to the more elaborate agreement. In the meantime, this letter agreement allows you, with a high degree of legal security, to test the relationship before committing to the time and effort necessary to develop the longer-term relationship.

At this point, I would again like to return to the idea discussed earlier of developing a distributor or agent brochure. Use of these brochures in conjunction with agreements, whether complex documents or letter agreements, is very helpful in establishing what I would call the "marketing approach to legal agreements." In this method you shorten the legal agreement by covering some of its terms in the brochure and then incorporating the brochure as part of the agreement. This approach not only allows you to show the potential distributor or agent that you have carefully thought out the relationship, but it also helps to shorten negotiations and begin the relationship on a positive note. Whichever approach you use, your agreements should include the elements described in the following section.

Elements of a Distributor Agreement[2]

DEFINE TERRITORY

Geography, Industry, and Customer Type

Territory can be defined by geography—France or Paris south of the Seine; by industry—the automobile or chemical industry; or by customer type—retailers only or government agencies.

The Right to Sell Outside the Territory

You can deny such a right, but may run up against antitrust laws found in such places as the United States and the European Economic Community. It would be better to define that the distributor cannot sell where:

- The exporter has other distributors.
- The distributor does not have offices and employees.
- The distributor does not have the capabilities to inventory, service and maintain the product.

DEFINE PRODUCTS

The exporter must determine which products the distributor would be allowed to handle. It should reserve the right to add and delete products upon proper notice. It should define what rights, if any, the distributor has to future products. Finally, the exporter can require the distributor to maintain facilities and spare parts to provide for maintenance and other post-sales activities.

STATEMENT OF NONEXCLUSIVITY OR EXCLUSIVITY

Generally, exclusivity should be avoided unless there are some very favorable concessions that the distributor is willing to make. When appointing distributors, think of your marketing rights to a given territory as a valuable commodity that should not be given lightly. Remember, once an exclusive distributor is appointed, you cannot appoint another distributor in the territory (and once you appoint a nonexclusive distributor, you cannot appoint an exclusive distributor).

If you must appoint an exclusive distributor, you should require the following of the distributor:

■ Distributor exclusivity to you.

■ A large initial order paid for upfront.

■ Annual quotas broken down by geography, product, industry and customer type.

■ Reserve your right to sell directly into the territory and to appoint agents.

■ Provide for favorable arbitration terms.

Finally, if you reach an impasse with your potential distributor over exclusivity, think about the following two strategies:

■ Begin with exclusivity that will become nonexclusivity if the distributor does *not* meet the quotas agreed to.

■ Begin with nonexclusivity, with an agreement not to appoint another distributor in the territory for the initial term. If the distributor meets the initial term quotas, it will become exclusive for all subsequent terms in which the quotas are met.

DEFINE TERMS AND RENEWALS

Define a specific term. This should be sufficient to determine whether the distributor will perform to the satisfaction of the exporter without tying up the market for too long. In general, you can treat renewals in two ways:

- Automatic renewals for the same term if one party doesn't inform the other party, within a certain time, that it wishes to terminate.
- Fixed terms with an automatic termination, unless a new agreement(s) is signed.

The first approach is recommended only if the company has established proper monitoring mechanisms and can react fast enough to terminate nonperforming distributors. The second approach has the disadvantage of requiring constant negotiations where the distributor may make additional demands.

DISTRIBUTOR'S RESPONSIBILITIES AND OBLIGATIONS

In this section, you define the distributor's rights and obligations to the exporter. Whether you use the complex legal instrument or the letter agreement, this is one area where you can considerably shorten the agreement by using a distributor brochure (see pp. 101–102). Areas to be covered here are:

- Distributor must have adequate facilities and capable personnel.
- Distributor must agree to make its best efforts to promote and sell your products.
- Distributor must agree to maintain adequate inventories.
- Define whether or not the distributor has the right to appoint sub-distributors or dealers.
- Define the advertising and promotions responsibilities of the distributor.
- The requirement that the distributor keep the exporter informed of market conditions in its territory.
- Distributor's responsibilities in regard to translations. Language of communication.
- Limitations on territorial expansion and competitive lines.

EXPORTER'S RESPONSIBILITIES AND OBLIGATIONS

- The exporter will produce and provide quality products, parts, and accessories.
- Sufficient supplies of the product will be available when distributor orders so that lead time will be minimized.
- Suitable warranties will be provided on the products. Distributor will handle warranty claims.
- The exporter will create promotion and advertising tools that will be made available to the distributor.
- The exporter will keep the distributor up on technical developments and product changes. Training will be made available to the distributor.
- The exporter will keep the distributor up on its new marketing and sales plans.

TERMS AND CONDITIONS OF SALE

Still another candidate for the distributor brochure, the exporter should consider the following:

Prices

Prices can be established by offering the distributor a percentage discount off of an international list price or by establishing fixed distributor prices. If the *discount from list price is chosen,* consider developing an international list price distinct from your domestic list price. The international price list can be higher (normally 10% to 20%) to cover the additional costs of doing international business (export licensing, travel, long-distance calls, etc.). Therefore, if a normal distributor discount is 30%, and your international list price is 10% higher, the distributor, in effect, would have a discount of 23% off from your domestic list price. (30% off of $110 is $77, which is a 23% discount from $100.)

Fixed distributor prices have the advantage of allowing you to tailor your prices to the volume of each market and to prevent your distributor from easily learning the different margins you apply to your respective products. The biggest difficulty of this approach would be if your product is in an industry where prices change rapidly, especially if prices are declining.

In either case, you should consider offering the distributor additional discounts if they exceed quotas. This can be accomplished either on a stairstep or forward-looking (based on projected volume) basis. In lieu of (or in addition to) lower prices, other incentives can be offered to distributors who meet or exceed their goals. These might be free training, an advertising allowance, free travel, or prizes.

Price Changes

Your agreement should provide a mechanism for changing prices. As a general rule, lower prices should be passed on to the distributor as soon as they become effective, perhaps even for orders already accepted, but not delivered, in order to motivate the distributor to schedule regular orders.

If you intend to raise prices, you should consider providing the distributor the opportunity to order at the lower prices for a short period of time (say 30 days from the price increase announcement). However, be sure that you also specify a delivery date to prevent the distributor from ordering at the lower price for delivery six months from the date the price change goes into effect.

Order Terms and Conditions

Define the form of your purchase orders and the means by which the exporter will accept the order. Also, define the terms for cancellation of orders and for returns of defective products.

Shipment

Define whether variations from standard packaging are allowed and if so, at whose cost. Define the terms of shipment (e.g., F.O.B., F.A.S., C.I.F., etc.), and when risk of loss is transferred to the distributor.

Payment Terms

With new distributors, payment before or upon delivery are common payment terms. You might also consider establishing a letter of credit mechanism if shipments are to be on a regular basis. Open account is not suggested, unless you have had experience working with the distributor, because it will be difficult to obtain security interests in the products outside your home territory (see Table 3-2, pp. 37–38).

INTELLECTUAL PROPERTY

First, register all important trademarks and servicemarks in the countries in which you will operate. Normally, in dealing with distributors, your major concern would be over how your trademarks are used by the distributor on their business cards, stationary and catalogs. This should be controlled very closely to assure that your distributor does not leave the impression that it is more than a distributor. Your agreement should require that before your distributor uses your trademarks in any way, you have the right to review such use with approval necessary in writing. You may also be concerned on how and where your products are presented in their catalogs and other marketing literature and can require submission of proofs of these documents subject, again, to your written approval.

WARRANTIES AND LIMITATION OF LIABILITIES

Clearly state your warranties and your policy on warranty service. It is probably best (and a good distributor should demand it) that warranty service be provided in the territory by the distributor. Then the distributor should deal with you on warranty claims.

Pay special attention to warranty durations. If the normal lead time for distributor sale is three months, and your warranty, say of twelve(12) months, runs from delivery to the distributor, you may put yourself at a competitive disadvantage. Consider, in this case, providing a warranty that runs eighteen (18) months from shipment, or twelve (12) months from sale to the end-user, whichever comes first. If possible, have the warranty run from the time the product is first placed into use.

This allows the distributor sufficient time to sell the product without requiring you to extend your normal warranty. Finally, make clear to the distributor that if they extend the time or quality of your warranty, that they are responsible unless they first obtain your written permission to do so.

Try to limit your liability to the extent possible, but in all cases limit your liabilities to no more than the amounts received from the distributor in the past six months, or year.

TERMINATION

Termination is discussed later in this chapter.

GENERAL TERMS AND CONDITIONS

Confidential Information

Define what you consider to be confidential and require the distributor to, at least, use the same standards of confidentiality as it would use with its own confidential information.

Force Majeure

Consider adding force majeure (acts beyond the control of the parties) language. Allow for termination with cause if the force majeure goes beyond a certain period. You may wish to include acts of government in your force majeure language.

Export/Reexport

If you are a U.S.-based or COCOM-based company, be sure to include the proper export/reexport language.

Notices

Define specifically how and to whom notices will be sent. Also, define when the notice becomes effective (Common law—when placed in the mails; civil law—when received). It is probably best to provide for notice at the receipt of a facsimile.

Governing Law and Arbitration

Your agreement should define which law and covenants governs the distributor relationship. Where possible, select your own law. Consider using arbitration in all cases, but particularly where you cannot achieve your own governing law.

United Nations Convention on the International Sale of Goods (1980)

Check with your attorney as to whether it applies. If it does, you may wish to opt out of the Convention, because it has not been properly tested in the courts (see p. 236).

EXHIBITS

These are probably the most important part of the agreement, and will certainly be the sections that are most frequently referred to by both the exporter and distributor. Typical exhibits are:

- Products and price list
- Territory
- Technical specifications
- Quotas
- Distributor brochure

ELEMENTS OF AN AGENT AGREEMENT

DEFINE TERRITORY

The previous section on "Elements of a Distributor Agreement" contains most of the elements that are also used in an agent agreement; however, in the case of agents, you may wish to pay special attention to defining your territory in terms of customers or projects. This will force your agents to focus on the key customers/bids and leave the remainder of the market open for using other agents, distributors and/or direct sales.

DEFINE PRODUCTS

See previous section on "Elements of a Distributor Agreement." With agents, you may choose to limit your product offerings to those which make sense to the projects defined with your agent.

STATEMENT OF NON-EXCLUSIVITY OR EXCLUSIVITY

If you are going to tie the agent to specific customers or projects, it may be practical to grant your agent exclusivity as to those customers and/or projects, to avoid customer confusion and problems of splitting compensation.

DEFINE TERM AND RENEWALS

One of the biggest problems of dealing with agents is determining their rights upon expiration or termination of the agreement. The following hypothetical case illustrates the problem.

Hypothetical Agent Termination

ABC, Inc., a US-based company, has tried for some time to win a large project with a Brazilian electrical utility. On April 1, 1995, it signed a one-year agency agreement with Pardo Ltda., a Rio de Janeiro company, to represent it in dealing with the electrical utilities. The parties agreed on three (3) jobs for Pardo to work on during the year:

- Light São Paulo—a U.S. $5 million job.
- Cia Energia, Rio de Janeiro—a U.S. $10 million job.
- Cia Electricidade, Porto Alegre—a U.S. $6 million job.

Pardo was to receive a 6% commission on each job, payable as ABC receives its money.

ABC won the Light São Paulo job on December 1, 1995. It was paid U.S. $500,000 up-front, with the bulk of payment due when the job is completed (around February 1997). It lost the Rio de Janeiro job because, ABC believes, poor representation by Pardo. The Porto Alegre job is pending an answer, with ABC's bid complete, and an answer is expected by August 1, 1996.

Pardo received U.S. $30,000 as part of the up-front payment from Light São Paulo. The agreement between ABC and Pardo expired on March 31, 1996, and on April 1, 1996, ABC appointed Cia Lamenza to take over the work on the São Paulo and Porto Alegre jobs, and to identify other prospects. Lamenza is also to receive a 6% commission payable as ABC is paid. ABC won the Porto Alegre job in February 1997. The agreement was silent on commissions to be paid after expiration.

With these "facts" in mind:

- Is Pardo entitled to any additional payments on the São Paulo job? If so, how much?

■ Is Pardo entitled to any payments on the Porto Alegre job? If so, how much?

This is a typical, but very difficult, result of not planning for what happens upon expiration or termination. From Pardo's point of view, they have a very good argument for additional compensation on the São Paulo job because they were of direct assistance in obtaining the job. Additionally, Pardo has a good argument for some compensation on the Porto Alegre job because they probably arranged the contract and assisted in assuring that it was bid in the proper manner. If the agreement is silent, a Brazilian court may award Pardo full commissions.

One issue that should be considered by both parties in appointing agents is the agent's importance and value in obtaining the original order vs. its continuing relationship with the customer. Once this is determined, the agreement should be drafted to reflect that decision. One solution might have been to place a value on obtaining the order (for the sake of discussion—earned commission of 50%), and a time limit for the order to close to determine whether the 50% is earned. In this case, if you use 50% for obtaining the order, and define obtaining the order that it must be closed within six months of expiration or termination, then the following result would take place:

■ São Paulo—Pardo would be entitled to U.S. $150,000. Because $30,000 had already been paid, the other $120,000 would be paid as ABC receives its money. Lamenza, the new agent, would then be entitled to $150,000 for continuing to service the customer.

■ Porte Alegre—No commisssion to Pardo because the order closed after the six-month period.

■ The agreement signed with Lamenza should define compensation due to Pardo, and limit Lamenza to that part not paid to Pardo.

AGENT'S RESPONSIBILITIES AND OBLIGATIONS

■ Assist exporter in sales and promotion in accordance with the exporter's orders and instructions.

■ Inform exporter of all pertinent news related to market conditions and other factors related to the subject matter of the agency.

■ Be loyal to the exporter, and cooperate with it in the achievement of its objectives without regard to its own personal interests.

■ Assist the exporter in collections.

■ Serve as the translator, where necessary, to serve the agency's subject matter.

■ To preserve confidentiality.

EXPORTER'S RESPONSIBILITIES AND OBLIGATIONS

■ To furnish the agents its price schedules along with a reasonable supply of its catalogs and brochures.

■ To determine the agent's discretion, if any, in adjusting prices.

■ To pay the agent's compensation in a fair and timely manner.

■ To define what happens upon termination or expiration.

■ To preserve confidentiality.

COMPENSATION

It is recommended that the term *compensation* is used rather than *commissions*. This is particularly true for U.S. companies that must be concerned about the Foreign Corrupt Practices Act.

It is also recommended that compensation be tied to collections to assure the agent's role and intent in assuring the exporter will be paid.

TERMINATION

Termination is discussed later in this Chapter.

NON-EMPLOYEE STATEMENT

When appointing agents, particularly in civil law countries, special attention should be paid to assuring that the agent will not be able to claim employee benefits upon expiration or termination. As suggested previously, this is best done by appointing corporations as agents and assuring, where possible, that your agent register as such with the local authorities. In any case, your agreement should always contain a statement that the agent is not an employee.

GENERAL

See "Elements of a Distributor Agreement" earlier in this chapter. Also, U.S.-based companies should include a provision in general terms and conditions that the agent agrees to abide by the U.S. Foreign Corrupt Practices Act.

EXHIBITS

- Territory—customer list
- Products and prices
- Compensation and how earned

MAINTAINING AND MOTIVATING DISTRIBUTORS AND AGENTS

Now that you have appointed your distributors and agents, you need to consider how to go about maintaining the good ones and motivating them to do a better job. My experience has taught me that this is better done with a whole lot of "carrots" and only an occasional use of the "stick." This section discusses some of the key techniques for retention and motivation.

DEVELOPING LOYALTY

Perhaps it goes without saying that a loyal distributor or agent is a motivated one. The best way to create loyalty is to make your *distributor or agent ("marketeers")* feel as if they are part of your company. This is primarily accomplished *by developing identification with your company and its products*. The first step in developing such identification is to make the marketeers aware of your goals and principles.

One way to convey these principles is by joining with others to make a statement of ethical business practices. Such an example is *The Minnesota Principles*,[3] which is an attempt to develop a set of international standards for trading partners. One of these principles is a Stakeholder Principle, which applies to customers. It reads as follows:

Customers

We believe that our customers are not only those who directly purchase our products and services, but also those who acquire them through authorized market channels. In cases where those who use our products and services do not purchase them directly from us, we will make our best effort to select marketing and assembly/manufacturing channels that accept and follow the standards of business conduct articulated here. We have a responsibility:

- To provide our customers with the highest quality products and services, consistent with their requirements.
- To treat our customers fairly in all aspects of our business transactions, including a high level of service and remedies for customer dissatisfaction.
- To make every effort to ensure that the health and safety (including environmental quality) of our customers will be sustained or enhanced by our products or services.
- To respect the integrity of the cultures of our customers.

Marketeers should also be kept informed as to the future planning of the company, and their ideas on products, marketing and general business enhancement should be solicited. The exporter should not assume that it understands all local markets and defer, when reasonable, to ideas from their marketeers. Finally, the exporters should place its marketeers on its mailing lists, making sure that what they receive is selective to reduce costs and so not to overwhelm the marketeers.

Other ideas to improve loyalty are:

- Provide free product samples and advertising items bearing your company name and logo. High quality pens are very well received as are items of clothing, particularly hats.
- Hold regional marketeer conferences, either in the territory, a popular vacation spot, or at the headquarters.
- Hold contests tied to performance where the marketeer either competes with itself or with others to achieve certain prizes.
- Assist in training on an ongoing basis.

GOOD COMMUNICATIONS

As already alluded to, motivating marketeers is, in part, created *by good communications*. Communications can be greatly enhanced by developing a "Distributor (Agent) Relations" function that is responsible for direct day-to-day contact with your marketeers. If possible, each marketeer should be assigned to one employee whose job is to represent it in dealing with the company. The marketeer should be visited on a regular basis if time and revenues allow. Additionally, free or inexpensive trips to the home base by the marketeer should be provided. One local company we support has made it a policy of inviting the top salesperson in each of its distributors for a free week of training and conferences to its headquarters in the U.S. This is not a high budget affair (they can fly coach, share hotel rooms, and have a small per diem), but it offers a real incentive for those in the field to have an international experience that would normally not be available to them. This company has found this to be a more effective manner of increasing sales than to provide the same program to the owners or top management of their distributors.

IMPROVE MARKET SHARE

What we are talking about here are *mechanisms to improve market share*. Perhaps the key mechanism has been already discussed—that of using training programs to develop skills. Still another mechanism is the development of joint advertising campaigns—on a local and international level. You should also work with your marketeer to develop local language catalogs, product brochures, and promotional literature.

One time-tested mechanism to improve market share is to work with your marketeer to provide other ways in which it can earn money with your products and after-sale services. Because your marketeer probably is determined to be the full service arm of your company in the territory, it should be encouraged to push the sale of upgrades, spare parts and components, and after-warranty service contracts. Additionally, you might want to encourage your marketeer to establish alliances with manufacturers of complementary products so that your products can be offered as part of a wider variety of goods and services.

Finally, some companies are able to convince their distributors to participate in *inventory control programs*. In such programs, distributors agree to keep certain levels of inventory (perhaps determined by product) in exchange for a somewhat larger discount. The distributor must then automatically order replacement products at certain times as their inventories need to be replenished, and agree to a certain volume of purchases within a certain time period. While its margin may decrease slightly, the exporter is better able to gear-up for production while keeping their own inventory levels down. Most likely the exporter will make up for lower margins with better economies of scale.

PRICING, FINANCE, AND CREDIT

Maintaining and motivating marketeers can also be accomplished through the use of pricing, finance, and credit. While this applies primarily to distributors, it can also be used, in certain cases, with agents. This begins with an attempt to understand credit conditions in the industry, and the territory. In high inflation countries, credit may be expensive and hard to come by and collections may be slower. In this case, the exporter may consider rewarding its financially secure distributors with better credit terms in exchange for a slight upward adjustment in pricing to cover its local cost of money. Additionally, the exporter should also be aware of, and consider the payment cycle of, large customers and governments. In the last half of 1994, the Mexican government slowed down its payments to reduce inflation and preserve foreign exchange. Anyone who has worked with Mexico also knows that the government pays very slowly, just before and after presidential elections. In any case, you should always consider rewarding distributor success with better credit terms.

As mentioned in the pricing section of the Elements of Agreement, the exporter should consider developing staircase, provisional or forward-looking pricing. Staircase pricing awards greater sales but is difficult to administer unless the staircase is continuous. Provisional and forward-looking pricing (which essentially establish a discount level at the beginning of the period based on estimated sales) are also difficult to administer unless there is a proven track record and the distributor is willing to accept lower discounts if they do not meet the quotas.

Also mentioned previously was the necessity to establish clear policies on price adjustments, including giving the distributor proper time to order before price increases, and immediately pass on price reductions.

The exporter should also be aware of government policies that may restrict imports of finished goods to protect local industry and create jobs. If your distributor is up against such policies, you may wish to consider allowing it to undertake some amount of final assembly to reduce tariffs and provide greater margins. This is discussed more fully in the "Technology Licensing" (Chapter 10).

EVALUATING PERFORMANCE OF DISTRIBUTORS AND AGENTS

At some point, ideally on a regular basis, you will wish to evaluate the performance of your international marketeers. Clearly the best and easiest way to do this is *by setting targets and evaluating performance based on these targets.* At the beginning of the relationship this is not so easy. The exporter, upon entering new markets, will have only a rough idea of what the market for its products and services will be. The distributor or agent is likely to exaggerate its future performance to obtain the appointment. Therefore, in setting the initial targets, the parties should look to a combination of establishing a target that meets the business needs of the parties but is realistic in terms of market size and conditions. Sometimes, when given a choice, it is better to appoint the marketeer who offers a more reasonable target, but has all the other elements of a good marketeer (see Tables 8-1 and 8-2) than to appoint a marketeer with a wildly optimistic target but who is lacking in some of the key elements. Setting meaningful targets is not only important in evaluating marketeers but is also critical upon termination or expiration of the relationship. This is discussed in the next section of this chapter.

Another evaluation technique is to *compare competitors sales with those made by your marketeers.* If your distributor or agent carries competitive products, you can ask them how they are doing with these products. If there is a problem, and they are good marketeers, they should tell you before you ask. If they do not carry competitive products, consider asking your marketeer to obtain the market intelligence in their home market.

Another good method of evaluation is by *setting and monitoring inventory turnover rates.* Suppose you agree that a distributor should have a target of U.S. $500,000 for a year, and the distributor places an initial inventory order of U.S. $125,000, with the idea that the inventory should turn over every three months. In that circumstance, the exporter should review its order patterns on a quarterly basis to assure that the distributor orders range in the U.S. $100,000 to $150,000. If they do not, the distributor either is not meeting its sales goals, or is allowing its inventory to be depleted, which may negatively impact its ability to make future sales.

Evaluation techniques also include *monitoring requests for direct sales coming from the territory.* If the customers are coming to the exporter directly rather than purchasing from your distributor, or ordering through your agent, something is wrong. Either your marketeer is not advertising correctly so that customers are unaware of its presence, or customers are dissatisfied with its prices and/or service. As a rule, requests for direct purchases should be referred to your marketeers in the territory, but the right to make direct sales should be preserved to enable the exporter to sell if the marketeers are not performing properly.

Besides requests for direct sales, *the exporter should look for other unusual order patterns.* It should be very concerned if the marketeer requests that an order be shipped directly to a customer outside the territory ("drop shipped"), because the exporter should be concerned about protecting its other marketeers and because, in such orders, inventory requirements are avoided and customer service may be minimized. If a distributor requests drop shipments within its territory, this should also raise concern. An occasional drop shipment to meet an unusually large order may be acceptable, but a continual pattern of drop shipments probably means that the distributor is not carrying adequate stocks and/or is using drop shipments as a means to increase its margins. (Distributors normally are given larger margins than agents because of their additional responsibilities.)

If possible, the exporter should also *spot check the customers, or potential customers, of your marketeers.* This can normally be accomplished on trips to the marketeer's territory where joint marketing visits are established. Additional evaluation techniques are in *reviewing the quantity and quality of the marketeer's advertising* and in checking the *willingness of the marketeer to accept training.* Good marketeers should be pleased to send samples of their advertising to the exporter, and be willing to increase their knowledge base through regular training programs. If not, this is a sign that they may not be paying proper attention to your product and service.

TERMINATING DISTRIBUTORS AND AGENTS

With all the proper methods described in this chapter, you should be able to appoint an excellent network of marketeers. However, no person or company is perfect and conditions change so that it is sometimes necessary to allow your relationships to expire or to terminate them before the end of the term. Special attention should be paid to termination (especially at the beginning of the relationship as a preventive measure), because termination is often difficult and if the proper measures are not taken, can be very costly to both parties. Usually, termination by the exporter is necessary because of poor performance or because the exporter wishes to move to another method of serving the market. However, as the following two examples show, you should always expect the unexpected. These examples are actual cases:

Example 1. You have had an excellent relationship with a distributor in a Central American country for almost a decade. The distributor is a family business run almost exclusively by the father. The father is killed in an auto accident. The widow and the children take over the operation, but are unable to maintain the level of sales, which then begin to decrease dramatically. The exporter decides to terminate the distributor and appoint another.

The country you are dealing in has a tough law on distributor termination for terminations without "just cause." Although significant reduction of business is considered just cause, the family notifies the exporter that it plans to bring a legal action to recover indemnities for failure to terminate for just cause. This case was settled by the parties because the exporter feared the possibility of facing the widow and her children in a local court.

While the settlement amount was small, it would not have to be paid except for the unique circumstances of the case.

Example 2. A U.S. company is about to acquire a German company to augment its existing lines and to give it a large presence in the European marketplace. The German company had a twenty-year successful relationship with a distributor in Belgium. The U.S. company does not need the distributor because it has a sales office in Belgium and desires to serve that market directly thorough its own sales force.

Belgium has one of the toughest distributor termination laws in the world. The U.S. company did not undertake proper due diligence and acquired the German company before it terminated its Belgian distributor. It is now responsible for terminating the distributor. It is not just cause in Belgium to terminate a distributor to replace it with your own sales force. In fact, the law was designed particularly to avoid that eventuality where a local company creates a market and goodwill, and then is terminated.

In this case, the U.S. company was forced to settle this problem with a payment to the Belgian distributor in the middle six figures in U.S. dollars. Proper due diligence could have avoided the problem by forcing the German company to terminate the distributor before the purchase of the company closed.

This example serves as a good bridge for the analysis that follows. If you are a small company, or if your middle or long-term strategic plans contemplate the sale of your company, you might consider the fact that *the improper appointment of marketeers may actually lessen the value of your company to perspective purchasers.* In Example 2 proper due diligence would have resulted in either the German company terminating the distributor beforehand, or in a reduced price for that company so that the buyer would have funds to terminate the distributor. In either case, the value of the German company to the U.S. company would have been lessened.

The following discussion is based on trying to prevent or limit termination problems, to the extent possible, at the time you enter into the relationship. It is based on asking, and answering, three questions. These are:

- At the beginning of the relationship, ask what conditions could exist in the future that would make it necessary or desirable to terminate your relationship with the marketeer?
- What are the commercial and legal obligations you are making to the marketeer? Where are they coming from? What might you be liable for?
- How can you plan ahead to limit those obligations?

WHY TERMINATE?

Before entering into a marketeer relationship, the exporter should consider what might be the reasons in the future where it would choose to allow its agreements to expire, or to terminate them.

One reason to move away from marketeers is when you wish to *replace them with your own sales office, or with your own manufacturing or assembly operations in the territory.* This is of particular concern in the large markets. You decide to enter the market through marketeers, but it is reasonable to assume that if the marketeer is successful, you will then consider increasing your margins by using your own sales force, and perhaps later, by making the products in country to supply that sales force. If this is within the realm of the possible, you might consider the appointment of a marketeer that can grow with your needs and desires in the marketplace. For example, should you desire your own sales force in the future, would it be possible to acquire the marketeer's company as part of your sales force in the territory? Is the marketeer sophisticated enough to be your licensee or joint venture partner? These factors should, at least, be considered upon appointment.

Another common reason for termination would be *to replace an existing marketeer with another marketeer.* Because penalties imposed by some countries for unjust termination are tied to the marketeer performance, it is relatively simple, in almost every country, to terminate the truly *poor performers,* although occasionally even a poor performer might try to convince a court that it has made considerable effort to build goodwill and therefore is entitled to something, even if it has not sold much of your product.

The more difficult cases would be with the *adequate performers.* These fall into two categories:

- Those who miss targets, but still generate sales. For example, a distributor who purchases U.S. $350,000 per year against a target of U.S. $500,000.
- Those who may be making their targets but, in the view of the exporter, which should be supported by significant data, are not performing up to the potential that exists in the marketplace. That is, they may be making the U.S. $500,000 target, but the exporter is convinced that another distributor could generate U.S. $1,000,000 in revenues.

In the first category, the marketeer may still be able to argue, and perhaps prove, unjust termination if they can show that the target(s) established were unrealistic, or that business conditions in the country resulted in their inability to reach a target. This will depend on general economic and specific industry conditions, but as a general rule, 50% of the target is probably somewhere near the line that distinguishes the "poor" from the "adequate" performer.

The second category is the most difficult. In these cases, if the law requires, it will almost always be necessary to pay termination indemnities. This will finally come down to a business decision for the exporter—Is it willing to pay those indemnities to appoint a stronger organization? In a later section methods of reducing termination indemnities are discussed.

Finally, the exporter may wish to terminate a marketeer simply because *it no longer wishes to be present in the market.* This may be because the market generates insufficient volume to justify the expense, because of a change in government, or because the existing government has imposed conditions (e.g., exchange controls or local content requirements), which make it difficult, or impossible, to operate in that market.

In some countries that protect marketeers, the simple decision of leaving the country may not be sufficient to meet the standards of just termination, and indemnification may still be sought by the marketeer. In this case an exporter may decide to ignore court-awarded indemnities (if they have no assets in that country), because it will be difficult to have a court decision in the marketeer's country recognized by a country where the exporter has assets. This approach works often, but presents a risk if the exporter should ever try to reenter the market.

UNDERSTAND YOUR COMMITMENTS

Another area to be understood before appointing marketeers, is *the nature and type of commitments you will be undertaking upon termination.* In some countries, these are quite limited. This section discusses those countries in which termination payments may be necessary. We will review both the form and substance of the commitments.

Form

A substantial number of countries have developed laws and regulations to protect marketeers from unjust termination. These laws and regulations are designed to protect local marketing companies against foreign exporters who use the local company(ies) for a period of time to develop the market and create goodwill for the products and services of the foreign company, only to replace them at the end of the period with their own local sales offices. In principle, these laws and regulations may serve as a mechanism to protect local companies against foreign intrusion. Unfortunately, and in reality, these laws have been greatly abused, and in some cases have resulted in foreign companies having to pay outrageous sums of money to replace marketeers with other marketeers, or to replace marketeers with their own sales force.

Just to be clear, it is possible, everywhere, to terminate marketeers. The issue is not the ability to terminate, but the monetary costs associated with it.

These laws and regulations are generally found in some Western European countries (including Germany and France), Central America, parts of South America, and parts of the Middle East. Although the United States has no federal laws on the subject, about half of the states have some regulations covering agents, distributors, or both. In general Asia is free from such laws and regulations, although countries like Korea do have some restrictions on the use of agents. Check with your attorney in each case.

Many countries have a specific piece of legislation or a regulation that covers the subject. Other countries (Argentina and Venezuela, for example) bring together specific parts of their civil, commercial and labor codes to reach the same results. A common name given to these laws and regulations are "Dealer's Acts."

Substance

In describing Dealer's Acts we will discuss what areas they cover, how just cause is defined, and what liabilities to the exporter might result from terminating a marketeer without just cause.

Coverage

Generally, Dealer's Acts cover agents, distributors, and all variants of those two market channels, including dealers, jobbers, manufacturer's representatives, original equipment manufacturers, and value-added remarketeers. There are some exceptions. For example, Brazil protects agents but not distributors (directly), while Belgium protects distributors, but subscribes generally to the EEC rules regarding agents, which are not as onerous.

Because most of these countries apply the civil law system, it is possible to prove the existence of marketing agreements through actions and oral statements, even in the absence of a contract. The Dealer's Acts generally cover both goods and services.

Because almost all Dealer's Acts are designed to protect against foreign companies, it is interesting to note that a local subsidiary of a foreign company usually are considered a foreign company. Therefore, a foreign company cannot avoid the Dealer's Act in Belgium by establishing a wholly, or majority-owned, subsidiary in that country, which then appoints the Belgian distributor.

Definition of Just Cause

Dealer's Acts allow for termination without indemnities if the marketeer can be terminated for *just cause*. However, just cause is difficult to prove, and must be based on one or more of the following reasons:

- Non-performance of essential acts or omissions of acts that substantially and adversely affect the customers of the exporter.
- Material breach of contract.
- Fraud and abuse.
- Gross ineptitude or negligence.
- Disclosure of confidential information.
- Misuse of intellectual property.
- Significant diminution of business.

Liabilities for Unjust Termination

If it is determined that the marketeer has been terminated without just cause, the exporter will be required to compensate the marketeer for this termination. In some countries, this may also apply on expiration:

Basic indemnification formulas. Depending on the country in which the termination took place, two general types of indemnification formulas are used. In some countries, an *expert* will be appointed by the court to determine the indemnity. The expert will examine the marketeer's efforts to accredit the exporter's products and services in the territory, examine the volume of sales, and try to place a value on the goodwill created by the marketeer in the territory. It is in the area of goodwill where the court will have considerable discretion to increase the amount of the liability to be paid to the marketeer.

In the other countries, *a monetary formula tied to sales or profits and the duration of the relationship* will be applied. A typical formula, for example, will look at the average profit generated by the marketeer from its business with the exporter in the past five years and then apply a one-year average of profit over those past five years, as follows:[4]

Duration of Relationship	Years Profit Awarded
1–5 years	1 year
6–10 years	2 years
11–15 years	3 years
16–20 years	4 years
20+ years	5 years

If the arrangement is less than five years, the court will award one year's profit based on the average profit during the duration of the relationship.

Purchase of unsalable merchandise. In most cases, the court will also determine a value for inventory remaining with the marketeer, and require the exporter to pay that value. The exporter will have the right to recovery of the unsalable merchandise.

Labor obligations. If the marketeer was forced to terminate personnel as the result of the unjust termination, the exporter may be responsible for the costs of termination of those personnel. In countries with strong labor codes, this can be a significant number.

Failure of exporter to pay. If the exporter decides not to pay the awarded indemnities, the marketeer and/or the court has four basic alternatives:

- Seize exporter's in-country assets.
- Try to enforce the judgment in a country where the exporter has assets.
- Prohibit exporter from appointing other marketeers.
- Close the border to future importation of exporter's products and services.

PLAN AHEAD

Termination problems can be lessened by planning ahead. This can be done by pricing your products or controlling commissions to create a termination reserve. This is a particularly good strategy in countries where time percentage formulas are used. For example, in Brazil, agents are entitled to one-twelfth of their entire commissions for the entire length of service (8.33%)[5]. In this case, the exporter can reserve one-twelfth of the commission paid as a possible termination payment.

In addition to creating reserves, the exporter may be able to reduce its potential liabilities by considering the use of some or all of the following twelve clauses in its marketeer agreements:

1. *Arbitration*

Take the issue out of the courts and put it in the hands of arbitrators who are more likely to make unbiased awards. The International Chamber of Commerce and the United Nations Commission for International Trade Law (UNCITRAL) Rules are good choices.

2. *Governing Law*

Try to specify the law of the country of the manufacturer, or a third country that does not have a Dealer's Act.

3. *Future Legislation or Regulations*

Have the agreement automatically terminate one day before any negative future legislation comes into effect.

4. *Bankruptcy*

Have the agreement automatically terminate if the marketeer files for bankruptcy or any other form of court protection concerning creditors.

5. *Material Default*

Define material default to include such things as continuing failure to meet quotas, late payments or non-payment, or misuse of intellectual property. Make a material default an automatic grounds for termination.

6. *Non-Exclusivity, and the Right to Sell Direct*

In this case, you may not need to terminate, but merely appoint another, and let your existing marketeer continue its operations, or keep your marketeer, but begin to sell direct. Be careful here, because some countries may determine those actions, under certain circumstances, to be an effective unjust termination.

7. *Assignment*

Automatic termination applies if marketeer assigns its rights to others without the exporter's written permission.

8. *Material Change of Ownership and/or Management*

Automatic termination, if either occurs. This can avoid the situation mentioned previously when the owner was killed and the widow took over.

9. *Reserve the Right to Terminate Without Cause*

Upon written notice; this normally would not work in Dealer's Act countries, but when coupled with an arbitration clause, and if the notice period is reasonable (3 to 6 months), it may be effective.

10. *Fix the Term, and Require New Agreement for Each Term*

This would be of considerable assistance in certain European countries, where nonexclusive marketeers become exclusive if, in certain circumstances, time has past and no other marketeers are appointed.

11. *Non-Employee Statement*

This is essential for agents, and may be of some assistance with distributors, in countries where termination costs of the distributor may become the responsibility of the exporter.

12. *Repurchase Requirements*

This is helpful in defining the method and price by which the exporter repurchases the products upon expiration or termination. It may also make good business sense if you no longer wish the former marketeer to have access to your products.

While these twelve clauses are helpful in limiting liabilities, they are far from perfect. Exporters must simply be aware that appointing marketeers may have the additional cost of termination, and should plan for it as a cost of doing business. You should plan ahead, but don't rest assured.

REFERENCES

1. See Business International Corporation *201 Checklists: Decision-Making In International Operations,* New York: BIC, 1980, 22nd Checklist, pp. 29–30.
2. A good model Distributor Agreement can be found in International Chamber of Commerce ("ICC"), *The ICC Model Distributorship Contract (Sole Importer—Distributor),* Paris: ICC, 1993, 21 pp.
3. Minnesota Center for Corporate Responsibility, *The Minnesota Principles: Toward An Ethical Basis For Global Business,* Minneapolis: University of St. Thomas, 1992, (no ISBN number), copies available through the Center. Call 612/962-4122.
4. Panama, Executive Decree 344 of 1969.
5. Law No. 4886 of December 9, 1965, as amended.

Chapter 9

METHOD 6: INTERNATIONAL FRANCHISING

INTRODUCTION

The European Economic Community Regulations defines a franchise as follows:

> "Franchise means a package of industrial or intellectual property rights relating to trademarks, trade names, shop signs, utility models, designs, copyrights, know-how or patents, to be exploited for the resale of goods or the provision of services to end users."[1]

Franchising is one of the most rapidly growing areas of international technology transfer. Long a standard way of doing business in the United States, where one-third of all retail sales are made by franchisers, franchising is now an important business component in nearly every country in the world.[2] Effective franchises have been created in hotels and motels, soft drinks, car rentals, fast foods, automotive services, recreational services, business services—such as print and sign shops, home maintenance, and numerous other areas.

While franchising is basically a form of technology transfer and licensing, it has some of the characteristics of distributors (e.g., sale of goods and services, after-sale responsibilities, training and stocking requirements). The essential part of a franchise, however, is the transfer of certain industrial or intellectual property rights related to trademarks, servicemarks, trade names, shop signs, utility models, designs, copyrights, know-how or patents that are to be exploited for the resale of goods or the provision of services to end-user customers. Overall, franchising has four common elements. They are:

1. Independent business parties: The franchisor and franchisee are distinct and independent from each other except for the franchise relationship, the major exception being company-owned stores.
2. The goods and services are sold or offered in a regularized fashion as part of a network established by the franchisor.
3. The use of the franchisor's trademark, tradename, servicemark or other intellectual property.
4. Compensation is received by the franchisor from the franchisee in various forms, including up-front fees, royalties linked to sales, and special fees for assistance provided by the franchisor.

As Philip Cateora, the author of one of the most important books on international marketing, states, franchising, when it works, is the ". . . effective blending of skill centralization and operational decentralization."[2]

METHODS OF FRANCHISING

There are five major methods used by franchisors in establishing franchise relationships.

DIRECT INVESTMENT—THE COMPANY-OWNED STORE

In this case, the franchisor establishes a direct investment in each country where it will commence operations, normally by establishing a subsidiary company that sets up its own store(s). This will be accomplished when the franchisor:

■ Desires to approach the market directly.
■ Is unable to locate good franchisee candidates.
■ Wishes to establish itself in the marketplace first and then sell its already-established stores to local companies at a profit.

While clearly the most expensive manner to establish franchise operations, this method allows for complete control, and also for the greater potential profit.

MASTER FRANCHISE

In this method, the franchisor establishes a relationship with one company and grants it the right to establish franchises in the selected country or territory, either on its own, or by giving it the right to sub-franchise. The master franchisee will be responsible for all of the duties of the franchisor in the territory, including collections of royalties and fees from the sub-franchisees, if any.

JOINT VENTURE

In this method, the franchisor creates a subsidiary in the territory, which is partially owned by other entities—at least one of which is a local party. The subsidiary then creates company-owned stores, licenses others, or undertakes a combination of the two.

APPOINTING OF FRANCHISEE(S) BY THE PARENT COMPANY

In this case, the parent company, or a regional first-line subsidiary, makes a direct appointment of franchisees on a case-by-case basis in one or several territories. No local subsidiary of the franchisor is created. This is probably the most common form of international franchising.

DIRECT LICENSING

This form of franchising is closer to a more traditional technology transfer. In this case, the franchise arrangement may cover only the use of trademarks, trade names, and servicemarks, and the sale of a key component of the product. This form is very common in the soft drink industry, where the franchisor grants use of the intellectual property, along with the sale of syrup, which is then used by the franchisee, normally a bottler, who manufactures the final product.

WHY AND WHEN TO USE FRANCHISING AS AN INTERNATIONAL STRATEGY

The franchising method is normally used when a company has some valuable intellectual property and methods it believes can be used across international boundaries. Additionally, it will be used when the company feels it is stronger in the development of the product than in the international skills necessary to market the product in other economic and/or cultural environments.

For a company to consider using the franchise method, it should consider the following *internal company characteristics:*

■ The company (except for the direct investment strategy) does not have the resources or desire to invest heavily in overseas markets.

■ The company has explored, and rejected, the distributor method.

■ The company has determined that traditional licensing will not work.

■ The company normally works through franchisees in its home country, and has developed the appropriate methods and techniques.

Franchising is also dependent upon *product characteristics* of the company. The use of franchises does not make sense if the company manufactures or sells components or products that alone do not lend themselves to franchising. For example, a manufacturer of computer peripherals will not normally establish a computer store, but could become a supplier to franchised computer stores. The same would be true of manufacturers of printing presses or food condiments. Most franchises are established in their home market as distinct operations that are primarily market-driven rather than product-driven. This would not, however, stop a potato grower or marketeer from establishing a separate company that creates a fast food concept based on potatoes as its primary offering.

Market characteristics also help determine whether to franchise. Franchisors of self-service laundries or cleaners may not be able to successfully compete in countries where labor-saving devices and time saving are unnecessary, due to the availability and low cost of labor. Culturally, the market may not be ready for the type of franchise envisaged. Pepsico's Taco Bell division had to give very careful consideration to taking its American-style Mexican food into Mexico City where consumers perceive the food differently and where there are many restaurant alternatives. Even if successful, as apparently Taco Bell is in Mexico, Pepsico also had to consider what their franchise might do in replacing numerous family restaurants that are major sources of employment in a country with high unemployment and under-employment.

Finally, *legal and financial considerations* must be examined. The United States and the European Economic Community have very strict laws that favor the franchisee. Canada has no national franchise legislation, but the Provinces of Alberta and Quebec do. In Japan, franchises are regulated by very tough laws. These laws sometimes make it difficult to establish controls over franchises and also protect the franchisee against such things as franchisor marketing studies that may exaggerate market potential.

Financial considerations include the problems of obtaining royalties and other payments from soft currency countries, and a greater financial exposure (than, say, straight distributors), if the franchise is inadequately funded or does not work. While distributors may be costly to terminate, it is even more difficult to close franchises that do not work because of the exposure to the value of intellectual property if the company is forced out of the market. A poor franchise might have to be taken over by the franchisor, which would then be pushed into a territory where it had no desire to make direct investments.

ADVANTAGES/DISADVANTAGES OF USING THE FRANCHISE METHOD

ADVANTAGES

■ Assuming that the company has already developed its franchise system in the home country, this strategy will then offer it the opportunity to enter into the international marketplace with a *low capital investment*. Many times the up-front fees paid by the franchisee will more than cover the initial costs of locating and appointing them. Thereafter, if all works smoothly, the company will then enjoy a steady stream of revenues that it can take to profit or use to build its markets in other territories.

■ Franchising allows a company to be present in markets where it is necessary for a local party to be very close to the customers. It allows for international skill centralization with local operational decentralization.

- Because the franchisee is more likely to make a larger investment than a distributor, they will tend to be more dedicated than a distributor, which may have multiple lines and less at stake.
- Franchising is a very effective method to ascribe the company's trademarks and servicemarks in the territory.
- Franchising is often the first type of retail business to enter into the emerging market economies. Because of lack of marketing knowledge and practice, the former republics of the old Soviet Union, China, Vietnam and Eastern Europe, are excellent candidates for franchises.

DISADVANTAGES

- If the company has not developed its franchise system, or if this system must be fine-tuned for the international marketplace (e.g., laundromats in countries where there are few washing machines or dryers), the cost to develop franchises may be very high in the preparation of control procedures and marketing strategies.
- Franchising requires substantial involvement of the franchisor (or headquarters in a company store) to encourage and enforce product quality, service and standardization.
- Franchisors may be subject to possible financial and/or legal exposure if franchisees are provided with improper information or are forced to close because of underfunding, poor products and services, or other reasons.
- Franchising is closely tied to an understanding of cultural considerations. Donut franchises have had difficulties in England because that country's citizens were unwilling to replace their traditional pastries with American-style donuts.
- Because franchisees do not export, and are much more likely to import, there may be problems in getting paid in soft currency countries or any country that applies exchange controls.
- Finally, as implied above, franchises are much more difficult to abandon once they are established, because more than just money is at stake. The franchisor must also consider the commitments made to the franchisee and the value of its intellectual property, which may be impaired by an unsuccessful attempt to reach a new market.

SELECTING FRANCHISEES

Before selecting franchisees, a company must do more advanced planning than it would do for agents, distributors, or traditional licensing.

Because franchisees deal directly with the end-user customer, and because the products associated with franchising are more culturally sensitive, the franchisor must have developed its own understanding of the local market and not rely solely on information provided by its potential franchisees.

Additionally, a franchisor needs to more carefully examine its potential franchisees than it might its potential distributors. Having adequate unencumbered capital and a good status in the community are important elements in franchisee selection. The Franchisee Profile of Table 9-1 offers some of the key elements to look for in the appointment of franchisees. Chapter 5 includes a Franchisor's Profile (Table 5-4), and some information that would be of use to potential franchisees.

Table 9-1
Franchisee's Profile

1. Sufficient unencumbered capital for up-front costs and operations.
2. Local reputation in the community.
3. Intense consumer market knowledge. Particular knowledge in store location.
4. Industry and product knowledge.
5. Ability to conform to operations and procedures of the franchisor.
6. Ability to work with the franchisor in resolving market and product-unique problems.
7. Ability to expand its operations, if successful. If this does not appear likely, exclusivity in a market should not be awarded.
8. Knowledge of local personnel practices and issues.
9. Ability to make optimistic, yet reasonable, market projections.
10. Understanding of the value and ability to protect the franchisor's intellectual property.
11. Willing to accept products and services from the franchisor.
12. Willing to participate in advertising programs.

ELEMENTS OF A FRANCHISE AGREEMENT

Franchise agreements will obviously depend upon the laws of the countries in which they will operate. However, all should include at least the following elements:

DEFINE TERRITORY AND SITE LOCATION

With franchisees, as distinct from distributors, the territory is almost always tied to a particular geography. However, such geographical rights could be for only one store at a particular location, or they could define a given geography but limit the number of stores that could be established in that territory. Site location is critical and probably must be determined collectively by the franchisor and franchisee. One United States fast-food franchise failed in the Japanese market because of its insistence in locating its store near highway exits. Although this strategy normally works in the spacious United States, it did not make a lot of sense in countries with short driving distances and rapid trains.

GRANT OF LICENSE

Besides territory and site location, the grant of license should consider:

■ Exclusivity or non-exclusivity. When a given geography is selected, it is normal to grant exclusivity subject to the establishment of a certain number of stores within a given time period. Provision should be made to move to non-exclusivity if the franchisee is unable to meet those commitments. The franchisor should also reserve the right to open its own stores if commitments are not met.
■ Rights to sub-lease, if any.
■ Franchisee's right to downstream refinements or improvements, if any.

TRADEMARKS, AND OTHER INTELLECTUAL PROPERTY

This issue of confidentiality is not as critical with the trademarks, servicemarks, and trade names granted to the franchisee. The critical issue is how they will use such items.

Confidentiality, however, is very important for the trade secrets associated with the franchise (e.g., content of food products, or sales techniques), and breach of such confidentiality should be a material ground for termination.

TERM

Clearly specify the term of the agreement. Consider the possibility of early termination if goals are not met, but give the franchisee considerable time to cure any problems. While automatic renewals are sometimes used with agents and distributors, they are more common with franchisees. However, the agreement should specify the conditions for renewal (e.g., not in default, current in monetary obligations), even if the renewal is automatic.

TRAINING AND ASSISTANCE

Clearly identify the training and assistance provided. If necessary, make a certain degree of training a prerequisite to opening the business. Define the cost of that training and assistance, and carefully monitor that the programs established are being followed.

PURCHASE OF GOODS AND SUPPLIES

Where possible by law, and desired by the franchisor, require the purchase of goods and supplies either directly from the franchisor or from designated suppliers. Where the law prohibits such requirements (EEC), or where the realities of business preclude it (e.g., high duties, sanitary standards, perishability, or heavy transportation costs), set every specific standard in quality, size, shape, contents of the products, and supplies that will be purchased by the franchisee from third parties.

ADVERTISING AND SALES PROMOTION

Require franchisee to participate in your advertising programs and, if relevant, charge it a fee to cover a part of global advertising. Also, require the franchisee to meet your advertising and promotion standards, and insist that all local advertising must be subject to your written approval.

ROYALTIES AND OTHER FEES

Royalties

These are normally tied to the gross sales of the franchisee, limited only by taxes and other government charges.

Other Fees Include

■ Franchise Fee—the basic fee to become a franchisee, which includes the right to establish the store(s) in the territory, use of intellectual property, and initial training. This is normally an initial payment.

■ Revenue-based Fees—charged on the overall revenues of the franchisee.

■ Advertising Fees—part of your global budget.

■ Training Fees—for continued training.

■ Product/Service Enhancement Fees—which are charged when products/services are enhanced or new products/services are offered to the franchisee.

RECORD KEEPING AND REPORTING

Establish the nature and type of records to be kept, and the times at which such records must be reported. Reserve reasonable audit rights.

QUALITY CONTROL

Establish quality standards, and how they are to be controlled. Reserve reasonable audit rights.

UNIFORMITY

Could be part of quality controls.

INSURANCE

Determine what is needed, and require franchisee to obtain and keep all the proper insurance.

ASSIGNMENT

Specify that assignment of any type is not allowed without written permission of franchisor. Grant franchisee right of first refusal to acquire the franchise upon attempt to assign, or for other reasons.

STORE/BUSINESS CONSTRUCTION AND MODIFICATIONS

If a store or business has to be constructed or modified before commencing operations, be sure that all style and quality standards are met. The same would be true for modifications necessary after operations are begun.

RESTRICTIONS ON BUSINESS

The franchisee's right to modify its business should be closely monitored to prevent distortion of your image, products or services. However, be aware and considerate of necessary local modifications which are needed to meet local considerations. In Japan, you may have to allow for smaller stores or adaptation of the products to meet local tastes (e.g., squid pizza). In Germany, you may have to allow beer to be sold while wine may be necessary in France.

MAINTENANCE OF THE FRANCHISE RELATIONSHIP

In no area of international business transactions is the question of maintenance so important as in franchising. There is no question that the franchisor must have a high level of commitment and significant level of control over the franchisee. The franchisee is likely to be the weaker part of the two, not only financially, but also in knowledge level. Additionally, there is far less possibility of the replication of the product or system for a franchisee than a licensee. Overall, a good part of what the franchisee pays the franchisor is for continued commitment and support.

Ideally, the franchisor wants the franchisee to learn its techniques, provide sufficient royalties and other payments, and carry the franchisor's message to the customers. This can only be accomplished if the franchisor has developed the proper techniques and "culturalized" them, to the extent necessary to the local market. There are no substitutes for clear, understandable procedures and organization guides, viable training and advertising programs, and consulting services. The franchisor must make sure the franchisee has learned all of its techniques and will continue to apply them throughout the relationship.

Franchising is a new industry, and global franchising is still in its infancy. The legal system has not yet caught up with the process except initially to provide protection for franchisees against unscrupulous franchisors. However, the law seems to be moving to provide assistance in supporting "reasonable" franchisor requirements. Recently, a French court upheld the termination by McDonald's of a French franchisee who failed to meet McDonald's cleanliness standards, even though it met the less stringent standards of the local health codes.[3]

Franchising is one of the most rapidly growing areas of international business transactions. The next few years will not only bring new laws, but also the development of international standards and codes of ethics. As the most information-intensive of all the transactions, it will be the most likely to continue its development in both form and content in the years to come.

The most important element to be considered in franchising is that both parties to the arrangement make deep and long-term commitments to each other. This makes international franchising a particularly challenging method of global business, but one in which the greatest opportunity is likely to exist.

REFERENCES

1. European Economic Community (EEC), *Regulation No. 4087/88-30* of November, 1988, 1(3)a.
2. Cateora, P. R., *International Marketing*, 8th ed., Homewood, Illinois. Irwin Publishing, 1993. pp. 331–332.
3. Daniels, John D. and Radebaugh, Lee H. *International Business: Environments and Operations,* (6th ed.), Boston: Addison and Wesley, 1992, p. 554.

Chapter 10

METHOD 7:
TECHNOLOGY LICENSING

INTRODUCTION

This chapter explores how *intangible property crosses borders through technology licensing.* It covers the following areas in regard to licensing:

- Methods of international licensing
- Why and when to use licensing as an international strategy
- Advantages/disadvantages of licensing
- Selection of licensees/licensors
- State objectives in technology transfer
- What to license
- Revenue sources
- Elements of license agreements
- Maintenance of a license relationship

The process of licensing across national borders can be defined as follows:

International licensing is normally a contractual arrangement in which the *licensor* (granting company) grants access to its technology, patents, trademarks, copyrights, trade secrets, know-how, and other intellectual property to a foreign *licensee* (receiving company) to be used by the licensee in exchange for a fee and/or other considerations. This grant may be in the form of a direct sale of the rights, or be limited to a certain period of time.[1]

Technology licensing is a viable alternative to the exportation of finished products through intermediaries (export trading companies, agents and distributors) or to the various types of equity involvement (joint venture and direct investment), which could be chosen as an international strategy. This strategy *can be selected on its own as a global strategy* or as part of a broader international strategy, which might include licensing in only selected markets while applying other methods to other markets.

Additionally, *licensing may also be a component of another international strategy.* For example, a license(s) may be needed to allow agents or distributors to use certain trademarks, servicemarks or copyrights. It is also often an integral part of an equity joint venture and sometimes the agreed-to value of the technology is used as part of the equity investment. Finally, many companies use intercompany licenses to protect the intellectual property of the parent company that is held by the subsidiary, and to allow for payments by the subsidiary to the parent of certain license fees.

METHODS OF INTERNATIONAL LICENSING

There are five common methods in which technology is transferred through licenses. These fall into two general categories — licensing alone and licensing as part of another *transaction.*

LICENSING ALONE

Sourcing

In this case, the licensor might provide technology and other resources (e.g., raw material and/or components) to a manufacturer abroad, which will manufacture either a completed product or more advanced components and send them back to the company for final assembly or sale in its home market or abroad. The foreign manufacturer is normally not charged a fee for the technology, and is not permitted to use it for other than sourcing purposes. It, however, either receives a fee for its work or is allowed to resell the components or finished products back to the licensor for a profit. (See discussion of Sourcing in Chapter 4.)

Licensing to an Independent Party

In this case, the licensor will license the technology to a foreign licensee to use the intellectual property and/or know-how to make its own products for sale in its home and/or other agreed-to markets. In exchange for those rights, the licensee will pay to the licensor a fee (normally called a royalty), which is usually based on the sale, by the licensee, of the products resulting from the technology. The licensor may also receive other payments, which could result from management, training and consulting fees. These will be discussed in more detail later in this chapter.

LICENSING AS PART OF ANOTHER TRANSACTION

Joint Venture

Licensing may be used with an equity joint venture in two general ways:

- As part of the transaction in much the same way as you would license to an independent party (that is, the licensor charges fees to the joint venture which is the licensee).
- As part of the licensor's equity contribution to the joint venture. Here the parties will agree to the value of the technology as part of the total worth of the joint venture. For example, two parties agree to create a 50/50% equity joint venture with a value of U.S. $2,000,000. The licensee may contribute its share (U.S. $1,000,000) in cash, real property and equipment. The licensor could value its contribution in cash, capital goods, components and technology licenses. In this case, for the sake of discussion, the parties agree to place a value on the technology of U.S. $200,000. This would mean that the licensor would receive its 50% for the license rights plus U.S. $800,000 in other contributions. Normally, if done in this manner, the licensor may not be entitled to additional royalties.

DISTRIBUTOR/AGENT LICENSE

The licensor may need to grant certain rights to distributors and/or agents for the purpose of allowing those entities to use its trademarks, servicemarks and copyrights in the use of business cards, stationery, brochures and catalogs. This license can be included as part of the distributor or agent agreement (it normally is), or by a separate document if the rights granted need to be distinguished from the general marketing rights. Companies using distributors and agents should be aware that the granting of those license rights might require the agreement to be registered and/or approved by a government agency in the home country of the distributor or agent.

INTERCOMPANY AGREEMENTS

Here the licensor will grant to its subsidiaries or affiliates abroad the rights to certain intellectual property. This is done for a number of reasons:

- To identify only those rights which the parent wants the subsidiary to obtain. For example, a marketing subsidiary will not normally obtain the rights to manufacture and may obtain only rights similar to those normally granted to a distributor.
- In some jurisdictions, the parent company may be able to charge a royalty or other payment to its subsidiaries and affiliates.
- In the case above, these royalties or other fees may allow the parent company to reduce its global tax exposure by charging fees to jurisdictions with higher taxes and by paying taxes on the fees in lower tax jurisdictions. This assumes that the subsidiary will be able to deduct the technology fees paid to the parent as a business expense (e.g., reducing corporate taxes owed in Germany [50%], and paying taxes on the additional income in the United States [36%]).
- In the case of the subsidiary being sold, only those rights expressed in the intercompany agreement can be sold with the business.

WHY AND WHEN TO USE LICENSING AS AN INTERNATIONAL STRATEGY

The international licensing strategy is normally used when a company has valuable intellectual property it believes is suitable in other countries, but the company is not ready to make a direct foreign investment and/or is precluded from importing into the country either because the government limits importation or because market size does not justify direct importation through the use of trading companies, agents, or distributors.

For a company to consider the licensing method, it should consider the following *internal company characteristics*:

■ The company lacks capital, management resources and knowledge of foreign markets, but is willing to commit some of its technical resources to assist licensees.

■ The company has, or is willing to spend the time and money to legally protect the technology in the countries in which it will license.

■ The technology(ies) involved are not central to the licensor's core business.

■ The company has developed a licensing system in the home country that it feels it can take abroad.

■ The company hopes to be able to take advantage of improvements made by its licensees and to obtain those improvements through cross-licensing.

Licensing is also dependent upon *product characteristics*. Large and cumbersome products are often good candidates for licensing as are those products that are very basic but have been technologically enhanced by the licensor. For example, a company that has developed a superior building product (such as a brick with a built-in coupling device) is unlikely to be able to export the finished product because of its cost and size, and because bricks are locally produced in about every country, and therefore may be subject to tariff and non-tariff import restrictions. To take its business abroad, this company is likely to be more successful in licensing the technology for manufacturing the bricks to foreign licensees.

Products subject to rapid technological change are also good licensing candidates, especially if the licensor is continuing to undertake significant R&D. This allows the licensor to keep technologically ahead of any licensee who might become a competitor, and to prevent the spread of the technology by the licensee.

Market characteristics must also be examined in the discussion to license internationally. For many large companies, licensing is designed as a means to enter secondary markets. By secondary markets, we mean:

■ Those in which the company has decided not to enter through foreign investment or marketing through intermediaries.

■ Those in which local companies or foreign competitors have a strong presence, so that import of furnished products would be difficult.

- Regions of the world that are not of primary interest on a country-by-country basis, but where a licensee could produce sufficient products to justify the relationship. For example, a licensee in stable Costa Rica could be selected to manufacture and market to its less stable neighbors in Central America and the Caribbean.
- Those in which the company would like to develop a market and establish its goodwill, which then could later be exploited through direct investment.

Finally, the potential international licensor must look at *legal and financial considerations.* Often the decision to license has been made since the company has no other alternative because the government restricts direct investment through controls on foreign ownership or because it restricts the development of a marketing network by a number of tariff barriers. Brazil and Japan have used this strategy. In both cases, the countries have large internal markets and public policies in favor of building local industry. While this policy generally worked in Japan, it has failed in Brazil because that country has also greatly restricted the ability of licensors to obtain reasonable royalties and subjected all payments abroad to strict exchange controls.

However prohibitive this "stick" may be, some countries that restrict imports do offer a potential "carrot." For licensors who are willing to accept limited royalties and allow for significant assembly or manufacture in their country (value-added), some governments will allow meaningful reductions on the tariffs and other import requirements (e.g., import licenses), on the component parts or finished products. This tends to give the combination licensor/licensee a competitive edge in the market, which could ultimately maximize royalties and the sale of components by the licensor.

ADVANTAGES/DISADVANTAGES OF LICENSING[2]

ADVANTAGES

- Licensing allows the licensor to enter into foreign markets with a relatively low financial risk. In most cases, the licensor will have already made the investment in developing the technology to be licensed. In fact, the income received from foreign licensing may assist the licensor in further developing the technology licensed, or new technologies.

- Licensing allows the licensor to team with a foreign company with adequate capital and a local marketing network to build products or to provide services that otherwise would not be sold or provided in that foreign market.
- Licensing may enable the licensor to achieve an equity participation in a country that would not permit the establishment of a wholly-owned subsidiary. This is a good approach where the value of the license is used as part of the equity contribution.
- Licensing can be used to test markets that the licensor may desire, at a later time, to enter with a direct foreign investment.
- The potential licensee has the opportunity to acquire technology more rapidly and/or less expensively than it would by developing its own technologies.
- Licensing can assist both licensee and licensor when both have significant development capabilities and are willing to cross-license their new developments.

DISADVANTAGES

- The biggest drawback to licensing from the licensor's point of view is the possibility of creating a future competitor. Once an understanding of the technology is acquired by the licensee, it may seek to exploit that technology in the licensor's home market or in other countries where the licensor enjoys a competitive position. To a certain extent this problem can be lessened by three considerations:
  1. Restrictions in the legal agreements.
  2. Licensing assembly or manufacture of only some of the components—requirement of licensee to purchase certain components from licensor. Licensee, therefore, will only be able to *assemble* a completed product.
  3. Licensing products that are not state-of-the-art, or products in which the industry or technology is rapidly changing.
- If the licensee fails to meet quality standards, it may cause serious harm to the image of the licensor. This tends to be a serious problem where the licensee is not adequately financed, or does not have enough trained personnel.
- While the licensor may be able to enter markets with low financial risks, it does run the risk of running into a number of licensee demands which could make the relationship very costly. This is especially true for small companies that may find their critical R&D

people constantly on planes to fix the problems encountered by the licensees.

■ As we will discuss later, the licensing parties may run into a number of problems in dealing with the government of the licensee's country, and occasionally with the government in the country of the licensor.

■ Licensing may bring short-term gains but may not be a good long-term strategy if the licensee later is able to block the importation of finished products into the country by the licensor.

■ Fees received from the licensee may be the easiest to tax and may be subjected to high rates of taxation. Check with your tax experts on the issue of tax withholding on technology transfer.

SELECTING LICENSEES

The decision to license is a complex and difficult one. Many licensing relationships do not succeed because the parties fail to understand each others real agenda. This is sometimes complicated by the fact that the reasons for licensing are not strictly commercial but are determined by government policies and actions. The following example is illustrative:

A United States company, in the late 1980s, wished to take advantage of the booming market for entry-level mainframe computers in Brazil. Because Brazilian government policies, at the time, precluded foreign ownership, and because import duties were high, the U.S. company decided to license a prominent local company to assemble their mainframes. The hope was to establish themselves in the market, obtain royalties, and sell components to the Brazilian licensee.

After a considerable search, the company decided to license a Brazilian computer peripheral manufacturer. This company had had considerable success in using foreign licenses to produce high-quality products. Although it had little experience in mainframes, it appeared as if the company was well funded and was willing to acquire the technical expertise necessary to be successful with this new endeavor.

But the U.S. company misjudged the real intentions of the licensee. The licensee's owner, on the strength of a possible license from a prominent U.S. company, created a new company and took it public. By the time the parties came to the negotiating table, the licensee's owner had already made millions of dollars and was less concerned with the success of the project. Once the relationship got under way, and problems arose, the licensee's owner lost interest and allowed the project to fail. The U.S. company then lost a window of opportunity from which it took many years to recover.

The **Licensee Profile** in Table 10-1 offers some of the key elements to look for in the appointment of licensees. Chapter 5 contains a Licensor Profile (Table 5-3).

Table 10-1
Licensee's Profile

1. Understanding of the licensor's products and technologies.
2. Experience as a licensee, and perhaps as a licensor.
3. Good local reputation in the community.
4. Sufficient funds to license technologies, acquire capital equipment, and for working capital.
5. Access to raw materials and components.
6. Sufficient in-country infrastructure.
7. Existence of, or willingness to employ, qualified workers.
8. Willing to keep licensor information confidential.
9. Willing to pay appropriate license fees and acquire services and components from the licensor.
10. Access to local markets.
11. Ability to keep up with the technical developments of the licensor and of the industry.
12. Ability to develop a network of suppliers.
13. Quality orientation.
14. Willing to consider nonexclusivity or to earn exclusivity.
15. Offers the possibility of improving the licensed product and cross-licensing those improvements to the licensor.
16. Potential to be a future equity joint venture partner of the licensor.

GOVERNMENT POLICIES: STATE OBJECTIVES AND STAGES OF TECHNOLOGY TRANSFER

As international business transactions become more complex, so does the government's interest in regulating them. This section briefly explores some of the government (state) objectives in technology transfer and provides a general analysis of the stages that governments go through in regulating technology transfer. You should seriously consider the role the government will play before entering into technology transfer discussions.

STATE OBJECTIVES FOR TECHNOLOGY TRANSFER

A few nations (primarily the United States) still have some fairly tough regulations on the *outflow* of technology. The U.S. may have military interests (sale of weapons technology, or of machine tools, which would be used to make weapons); economic interests (to prevent competition); scarce resources; and significant foreign policy considerations, (e.g., prevent apartheid and promote nuclear nonproliferation), which it applies to the licensing of technologies abroad. Japan is another country with great concerns on the outflow of technology.

Most regulations applied by governments, however, are in the area of *incoming* technology. Here, the state's interests are varied and sometimes complex. Of first concern is to assure that the incoming technology will truly assist in *the modernization of national industry.* Throughout the 1960s and 1970s, many governments in the developing world adopted the strategy of import substitution. Technologies that did not create replacement of imports were heavily regulated to assure that they were subject to lower royalties and higher taxes. Some governments tried to regulate incoming technologies so that they were in line with what the government perceived was necessary to defend, or create, a certain lifestyle. The emphasis was to deny technologies which created needs and desires for products and services which were beyond the needs of most consumers (e.g., infant formula or gas-guzzling automobiles). Emphasis was placed on the "appropriateness" of the technology to the level of development and ideology of the state.

Governments also restrict incoming technologies for *balance of payments and hard currency considerations.* Restrictions on the amounts of royalties and the availability of hard currency to remit abroad are placed on technologies that already exist in the country, or for products deemed unnecessary. Additionally, some countries place currency limitations on needed technologies to allow those technologies to be developed locally. The goal is to create a protected local market before foreign technologies are allowed to enter.

Finally, restrictions are placed on incoming technologies *to assist in the improvement of the local intellectual infrastructure.* These restrictions are not in the form of monetary limitations, but rather in the form of additional requirements on the licensor. These restrictions are in the area of quality guarantees; contributions to R&D of the licensee; required training of licensee employees and requirement that the technologies transferred would result in products and services that could be marketed globally.

STAGES OF TECHNOLOGY TRANSFER

A handy guide to understanding such government restrictions would be by determining where the government might be in its stage of technology transfer.

Early Development Stage

In this stage, the country is largely an exporter of raw materials and foodstuffs. Almost all industrial products are imported and it is just beginning to develop local industry. At this stage, there tends to be *little or no regulation of technology transfer.* Licensors are relatively free to import any type of technology, including that which is not state-of-the-art, without government approval or registration. In fact, the government may have not yet even developed the mechanisms to evaluate technology.

The main concern of the government at this point will be in developing basic infrastructure (roads, sewer systems and communications), and its emphasis will be on job creation. With that in mind, the government will be less concerned whether the technology is oriented towards assembly or manufacture unless it is trying to develop downstream operations in areas where it exports raw materials.

Growth Stage

In this stage, the country will have already developed certain basic manufacturing and have developed a basic infrastructure. The government will now move towards the regulation of technology in a meaningful way. This, especially in larger countries, tends to be *the period of the most government regulations.* In this stage, look for:

■ *The development of technology priorities.* The government will identify the needed technologies and provide incentives, or lack of disincentives, to acquire them. An example of the incentives might be higher tariffs on finished goods for the competitors of companies that agree to license assembly or manufacture in the country. Technologies that do not fit those priorities may not be approved.

- *Local content requirements.* Require that a certain degree of local components and labor must be achieved within a certain period of time before the license will be approved.
- *Purchase over lease.* The licensor is entitled to royalties for a certain period (normally 5 years), after which time the licensee acquires full rights to use the technology for its own purposes.
- *Payment limitations.* Restrictions on the amount or percentage of royalties and other payments. Normally, this is applied to royalties and other payments that will be made in hard currency.
- *Education and quality requirements.* Discussed on pp. 151–152.
- *Requirement to keep the technology current* and/or to require license of new technologies.

Mature Stage

At this point, the government has gone a long way towards reaching its technology priorities and has developed a significant intellectual base and government infrastructure. Here the emphasis will shift back towards deregulation of technology but the government may maintain a watchdog function over technology transfer. Examples of a country in the mature stage are:

- Recognition of the need for different types of international alliances and freedom of trade and technology flows.
- Emphasis on quality for the domestic market and the need to develop products which can compete globally.
- The development of more balanced government policies:

1. Approval criteria simplified or ended. Registration replaces approval. Registration is for the purpose of developing a national data base.
2. Government has developed personnel and/or agencies to critically evaluate technologies on behalf of locals. It will assist the private sector with information on technologies already available in country to prevent the introduction of repetitive technologies. However, this will only be advisory.
3. Total removal of limitations on payments or the ability to pay "world prices" for the technology transfer.

Before leaving this section, I would like to apply this analysis to two countries. The first is Mexico, which has gone through the first two stages and is now at the mature stage. Prior to the early 1970s, Mexico did not have onerous requirements on technology transfer. In 1972 and 1973, it passed its Transfer of Technology Laws, which set priorities, limited royalty payments, and set up various quality and training requirements. In the early 1990s, Mexico abolished its Transfer of Technology Laws. Now only agreements that grant the foreign licensor the ability to intervene directly in the Mexican company's decision-making process need to be approved by the government. All other transfers must merely be registered. All royalty guidelines have also been abolished.

The second example is Russia (and the other former Soviet Republics). *In this case, we may find examples of all three stages of technology transfer.* In the realm of certain products and services, Russia, in many ways, is equal to, or behind, the current levels of technical development of such countries as Mexico and India. This includes a wide range of consumer goods and many of the basic services associated with international business (e.g., banking and finance, transportation, accounting and law), and those associated with the tourist industry (e.g., hotels, restaurants, airline reservation systems, and tourist promotion technology).

Yet in other areas, Russian products and technologies are state-of-the-art, or even more advanced. This includes ferrous and non-ferrous metallurgy, certain areas of chemistry and chemicals, some instrument building, farm machinery, and some areas of medicine. It will be interesting to see what types of technology transfer policies will be developed in that significant market. In the meantime, companies should be aware to expect the unexpected in dealing with the Republics of the former Soviet Union.

WHAT TO LICENSE

Identifying the technologies to be transferred is only part of the licensing decision. Both licensor and licensee must also consider what rights to those technologies are to be granted. Rights granted can range from simple *use of a finished product* to the complete *sale of the rights to the entire technology.* This section explores the rights commonly granted in licensing transactions.

RIGHT TO USE

In this case, the licensor may only be granting the licensee the right to use the product for its own recreational or commercial use. The best example of this type of right is in the area of computer software. The software company normally grants only the right to use the software provided on a certain computer (sometimes spelled out by the serial number on the machine). This right might include the right to make a backup copy of the software, but definitely does *not* include the right to make additional copies for other sale or use. The right to use (only) may also be important in licenses granted in sourcing situations.

ASSEMBLY VS. MANUFACTURE

To be considered here is whether the licensee is being granted merely the rights to assemble provided or acquired components or whether it will receive the technology and rights to undertake "significant transformation" of raw materials into components and/or the finished product.

To illustrate the point, consider assembly vs. manufacture of a twist-action writing instrument (pen or pencil). An assembly situation might be one in which the licensee is provided with the right to acquire or purchase from the licensor the finished components, and then given the right to assemble the components into a finished product, which it then places into a container suitable for marketing. A manufacturing situation is one in which the licensor provides the licensee with the technology sufficient to manufacture the components (say the instrument and its ink or lead source) from raw materials, and to design and complete the finished product from the manufactured components.

Licensors looking to protect their technologies will try to limit the licensee's right either to straight assembly of all components or to the manufacture of certain local components that it will assemble in combinations with other components supplied by the licensor or acquired through third parties. In this circumstance, the licensee never acquires the right to replicate the product in its entirety, and is therefore less likely to become a future competitor of the licensor.

A variant of this approach is to begin with assembly rights and allow the licensee, upon reaching certain milestones (which normally include a certain level of payment to the licensor), to acquire more and more manufacturing rights. An example of this would be a *staged technology transfer:*

■ *Phase I*—Licensee markets and services finished products provided by the licensor. In a sense, the licensee is a distributor who is testing the market for the product.

■ *Phase II*—Licensee now is responsible for final testing and assembly of components and finished product provided by the licensor.

■ *Phase III*—Licensee free to source components from third parties.

■ *Phase IV*—Licensee begins to manufacture some of the components along with the assembly of finished product.

■ *Phase V*—Licensee now manufactures all but one or two critical components, which continue to be provided by its licensor, and assembles the finished products.

■ *Phase VI*—Licensee now has all rights to manufacture components and the finished product.

These six phases will normally take place over several years, and the parties can agree to stop at any intermediate phase if a new product or technology is introduced by the licensor.

THE RIGHT TO MARKET AND SELL

The sourcing relationship described earlier in this chapter is one in which the licensee may have the right to assemble and/or manufacture, but *does not* have the right to market and sell (except to the licensor or customers designated by the licensor). Whatever assembly/manufacturing rights agreed to between the parties, they will need to determine where the licensee is able to market the products that result from the technology. Antitrust laws in some countries (mainly the United States and EEC) prohibit absolute restrictions on the sale of products. However, the licensor can make reasonable restrictions on the licensee's marketing rights. These include:

1. No marketing where the licensor has other licensees.
2. Limit restrictions on marketing and sales to the home country of the licensor. These differ from relationship to relationship. Check with your attorney.
3. Limitation on sale of the products where the licensee does not have sales offices and/or cannot provide installation and after-sales service.

HAVE MADE/SUBLICENSE

If the licensee is incapable (particularly at the beginning of the relationship) to complete all of the assembly or manufacturing processes, the licensor may consider whether to add "have made" or sublicense language to the assembly and/or manufacturing rights granted. The language would allow the licensee to source some, or all, of its production from third parties. While "have made" and sublicense rights may increase the speed in which products enter the market, and reduce the licensee's capital costs, the licensor should be careful not to grant those rights if the licensee plans to use them only to become a contractor rather than a true licensee. Licensees that contract almost everything out may never develop the technological expertise needed to properly service the market and unless they can carefully control costs, they may never be competitive in the marketplace.

RIGHTS TO UPDATE AND ENHANCEMENT/FUTURE PRODUCTS

One of the key licensing issues is that of whether the licensor grants to the licensee the rights to the technology at a particular time (static license) or the right to the continuous updates and enhancements (dynamic license). A static license has the advantage to the licensor that the licensee is less likely to become a future competitor. It may also make sense to use a static license, at least at the beginning of the relationship, if the licensee has not yet developed sufficient technical capabilities, or the products or services resulting from the technology are, and are likely to remain, appropriate to the licensee's marketplace.

The licensee, however, may demand a more dynamic license, or its government may require it (a typical demand for countries in the intermediate stage). In some cases, this demand may be reasonable in light of the up-front expenditures that must be made by the licensee, or because the level of royalties and other payments are sufficient to require a longer-term payoff to the licensee. In other cases, the demand may be in line because the market size complexity and/or competitive nature may require the licensee to be on top of all developments. Two compromise strategies commonly used are:

1. Begin with a static license but allow, in the initial agreement, for updates and enhancements if certain goals are met or conditions occur. Examples of goals might be the payment of a certain level of

fees or the assembly/manufacture of a certain number of units. For conditions, the examples might be proof of the availability in the country of more modern versions by their competitors or the licensee's availability to manufacture, sell, and service the more advanced product.

2. Begin with a dynamic license, but tie the license only to certain versions of products or to certain products in the line. When new products are developed by the licensor, then a new agreement will be necessary.

REVENUE SOURCES

For the licensor, there are three general ways in which to obtain revenues from the licensee. These are royalties and other fees for the use of the technology; sale of products and components; and sale of services such as management contracts, training and consulting. A good licensing relationship should allow the licensor to obtain revenues from all three sources.

ROYALTIES AND OTHER FEES FOR THE USE OF THE TECHNOLOGY

A royalty is normally a fee associated with the production and/or sale of products and services that result from the use of the technology. It may be a fixed payment per unit (unit charge royalty), or it may be a percentage of the sales price of the products or services (percentage royalty). In designing royalty fee schedules, the parties should consider the following:

■ When will the fee be paid? Should it be paid upon production or upon sale? If the licensee is able to keep its inventory to a minimum, this would not be a critical issue. However, if the licensee develops significant inventory, it is clearly better for the licensor to be paid on the basis of production.

■ Make sure you understand *on what* the royalty percentage, or per unit fee, will be paid. In the case of a percentage payment, will the royalty be based on the net sales price of the product to the customer (less taxes and shipping costs), or will it be paid in proportion to the value added to the product or service by the licensee? For example, assume we have a 5% royalty that would be applied to U.S. $2,000,000 in net sales. These net sales were generated by the licensee with a 50% value added by it to the product. In the case of a straight royalty based on net sales, the royalty due would be U.S. $100,000. In the case of value added, the royalty would be U.S. $50,000 ($2,000,000 × .05 × .50 = U.S. $50,000).

■ Determine what is meant by value-added. Value-added normally includes not only the value added by the licensee itself, but also include any value added for components and services sourced in the licensee's country.

■ Who will be responsible for the payment of withholding taxes on royalties paid to the licensor. In order to tax the revenues of foreign licensors, many countries place a withholding tax on royalties. These generally range from 5% to 40%, with 10% to 25% being most common. If local law allows, the licensor may require the licensee to withhold and pay those taxes. If local law does not allow for licensee payments of licensor's withholding taxes, the parties may consider increasing the royalty amount to provide the licensor with the after-tax royalty level it requires.

■ Be sure to establish in the agreeement between the parties the appropriate accounting procedures and audit rights to be able to assist the licensor in obtaining its full royalties, and the licensee to assure it obtains its full local tax benefits.

In addition to the royalties, the parties may consider other fees for the use of the technology. Most important would be an initial or up-front fee. An up-front fee for technology transfer is often demanded by the licensor. This fee could be structured as a nonrefundable fee or it could be an advance on future royalties, or it might be used to reduce future royalties. In any case, the up-front fee is normally designed with the following factors in mind:

■ It will be used to cover some, or all, of the up-front costs of the licensor in transferring the technology.

■ It will be used to show the seriousness of the licensee.

■ It will be used as a hedge in case the licensee is unable to commence production, or is unable to reach adequate production levels. Therefore, the fee should be due at the latest when the technology is delivered and never be tied to the commencement of production.

What to charge as an up-front fee is clearly subject to the bargaining power of the parties, but in situations where there are strict government controls on technology fees, a large up-front fee should be seriously considered. For example, Brazil, for years, limited technology transfer royalties to five percent (5%) on the Brazilian value added to the net sales price. However, the law did allow the licensing parties to agree to up-front payments as long as they did not exceed reasonable calculations of technology payments over 5 years, and were present valued.

Assume the licensing parties were about to sign a five-year agreement at a royalty of 5% on the Brazilian value-added. Assume the value added was reasonably estimated to be U.S. $30 million (e.g., $2 million in the first year; $4 million in the second; $6 million in the third; $8 million in the fourth; and $10 million in the fifth), then the royalties over the period are estimated to be U.S. $1.5 million (5% of U.S. $30 million). If a 5% interest per year figure was used, the present value of U.S. $1.5 million over 5 years is .7835 resulting in an up-front royalty of U.S. $1,175,250. This amount would be subject to withholding tax and the agreement would have to be royalty-free thereafter. However, the ability to collect this amount in advance might make the transaction quite palatable to any prospective licensor.

SALE OF COMPONENTS AND PRODUCTS

The limitation on the amount of royalties that could be charged, plus the heavy taxes associated with such royalties, have caused licensors to look at other means of obtaining revenues through licensing. This has pushed licensors towards arranging transactions in which they will sell components and some finished products to the licensee (e.g., the license is for products A and B in which components are sold by licensor, and the licensee also purchases from the licensor completed products C, D, and E to have the complete product line). This results in a double benefit for the licensor in that it is able to sell more products while reducing the possibility of the licensee becoming a competitor. It also serves the licensee's interest in keeping its royalties and production costs down.

Another way for a licensor to maneuver around the royalty restrictions and tax problems is to reduce, or eliminate, royalties and raise the price of capital equipment, components, and finished products sold to the licensee. However, this approach may not work in countries that have high import duties because the additional cost of the duties may exceed the royalties desired. This will depend on many factors such as the ultimate destination of the goods, but should be considered as one approach to the licensing relationship.

SALE OF SERVICES

In addition to straight royalty fees and sale of products, the licensor may also consider what revenues can be obtained from the sale of services to the licensee. Said services normally fall into three categories:

- *Management Services.* The licensor agrees to provide personnel to assist the licensee in managing either the technology transfer, or perhaps the plant itself.

- *Training Services.* The licensor may provide the licensee a certain amount of free training to assist in the original technology transfer. After that point, the licensee must pay for any additional training. While this may be a viable source of revenue, the licensor should consider not to price this so high that the licensee will not take advantage of the training offered, thereby perhaps placing the quality of the products in jeopardy.

- *Consulting Services.* The licensee may require a certain degree of consulting from the licensor to respond to production problems or to improve production or marketing capabilities. Consulting services can also be used for marketing and sales of the products and services.

ELEMENTS OF THE LICENSE AGREEMENT[3]

Unlike distributors and agents, it is not wise for the licensing parties to consider developing letter agreements to cover the licensing relationship. Instead, this arrangement requires complex agreements that attempt to cover all known eventualities. The key elements of a License Agreement include:

PARTIES TO THE AGREEMENT

License agreements should have a clear definition of the contracting parties. The licensor should be specifically identified to be sure that it has the right to the technology to be transferred. The licensee should be the party who is actually going to put the technology to use. If the licensee is not going to undertake the actual assembly and/or manufacture, those parties must be identified or the licensee should have the appropriate "have made" or sublicense rights.

PREAMBLE OR RECITALS

The Agreement should describe the parties and the technology to be licensed. It should identify, generally, the respective roles of the parties. In cases of heavy government regulation, it should also state in what manner the transfer of technology will be beneficial to the receiving country.

DEFINITIONS

This is an extremely important part of the agreement, which normally defines such terms as what is meant by assembly, manufacture, improvements, models or products covered, technology, technical assistance, term, territory, training, and value added.

EXHIBITS OR ANNEXES

This part defines the exhibits, or annexes, which are to become part of the agreement. These might include:

1. Product description
2. Technical specifications
3. Territory
4. Royalty schedules
5. List of patents
6. List of trademarks
7. List of other intellectual property
8. Management agreement
9. Training plan and rates
10. Consulting rates
11. List of capital equipment needed, or to be acquired
12. Component Purchase Agreement

LICENSE GRANTS

This section should define exactly what rights are being transferred and how and when the transfer will occur. It should cover assembly or manufacture, exclusivity or non-exclusivity, and what happens if the technology granted or licensed is not used within a certain period of time. It also might cover what happens if the licensee discontinues exploitation of the technology.

TERRITORY

In this section, the territory should be defined in regard to three factors:

1. Assembly or manufacture rights, which could be tied only to the licensee's home country.
2. "Have made" and sublicense rights, which can also be strictly limited by the agreement.
3. Marketing and sales rights, which could be subjected to some reasonable commercial limitations.

ASSEMBLY/MANUFACTURING PHASES

This is needed if the technology is to be provided in phases. Conditions should be set for moving to each new phase.(See pp. 155–156.)

TECHNICAL ASSISTANCE AND TRAINING

This section should define the technical assistance and training that is to be provided by the licensor without additional cost, and refer the reader to the appropriate exhibits or annexes that define the additional costs for such technical assistance and training.

QUALITY

The agreement should define the quality standards required by the parties. For the licensee, this would relate to the quality of the technology. For the licensor, this would relate to the quality of the products.

REMUNERATION

The royalties should be specifically defined, considering whether they are to be based on units, or figured on the net sales price. If a percentage of net sales price is used, the factors that go into defining net sales should be included. The terms of royalty payments should also be included (e.g., monthly, quarterly, etc.), and proper reporting procedure and audit rights should be established. If a unit charge royalty is established, the parties should also build in an inflation factor, and define whether the unit royalty is earned when the product is produced, or when it is sold.

In regard to up-front fees, the amount and payment dates should clearly be established. The licensor should demand a substantial part of that fee upon actual transfer of the technology but make the fee subject to stages which could include such factors as technology transfer date(s), provision of training, provision of technical assistance and factory start-up. Fees for additional management training and technical assistance should also be defined, as should their payment terms.

WARRANTIES

The warranties that apply to the technology itself, as well as products and components supplied by or through the licensor, should be clearly defined. If there are any warranty disclaimers, they should also be stated in this section. As to the technology itself, the agreement should clearly specify that the warranties apply only to the extent that the technology is used in accordance with the instructions of the licensor.

CONFIDENTIALITY

Both the licensor and licensee should be held to a very high standard of confidentiality. If "have made" or sublicensing is provided for, the parties should determine what needs to be disclosed to the manufacturers and/or sublicensees and assure that they are held to the same confidentiality standards. It is recommended that the agreement state that violations of confidentiality are grounds for termination of the relationship.

LIABILITY

It is reasonable for the parties to attempt to limit their liabilities to each other in some way. Normally, this is either a fixed monetary amount or is limited to the amount actually received in the case of the licensor.

TERM AND TERMINATION

The term of the agreement should be defined as should the conditions for extending the agreement, if any. It is recommended that the parties should mutually agree, in writing, to any extensions and/or renewals.

Termination can be tricky, but should include at least the following considerations:

- Ability of the parties to terminate in the case of insolvency or bankruptcy.
- Ability to terminate if the technology is not used, or exploited, for a certain period of time.
- Ability to terminate upon material breach. It is helpful to define materiality (e.g., non-payment of fees, misuse of the technology or violation of the confidentiality provisions).
- The provision of a cure period to resolve problems before termination becomes official.
- A statement of which obligations (e.g., confidentiality) survive the expiration or termination of the agreement.

IMPROVEMENTS/NEW PRODUCTS

Determine, and make clear, which improvements, if any, to existing products will be part of the agreement. Define whether new products should be included or if a new agreement is required. If necessary, use product characteristics or other criteria to define what is meant by a new product.

GRANT-BACKS

If the licensor is willing to grant improvements and/or new products to the licensee, the licensee should be willing to grant rights to the licensor for all improvements made by the licensee. If grant-backs are provided for, the parties should determine the conditions associated with them. For example, right of first refusal, exclusive or non-exclusive, whether or not royalties and other fees would apply, and which territories the grant-backs apply to. In countries with strong antitrust laws, the parties should check with their attorneys before drafting the grant-back rights.

PURCHASE OF FINISHED PRODUCTS, COMPONENTS, AND SUPPLIES

Because this may be a critical part of the commercial relationship, the terms and conditions of the provision of finished products, components and supplies should be clearly spelled out. It is recommended that this be accomplished as a separate agreement that could be attached as an exhibit to the license agreement, e.g.,The Component Purchase Agreement.

The parties should also consider whether this will be a two-way proposition. For example, in a sourcing situation, sales of products and/or components from the licensee to the licensor may be the entire purpose of the licensing relationship. Additionally, the parties may find that the licensee is more efficient in producing certain components and the licensor may wish to purchase those components from its licensee.

DISPUTE RESOLUTION

The agreement should describe the conditions under which disputes would be resolved. It is probably a good idea to include some form of conciliation procedure before submitting the dispute to arbitration or litigation. If arbitration is selected, the parties should determine the rules and whether the arbitration is to cover all items, or only technical issues.

CONDITIONS PRECEDENT—GOVERNMENT APPROVALS, AUTHORIZATIONS AND/OR REGISTRATIONS

The parties should consider what must occur before the agreement becomes effective. Such conditions fall into two general categories. The first would be the actions that must be taken by the parties themselves. For the licensee, this might be the requirement of proof that the licensor has the legal right to transfer the technology. For the licensor, it could be such things as a licensee commitment of capital, a proper manufacturing facility being in place, and/or payment of certain up-front fees.

The second set of conditions would be the necessary government approvals, authorizations, and registrations. These could include:

1. Registration of the technology in the licensee's country, and other countries covered by the license.
2. Approval of the up-front fees, royalties and other charges, and right to remit those fees in hard currency.
3. Agreement as to local content.
4. Permission for foreigners to enter the country to assist the licensee.
5. Agreement to reduce tariffs and other charges on finished product once the assembly and/or manufacture commences.

FORCE MAJEURE

By *force majeure,* we mean those acts and causes outside the control of the parties that cannot be avoided by exercise of due care. The agreement should decide if these include acts of government. They should also decide what happens in the event of a force majeure and the length of time in which a force majeure must exist before the agreement can be terminated.

GENERAL PROVISIONS

Additional general provisions which may be necessary, include the following:

1. Assignment rights—these should be severely limited.
2. Notices—form and timing.
3. Amendments—when allowed, and must be written.
4. Independent contractors— neither party is owned by the other.
5. Governing laws and court(s) of jurisdiction.
6. Non-waiver of rights—that is, if something is waived in the past, it is not automatically waived in the future.
7. If one of the parties is a U.S. company, statements regarding its export administration and foreign corrupt practices laws.

MAINTAINING THE LICENSE RELATIONSHIP

Finding and appointing license partners is just the beginning of your relationship. Because licensing is more complex than working with straight marketeers, both licensors and licensees should not enter into relationships with each other unless they feel relatively comfortable that there is a good chance to build a long-term relationship. How to maintain that relationship is the subject of this section.

DEGREE OF INVOLVEMENT AND COMMITMENT

As stated at the outset of this chapter, companies enter into licensing relationships for many reasons, which can differ from an occasional transaction to a full-blown international strategy. If licensing is viewed by the licensor to be an occasional strategy that presents the opportunity to acquire some marginal revenues and/or to address less critical markets, the licensor should focus the bulk of its activities in the selection and appointment process, and try to key in on opportunities that exist from only the more sophisticated licensees. The basic reason for this is that licensors of this type are unlikely to have, or acquire, the resources necessary to properly manage less sophisticated licensees. Under these circumstances, the licensor may be willing to appoint an individual or small team of persons who have licensing as their responsibility, and perhaps make available members of their technical team for occasional consultation and training. The licensee, however, will have to be pretty much self-sufficient.

In circumstances where licensing becomes an integral part of a company's international strategy, particular care will have to be taken in defining how licensing is managed; to what degree the licensor wishes to get involved in the licensee's activities; to the creation of the principle of fairness in regard to royalties and other payments; and to how misunderstandings and disputes will be managed and resolved.

MANAGING LICENSEES—THE INTERNAL MANAGEMENT ISSUES

The management of licensee activities can be done from three possible groups: the international division; a distinct licensing function (which may also manage licensees in the home market); or from the operational division, which has responsibility for the technology and the products. All have their advantages and disadvantages and the company may eventually decide to create a matrixed solution.

The international division should be staffed with people who are savvy in the cultural and other variables of selecting and appointing international licensees, but would probably not have the technical expertise to deal with the licensees on a day-to-day basis. A licensing function could be developed with the purpose of optimizing licensing as a corporate strategy, and it should develop considerable expertise on how to deal with licensees. However, it will be difficult for such a function to fully manage the licensor function when it comes to providing technical assistance to the licensees. The operations division may be able to resolve technical issues and problems, but it may lack the expertise in cultural and political aspects, and may take a more parochial view as to how the licensing process fits into the overall strategic plan of the company.

To solve this potential management problem, the company should consider the following points and suggestions:

■ Have members of all groups involved in the selection and appointment process. Avoid international "deals" teams that find and appoint the prospects and then turn them over to operations without that group being sufficiently involved at the outset, or having "bought into" the deal.

■ Appoint one individual or office that is to serve in liaison with the licensee. This point of contact should then work with all the appropriate groups in the company to evaluate and serve the needs of the licensee.

■ Develop a system that rewards all involved groups as to revenue and/or profit credit.

■ Have top corporate management communicate its feelings regarding each license relationship to the involved parties, and identify one individual in top management to resolve any problems between the functions or departments.

LICENSOR INVOLVEMENT IN LICENSEE ACTIVITIES

Ideally, a licensor would like to limit its relationship to collecting royalties and selling products and components. Realistically, the licensor is likely to be more heavily involved in the licensee's activities, especially if the technology is complex, the licensee needs continuing technical assistance, and/or the licensee is having marketing problems. The licensor needs to decide whether it will take a proactive or reactive response in dealing with its licensees. The proactive response may include management assistance, periodic visits, progress reports and, in extreme cases, actual involvement in the activities of the licensee through board membership, or through the provision of personnel on the licensee's site. The licensor needs to determine which, if any, of the proactive alternatives it is willing to offer. This will obviously depend on the trade-offs involved, but even in situations where the licensee is willing to pay for these services, the licensor needs to think hard before committing human resources that can be used in other ways.

THE FAIRNESS PRINCIPLE

Despite the best legal agreements, the balance of benefits between the parties may have to be reassessed and adjusted as the relationship continues. Although licensing may not be part of an equity joint venture in which profits are formally shared, it is a collaboration between the parties in which both parties must benefit. High royalties and/or component prices may have to be readjusted downwards if the licensee perceives, and can show the licensor, that it is not receiving its fair share. In this case, they may examine if lower royalties and prices could result in larger volumes which ultimately would generate more revenues and profits for both parties.

Licensors will soon lose interest in licensees that are not providing it with sufficient revenues and profits to justify the relationship. If the bulk of the benefits are going to the licensee, royalties and products and component price may need to be revised upwards, or if that is not legally possible, some other methods must be developed to equalize the relationship (e.g., consulting and/or training agreements). If neither party is benefiting from the relationship, the parties will need to meet to reassess how to put it back on line or to discuss the best manner to establish a friendly separation. In any case, what I am saying is that a licensing relationship cannot simply be managed from the legal agreement, but that the parties should develop methods to keep the relationship in balance. This is the theme pursued in the next section.

RESOLUTION OF MISUNDERSTANDINGS AND DISPUTES

The section dealing with legal agreements discussed some methods of dispute resolution that include third-party involvement (e.g., conciliation and arbitration). Most misunderstandings and disputes, however, will have to be handled between the licensor and the licensee. To accomplish this in the most efficient manner, consider the following suggestions:

- Each party should identify at least one individual who will remain with the project through completion. This individual should attempt to learn and understand the other's side, language, company policies and cultural variables.
- The companies should make a special effort to understand the internal workings of their counterparts. They should share organization charts, company brochures and other like information.
- The parties should communicate regularly by telephone or memos. If possible, a communication schedule should be established, and adhered to.
- Misunderstandings and problems should be communicated immediately and not allowed to fester.
- All parties must continually keep in mind the fairness principle.

I hope, this discussion on licensing has provided some insights on how to select and appoint licensing parties and manage licensing relationships. We will now turn to a discussion of international alliances and equity joint ventures.

REFERENCES

1. For an excellent overview on Licensing, see Richard Schaffer (et. al.), *International Business Law and Its Environment* (2nd ed.), West; Minneapolis, 1993, Chapter 15, pp. 425–452.
2. See Business International Corporation (BIC), *201 Checklists: Decision-Making in International Operations*, New York: BIC, 1980, Checklist No. 28.
3. *Ibid*, Checklist No. 31

Chapter 11

METHOD 8: INTERNATIONAL ALLIANCES AND JOINT VENTURES

INTRODUCTION

This chapter explores various types of international alliances, including the equity joint venture. An international alliance could be said to exist when:

- Two or more parties contribute tangible and/or intangible assets towards the mutual conduct of business activities.
- An organization of some type is created between the parties (equity or non-equity).
- At least one of the parties is foreign to the targeted market(s).

International alliances can be established between competitors, companies with complementary products and/or services, customers and/or suppliers. They can also be established for an individual project, or as a long-term vehicle to address a particular industry or market.

In today's world, international alliances make more sense than at any time in the history of international trade. The reasons for this include:

- The expansion of international competition, which makes it more and more difficult for a company to approach the global market with only its own resources.
- The reduction of product cycles, which make it necessary to move faster to establish markets, make sales, and pursue international strategies.
- The growing cost of research, product development and marketing, which force companies to find ways in which to increase efficiencies for both domestic and international markets.

The following pages explore international alliances from two perspectives. First, we will examine the non-equity versions of international alliances. These include cross-licensing (R&D partnerships); the joint marketing and sale of products and services; and the development of non-equity consortiums to respond to certain international projects. The second part of this chapter will explore the equity joint venture. In this case, the parties actually create a specific company of a particular nationality in which ownership is shared by the parties through the issuance of shares or quotas.

NON-EQUITY INTERNATIONAL ALLIANCES

The three most common non-equity international alliances are:

RESEARCH AND DEVELOPMENT PARTNERSHIPS AND CROSS-LICENSING

In an R&D partnership, two or more companies will, by contract, agree to pool their research and development resources to create or enhance technologies and/or products. This can be either companies of different nationalities, or companies of the same nationality, who enter the partnership to develop global products and/or to reach international markets. The products that result from this technology pooling will then normally be distributed by each partner individually within their own international marketing networks, although the R&D partnership could also cover joint marketing. Another version of technology-sharing is the cross-licensing of existing technologies. In this case, the companies find ways in which to combine their technologies to more rapidly be able to develop products and solutions to sell in the global marketplace.

JOINT MARKETING ALLIANCES

Joint marketing alliances can be of two types. The first is discussed in Chapter 8 under Co-marketing ("piggybacking"). In this case, one company piggybacks on the other's international marketing network. In effect, one company becomes the distributor and/or agent of the other. In the second case, both companies agree to handle the products of the other within their respective international marketing networks. This strategy can work very well where the companies market in different territories, or even within the same territory, but to different customers. Again, this can be structured in a distributor or agency-type of relationship.

CONSORTIUM

In a consortium relationship, several participant companies come together to pool their resources to bid on a significant project or group of projects. Normally, each company would have a different specialty which, if bid or offered alone, could not win the project(s), but together with other companies with different specialties, could result in offering a viable and complete solution to the customer. Consortia are also sometimes created for the production of specific products.

In creating a consortium, each company retains its individual identity, but together create a *business organization* that does not fit into the standard partnership or corporate form. In fact, no specific "legal entity" is created.

Consortia (sometimes also called Associations in Participation) are accepted in most legal systems if they meet the following characteristics:

- A contract is signed between the members in which the parties may, if they desire, subject themselves to the control of the organization that they have jointly formed. The contract should include:
  1. A name of the consortium.
  2. The location of its head office.
  3. The name of the jurisdiction to which it will be subject.
  4. Its purpose.
  5. The rights and obligations of each of the participants.
  6. Provision for management of the consortium.

7. The representation of the parties in decision-making.
8. The procedure for making decisions.
9. Provisions for dealing with earnings and the division of profits and losses, if any.

■ The consortium contract, and any modifications to it, often must be filed with the appropriate government agency, or commercial registry.

The consortium is not considered a legal entity in the manner of a partnership or corporation, and is not treated as such for tax purposes. Each party to the consortium will be responsible for their own taxes. Additionally, the consortium avoids the problems of partnerships in that, if one party pulls out or is adjudged bankrupt, the consortium may continue to exist between the remaining participants. A partnership would have to dissolve.

The following example shows how a consortium works. Various electrical utilities in certain Brazilian states and cities desired to purchase, through the formal bidding process, modern energy management systems, which allowed them to move energy around their grids so that sufficient power would be available during peak demand periods. Each electrical utility would bid their own projects and it was estimated that there would be 2 to 3 bids per year. Each bid was in millions of U.S. dollars, and normally required construction of buildings and infrastructure; sophisticated computer systems; energy management software and know-how; and local service, maintenance, and warranty services. Local laws also required that success of winning the bids was particularly dependent upon, at least, some level of local (Brazilian) products and services (local content).

To meet these conditions, a consortium was created that included several Brazilian and foreign companies that could bid a complete solution. Brazilian parties were selected in the construction, in computer peripherals, remote terminal units (RTUs), and in the service and maintenance areas. Foreign parties came into the consortium to provide mainframe computers and energy management software products, technical knowhow and training. The resulting consortium was established to bid certain of these projects over a five-year period. For the most part, it bid against other like consortia. In fact, while this consortium was U.S.-Brazilian, the competitive consortia were other U.S.-Brazilian, European-Brazilian, or Japanese-Brazilian in make-up. The customers were then able to choose from several business associations that offered complete solutions rather than have to face the coordination necessary if they selected individual bidders in each specialty. The consortium companies did not have to create a Brazilian corporation and at the end of the five-year period, this consortium wound up its business in a fairly simple fashion.

Consortia have also been created for the purpose of jointly producing products, either to meet the specific needs of an individual customer or on a longer-term basis, to provide a source of products to all participants. My experience indicates that the production of products over the longer-term is best served through the creation of an equity joint venture. However, filling short-term needs may work very well through consortia.

THE INTERNATIONAL EQUITY JOINT VENTURE

The definition of an international equity joint venture is similar to the definition for an international alliance, except that an actual company is formed and registered with the appropriate government agencies. To reiterate, an international equity joint venture could be defined as follows:

- Two or more parties contribute tangible, and perhaps intangible, assets towards the conduct of business activities.
- These assets are used to form a legal entity (partnership, limited partnership, limited liability company or a corporation).
- The legal entity formed is a distinct company with its own shares or quotas,* board of directors, officers and employees. It has its own budget and conducts business as a distinct entity.
- At least one of the parties is foreign to the targeted market(s).

International equity joint ventures ("IEJVs") come in many types and styles. The five examples below are illustrative of the types of IEJVs that have been created:

- Two or more foreign companies of the same nationality creating an IEJV in a third country. Two U.S. corporations, Honeywell and Control Data, created a company in Portugal (MPI) to manufacture products needed by both foreign companies in their global markets.
- A foreign and domestic company creating a joint venture in the domestic country. This is a very typical form of IEJV.
- Two or more companies of different nationalities creating an IEJV in a third country. For example, a U.S. and Japanese company creating a joint venture in India.

---

*Quotas are sometimes issued instead of shares in limited liability companies.

■ A foreign company and a domestic government company (or parastatal company, that is, partially government-owned). This type of relationship has become common as the result of the privatization of many companies that has occurred in Great Britain and various Latin American countries.

■ A foreign company, or companies, that creates an entity abroad, and then makes a private placement or takes the company public in the country where the company is located, or in global financial markets. This results in the creation of an IEJV.

CHARACTERISTICS OF A JOINT VENTURE

Separate Legal Identity

As stated before, the company formed has a separate identity. Its shares are normally held by its participants, but the company will have its own officers, directors and employees. Normally it will have its own facilities and will be operated as a distinct company.

Ownership and Control Is Divided Among the Parties

While ownership is usually divided in the form of shares or quotas, with the company with the largest or majority shares in theoretical control, it is also necessary to look at other forms of control. A minority party may have considerable influence or control by virtue of being the major technology supplier; the provider of key management; the major customer of the IEJV, or simply because one of the minority participants is a larger player in the international marketplace. This is further discussed under the "Major Issues" section.

Formed Through a Combination of Resources

IEJVs are normally formed where no single party possesses all of the assets needed to best exploit the available opportunities. To best explore how these resources are combined, we will examine the creation of a sample joint venture between a global company located in the United States and a local partner located in a developing nation. The IEJV will be located in the developing nation and its purpose will be to finally assemble and sell the products in the developing nation, and those nations in the same geographical area.

The expatriate partner would normally contribute:

- Capital—which might include cash, lines of credit, and capital equipment.
- Technology—various forms of intellectual property, which could include assembly, technology, and marketing know-how.
- Management expertise.
- Training and consulting.
- Finished product and/or parts and components.

The host country partner may also contribute any of the items mentioned above, but may also contribute:

- An existing physical presence in the country, including use of real estate and other property.
- Knowledge of language, culture and local business conditions.
- Rights from the host country government to undertake the proposed activity.
- Access to special government benefits.
- Lower cost sources of labor and/or raw materials.
- Marketing and sales contracts or expertise.

ADVANTAGES OF INTERNATIONAL EQUITY JOINT VENTURES[1]

SHARING AND REDUCING RISKS

Companies will enter into IEJVs when they believe that the project is too large or risky to be handled alone. This would be especially true in markets that do not justify full-blown subsidiaries, or in markets where the costs of doing business are high.

CREATE ECONOMIES OF SCALE

Economies of scale can be produced when less efficient local production techniques, coupled with low labor costs, can be combined with foreign technology to achieve efficient production techniques at low cost. This is particularly valuable in the IEJVs between parties from developed and developing nations.

IEJVs also allow smaller or medium-sized companies to combine resources to permit these companies to compete more favorably with their larger competitors.

ACCESS TO MARKET/BETTER PENETRATION OF MARKET

Some countries may require a local presence, which normally includes at least some local assembly or manufacture, before products are allowed to enter the market. Even if this is not the case, a local presence, and the existence of local stocks, might be advantageous in reaching government customers and in bidding government projects in countries where local companies are given preference. A foreign company might also achieve better market penetration if it uses the same resources to establish two 50%/50% IEJVs in two separate countries rather than establishing one wholly-owned subsidiary in a single country.

ESTABLISHING MORE EFFECTIVE RELATIONSHIPS WITH HOST GOVERNMENTS—REDUCING FOREIGN IDENTITY

It is worth mentioning a few areas where establishing a more effective government relationship can assist the foreign party. They include:

■ Reduced risk of expropriation/nationalization.
■ Prompt political acceptance and local identity.
■ The satisfaction of local legal requirements for ownership and/or local content.

EXCHANGE OR POOLING OF TECHNOLOGY

When IEJVs are created between technologically sophisticated parties, the result could be the creation of new and/or better technologies. General Motors and Toyota created a joint venture to manufacture lower-cost small cars in the United States. The joint venture allowed General Motors to learn Toyota's production techniques for the manufacture of high quality, but lower cost, motor vehicles. Toyota received technology associated with design and style which has assisted it in developing automobiles which are suitable to American tastes. Additionally, it had some access to GM's marketing network and was able to improve its marketing techniques.

TAPPING LOCAL CAPITAL MARKETS AND USING
CONCESSIONARY FINANCING

The more countries where a company has a presence, the more likely it will have access to local financing. This allows companies to achieve a more global financing strategy, borrowing in currencies at rates that are most favorable to its global position. Additionally, companies willing to invest abroad might find, in some countries, attractive government-supported financial packages and incentives. These are discussed further in Chapter 12.

ACCESS TO NATURAL RESOURCES

Countries with critical natural resources may give preference for their exploitation to local companies. This is true even for a few products (red cedar shingles) in the United States. Additionally, even abundant natural resources may be cheaper for local companies. Mexico, for example, as part of its National Industrial Development Plans, during the 1980s, provided electric energy, residual fuel oil, natural gas, and basic petrochemicals at a discount to companies, Mexican or foreign, that produced products in areas designated for development, and especially to companies that were willing to locate in designated geographical areas.

BETTER LABOR RELATIONSHIPS

Having a local partner in the host country is sometimes instrumental to creating and preserving better labor relationships. The local partner will understand the workplace environment and how to deal with difficult labor problems. It will also know how to motivate and incent the local workforce on all levels.

PROVIDE IMMEDIATE MARKET STRENGTH WHEN LOCAL PARTNERS
HAVE ESTABLISHED DISTRIBUTION AND CONTACTS

As stated previously, Japanese automobile manufacturers have used their IEJVs with American auto manufacturers to establish a larger presence through the use of the dealer network. Ford and Mazda have also used their IEJV to establish a market for Ford's light pick-up trucks in Japan. Similar marketing arrangements exist in the liquor industry and among various producers of food products.

DISADVANTAGES OF INTERNATIONAL EQUITY JOINT VENTURES

PROFIT SHARING

With the sharing of risks, comes the sharing of profits. This issue, however, becomes even more problematic when one partner desires the IEJV to be profitable while another partner would prefer to make its profits from selling to, or buying from, the IEJV. This problem is most likely to occur when a larger foreign company links with a smaller domestic company.

Still another issue over profits comes when one partner desires to distribute profits to the shareholders while the other wishes to put the profits back into the business. This problem will be discussed in more depth in the next section on major IEJV issues.

CONTROL OVER TECHNOLOGY

If one party to the IEJV is the major contributor of technology, it will often seek to maintain control over that technology while the other partner may wish the technology to be controlled by the IEJV itself. Even if this problem can be resolved, there are likely to be disputes over how the technology is exploited. For example, the foreign partner may desire that the IEJV produce a more sophisticated product for export while the local partner may desire to produce a less sophisticated, or "appropriate," product for the local market.

DIFFERENT GOALS

It is appropriate to compare an IEJV to a marriage. At the beginning of the marriage, both partners, besides being in love, may seek the same goals. As the marriage progresses, one partner's goals may evolve in a different direction or both partners may wish to pursue different courses.

One IEJV started with an agreement that a substantial amount of the production would be exported. This suited the foreign partner, who needed "export credits" from the host country to sell its other products in that country. At first, the domestic partner went along with this approach because the IEJV was weak in marketing and desired that the foreign partner be responsible for the largest portion of the offtake. However, once the IEJV established a viable marketing function, and realizing that considerable demand existed in the host country for the IEJVs products (and at good prices), the domestic partner continued to push for a shift towards domestic sales. As happens in many IEJVs, one company eventually bought out the interests of the other. In this case, the domestic company bought out the foreign company.

DIFFERING MANAGEMENT STYLES, CONTROLS AND RESPONSIBILITIES ARISING OUT OF DISSIMILAR SIZE AND CULTURAL DIFFERENCES

Partners to IEJVs must decide how the entity will be controlled. Here, there are three reasonable choices. These are: The foreign partner controls the IEJV; the domestic partner does; or the partners agree to have the IEJV create its own controls. If anything else exists, the partners are normally asking for trouble. One IEJV was created between a large global company and a small family-owned company. Both companies were very good at what they did but had entirely different goals and management styles. The small local company had 80 employees, 21 of which were family members, including an uncle who had never been at the company's facilities (he lived in another city), and a 10-year old nephew of the local company's president. The purpose of this company was to meet the needs of the extended family and, given the high local income taxation, it was determined to be better to have all family members on the payroll at lower individual salaries.

This situation was absolutely intolerable for the global company, which initially agreed to allow the domestic company to control the IEJV, but could not resist repeated visits by employees of its human resources department with their strong anti-nepotism bent. The result of this was first a serious decline of morale followed by a decline in production quality and quantity. Eventually the partners dissolved the IEJV and went their separate ways.

CHANGING GOVERNMENT POLICIES

The marriage analogy also applies here, but in this case, the marriage may be of the "shotgun" variety, arranged by the government of the host country, or at least by its policies. During the 1970s and 1980s, many governments, particularly in the developing world, pursued policies that made it necessary for foreign companies to establish a local assembly or manufacturing presence. To reduce costs, many foreign companies responded to these policies by entering into joint ventures with local companies. When these countries moved towards market economies in the late 1980s and 1990s, the purpose for the IEJV for the foreign partner's point of view lessened or dissolved.

With lower tariffs and direct access to markets with finished products, the original purposes of the IEJV no longer existed. As this occurred, the IEJVs became more difficult to manage and many of the foreign partners pulled out. While there are still many valid reasons for IEJVs, potential partners "foreign" to the entity should carefully consider entering into IEJVs if a major purpose is to satisfy government requirements.

MAJOR ISSUES IN FORMING AN INTERNATIONAL EQUITY JOINT VENTURE

Before an IEJV is formed, the prospective partners should examine a number of critical issues, which, if understood and handled adequately, could result in limiting problems at a later date. This section covers five significant issues. These are: (1) how the partners will be compensated; (2) the control issues; (3) calls for additional capital; (4) staffing of the IEJV; and (5) termination issues.

PARTNERS' COMPENSATION

Eventually, all partners will desire to be compensated for their efforts in the IEJV. The forms and manner of compensation, however, can raise considerable concern as the joint venture progresses. In some cases, the IEJV itself will be designed to maximize profits. In this situation, the parties need to consider how, and when, such profits will be distributed. Normally, profits will be distributed in relationship to each party's percentage of ownership. However, the shareholders should also recognize the respective roles of each party in the operation of the IEJV. For example, if one party contributes a larger share of the management, marketing efforts and/or technology after the IEJV commences, that party may be entitled to, or demand, a higher proportion of the profits. To the extent that this can be recognized during the formation of the IEJV, it should be provided for and the IEJV documents should, in any case, be flexible enough to allow for changes in IEJV compensation as the operation changes through time.

When IEJV profits are distributed is another potential problem area. This is especially true when one party may be looking for longer-term gain, while another one is oriented towards shorter-term gain. The first company may desire to defer profit distribution in order to use those funds to expand the business while the other company may desire more immediate distribution of funds to meet the current needs of the investing company and its shareholders. This is of particular concern when one contributor is an individual or a smaller family-owned company while the other is a larger, more global organization. This problem can be partially solved through the creation of a dividend policy at the outset that can be adjusted after a number of years. This will be further detailed in our discussion of IEJV agreements.

In other cases, the IEJV will not be designed to maximize its own profits, but rather to maximize the profits or goals of its owners. In this case, to the extent allowed by the local taxing authorities, the IEJV would be designed as a breakeven proposition, and may even be designed to lose money in its early years.

Illustrative of this point is a joint venture that was designed to break even. The foreign investing party desired to make its profits directly through the sale of components, management contracts, and license royalties and fees. The local investing party desired to make its profits from the IEJV through management services, and by the purchase of the bulk of the output of the IEJV which the local company was to sell at a considerable profit in the home country.

CONTROL

The most common manner of controlling an IEJV is through equity control. However, equity control does not always indicate effective control. The following are some methods in which a minority equity party can establish and maintain effective control of an IEJV. For the sake of discussion, let us assume the minority equity party holds 40% of the shares while the majority party(ies) holds 60% of the shares:

- The minority party provides the key technology to the IEJV.
- The minority party provides the key manufacturing parts and components to the IEJV.
- The minority party manages the IEJV.
- The equity of the majority parties is split among many partners or is traded on a local or global stockmarket.

Typically, relatively equal parties to an IEJV will attempt to balance control either by the creation of a set of checks and balances or by a 50%/50% split in equity. This works part of the time, but also fails frequently.

The most famous example of a "balanced" IEJV that failed is Union Carbide India Ltd. ("UCIL"). UCIL was created with Union Carbide owning 50.9% of the equity while local Indian investors owned 49.1%. The Indian shareholders were given control of the board of directors and appointed the majority of the management. While the critical technology was provided by Union Carbide, the Indian partners suggested that it be adapted to Indian safety standards, and modified to provide for more Indian content in the construction of the plant. Both, Union Carbide claimed, were also requirements of Indian law.

Toxic MIC gas leaked from the plant in Bhopal on December 3, 1984, resulting in numerous deaths and injuries (which continues to this day if one examines the long-term environmental degradation of Bhopal, including an abnormally high number of stillbirths). Charges and countercharges continued throughout the entire litigation process. While we will never know who was really at fault (Union Carbide claims sabotage), because the case was settled for U.S. $470 Million in 1989, the Bhopal IEJV stands as one of the greatest failures of the IEJV process.[2]

The conventional wisdom that 50/50 IEJVs do not work was seriously questioned when two specialists with McKinsey & Company examined 49 alliances of the top companies in the U.S., Europe and Japan, and found:[3]

- 51% were successful for both parties; 16% for one party, and 33% resulted in failure for both. Success was defined as both having at least recovering their financial costs of capital, and in making some progress on their strategic objectives.
- Alliances were more effective for related businesses or new geographic areas.
- Alliances between strong and weak companies are least likely to succeed.
- Alliances with evenly split financial ownership are more likely to succeed (50/50%), than those in which one owner holds majority interest. Percentages of ownership are less important than establishing clear management control.
- More than ¾ of alliances have terminated with the acquisition of the IEJV by one of the owners.

Therefore, the issue of who controls the IEJV may be more important than ownership percentages. In dealing with the issue of control, it is probably best when initiating the IEJV, to determine which party should logically control it in the early years. If the project is one where technology is critical to success (e.g., Bhopal—Union Carbide), it may make practical sense to have the technology supplier control the IEJV until the technology is fully absorbed by it. If the project is one where finished, or near-finished, products are being introduced into a new geography, and the local party is well placed to market in that geography, then the local partner should control the IEJV. The parties might also consider including in the IEJV agreements, a provision that calls for control of one party for a certain period of time, but with a gradual shift of control to another party as the entity becomes firmly established.

CALLS FOR ADDITIONAL CAPITAL AND/OR GUARANTEES

Determining the financial needs of the IEJV is not always easy. There is always hope that the IEJV will generate enough capital for its own needs and that additional equity and/or debt will not be required. However, in the real world, this is often not the case. To prepare for the eventuality of the need for additional capital or debt financing, the parties should determine at the outset what their policies will be. In regard to additional capital, the following should be considered:

■ Is the capital needed for growth or survival?
■ If needed for survival, at what point do the parties agree to "pull the plug"? What does "pulling the plug" mean?
■ If needed for growth, how do the parties assess growth opportunities?
■ If one party wants to grow and the other does not, can the party seeking growth provide the bulk or all of the growth equity in exchange for reorienting the ownership percentages in favor of the investing party?
■ To what extent will the parties provide for third-party investors to cover growth needs? If this is acceptable, in what form would the equity be achieved (e.g., take public and/or sell to one or a few private investors)?

In the area of debt financing, a similar set of questions might be posed, but the parties may also consider to what extent, if any, they would be willing to guarantee the debt acquired by the IEJV. This is commonly required of IEJVs, particularly in their early years.

MANAGEMENT AND STAFFING

To succeed an IEJV must be properly staffed and managed. Staffing of non-management employees is normally accomplished in the local market. Top management, however, is a different matter. If the foreign party uses its management in key IEJV positions, it will obtain near effective control of the venture, but the IEJV will begin with expatriate management that may not be as effective in the initial years of the venture.

If top management comes from the local partner, it will give that partner near effective control of the venture, and a strong local presence, but may put in place individuals who are not as familiar with the technologies and products. Generally, a compromise is established where the various parties contribute the management with, perhaps, some management being recruited from outside the companies. The problem with this approach is that it often results in creating a management team that is pulled in different directions to the satisfaction of none of the parties. Therefore, it is important, at the outset, to determine clear management control. This may mean that one party concedes management to the other, but this might be preferable to mixed management. The decision of who manages must be made on the basis of the real needs of the IEJV. If technology is critical, the party providing technology should provide management in the early years. If local production or market conditions prevail, management should come from the local partner.

TERMINATION

As I have stated previously, in regard to agents and distributors, the time to plan for termination is when the relationship is being established. Because many IEJVs wind up being acquired by one of the partners, the parties should consider the possibility of building into the agreement buy-sell provisions that allow the selling party to recoup all of its financial investment, plus a reasonable amount of growth and its technology, if the seller is a party that contributed technology.

If the IEJV is to be terminated and/or liquidated, the parties should contemplate what happens to the contributed, or otherwise acquired, technology and critical equipment. Provisions should be built into the agreements allowing the parties who contributed the technology at least the right of first refusal to reobtain the technology and equipment as part of the liquidation procedure. If, for no other reason, this will prevent the technology and equipment from being acquired by a third party competitor in the liquidation proceedings.

INTERNATIONAL EQUITY JOINT VENTURE AGREEMENTS

Creating an IEJV is one of the most complex legal relationships that can be entered into, requiring a number of detailed legal agreements. This section concentrates on the International Equity Joint Venture Agreement, which is the base agreement to be used in designing the relationship. However, be aware that several other agreements will also have to be designed and executed, depending on the nature and complexity of the IEJV. In addition to the Agreement to be discussed, the parties should consider the need for the additional agreements defined below.

ADDITIONAL AGREEMENTS

Company Statutes

These are normally articles of incorporation and by-laws. These documents can be quite useful in defining how the IEJV will work on a day-to-day basis and in determining the issues of control through such devices as high-vote majorities (e.g., in an IEJV that has 5 board members [3 vs. 2], those issues which must be approved by 4 board members).

Management Agreement(s)

If the IEJV will be managed by one of the parties (or outsiders), and they will not become employees of the IEJV, these agreements may be needed to define costs, responsibilities, and other critical matters.

Supply Agreement(s)

If one or more of the parties to the IEJV are going to provide supplies, components or products to the IEJV, an agreement(s) defining how this will be done would be necessary.

Technical Assistance/Training Agreement(s)

If one or more of the parties are to provide technical assistance and/or training to the IEJV, which is not part of their equity contribution, such agreements will be needed.

License Agreement(s)

These can be:

■ Know-how licenses.
■ Trademark/Trade name licenses.
■ Patent licenses.

Again, if these licenses are not part of the equity contribution of the parties, then separate agreements are necessary.

Often, the previously mentioned agreements are included as exhibits or attachments to the International Equity Joint Venture Agreement, and they may be directly tied to that agreement. For example, management and license agreements may automatically terminate if the IEJV is dissolved and/or liquidated.

THE INTERNATIONAL EQUITY JOINT VENTURE AGREEMENT[4]

In designing the IEJV, special attention should be given to the International Equity Joint Venture Agreement (IEJVA). What follows is a checklist and discussion of the key areas to be covered in the IEJVA.

Parties

The IEJVA should clearly define the parties to the joint venture.

Name of the Joint Venture

Careful consideration should be given to the name of the joint venture. It is especially important to create a name that is distinct from the names of the partners if the joint venture is to truly be a distinct entity. There is a tendency to name a joint venture after the parties or one of the parties or a mixture of the two parties' names. This tendency should be discouraged unless one of the parties has an overwhelming majority of the equity (say 75% or 80%), and will truly manage the joint venture. In one case I was involved with the 50%/50% joint venture was named after the foreign company (say ABC of France). This led the general public to believe that the joint venture was a subsidiary of the parent company while it was being managed, for the most apart, by the local partner.

When production and quality problems arose, the foreign party received the brunt of the criticism in the local market.

Purpose of the Joint Venture

Determining the purpose of the joint venture may seem to be a small matter, but it is one that requires considerable thought and discussion. It has practical importance in that in most civil law countries (Europe and Latin America), the defined purpose may be all that the law will allow it to do without amending the corporate charter. That is, saying merely that the purpose of the joint venture is the *manufacture* of widgets may not give it the right to *sell* widgets.

Defining the purpose of the joint venture should come from intense discussions of the parties. This is an excellent checkpoint to prevent further problems. If the parties cannot agree on the purpose of the joint venture at the outset, then the chances are very high that problems will exist in the future.

Legal Form of the IEJV

Agreement needs to be reached on the legal form of the IEJV (e.g., limited liability or stock corporation), and the jurisdiction where it will be located.

Government Approvals

The joint venture should not commence operations until all government approvals have been achieved. Government approvals that might be sought, depending on the jurisdiction, include:

- Duty exemptions for capital equipment that will be imported from abroad.
- Permission to make foreign investments.
- Permission to import parts, components and products needed for the joint venture.
- Approval of the equity breakdown.
- Approval of any technology transfer agreements.
- Approval to bring into the country and employ foreign professionals.
- Approval of local content requirements.

Not all approvals will be necessary in all cases, but it is wise to know what approvals will be critical to the success of the joint venture.

Term

The parties may wish to select a term for the joint venture and place that term in their agreement. Reasons for setting a term could be:

■ It is required by the local law.
■ The joint venture may be for a limited duration.
■ You may wish to establish a threshold for termination if the purpose of the project is unattainable.

Obligations of the Parties

The obligations of each party to the joint venture should be identified and spelled out in some detail. The key obligations would normally include:

Equity Contribution

Here you need to determine how much equity the partners would include and in what form. Cash equity needs to be controlled for inflation and devaluation purposes. Additionally, the parties need to establish either a schedule or series of events that trigger the payments of the cash obligations, as usually the full amount pledged is not needed at the outset. For other than cash equity, you need to agree on how this equity will be valued. Examples of non-cash equity include:

■ Real property and fixtures
■ Personal property
■ Capital equipment
■ Components, products and spares
■ Training and services
■ Technology and intellectual property rights
■ Other intangibles, such as goodwill

You also want to assign percentages of ownership in relation to equity contributed. This does not have to be done in direct relation to value.

Financial Liabilities for Future Needs

In addition to the agreed financial contributions, the parties need to determine how the future equity needs of the joint venture will be fulfilled. This has already been discussed in some detail earlier in this chapter.

Services and Management: Future Contributions

Any or all of the parties may agree to provide services to the joint venture, either by as part of its equity contribution, for free or expenses only after the joint venture is established, or for a fee which should be established in the agreement or to be determined in the future. The same would be true for training and management services. Future contributions should be clearly defined and detailed.

Negative Covenants

In addition to the positive obligations of the parties, it is also necessary to include any negative covenants which the parties feel are necessary. These might include:

- No updates and enhancements on technology provided, or a general reference to no new technology.
- Limitations on the pledge of credit for additional financial needs of the joint venture.
- Limitations of liabilities.

Management and Control

As stated in the last section, management and control of the IEJV is one of the most critical areas for determining success. The issues of management and control can be looked at from a number of different areas:

- Formal control—shares, shareholders and directors.
- Appointment of officers.
- Appointment of the management team.

Formal management and control is control of the IEJV through share ownership, control of shareholders' meetings, and by appointment of directors. Normally, the number of shares issued to each party is a fairly good measure of control. However, there are numerous mechanisms to differentiate the raw number of shares from control. Different shares could be issued, some with voting rights and some without. In this case, it is possible for a minority party to control the IEJV. Shares can also be differentiated as to risk. In a situation where one party wants to assure itself a steady stream of revenues, it can be issued preferred shares with guaranteed dividends. The remaining shares could be issued as common stock with a dividend policy that restricts payments until the IEJV has met a number of goals.

The power of the stockholders meeting can be altered by the creation of certain super (high vote) majorities to prevent majority rule on certain critical issues. For example, in a 60%/40% joint venture, 65% of the votes could be required on such items as recapitalization, approval of annual budgets, activities outside the ordinary course of business, and change of corporate purpose. The same method could be applied to the board of directors. Using the same 60%/40% split described, the number of directors could be set at 3 for the 60% party and 2 for the 40% party, but 4 directors votes could be required for the approval of such items as the ones previously mentioned and other items that the parties deem important.[5]

Because the IEJV will normally be formed as a company, it will require the appointment of a certain number of corporate officers. These officers (president, vice-president, secretary, and treasurer) will normally run the company on a day-to-day basis, and will make critical decisions that normally must be ratified by the shareholders and directors. In addition to the officers could be the appointment of critical members of the management team including, perhaps, the directors of operations, finance, personnel and the company's legal counsel. Selection of these officers and key management personnel is critical to the IEJV's success or failure.

Use of Funds

The IEJV should have several provisions relating to the use of the funds contributed to, or earned by, the joint venture. The parties should clearly define the uses to which the initial and subsequent capital contributions are to be used by the joint venture. Additionally, a budget for the initial year should be established and projected budgets for future years should be developed. Finally, financial delegations of authority should be established.

This section may also be the appropriate place for the determination of the dividend policy. Two factors to be considered here are:

When Will the Dividends Be Paid?

This can be tied to accomplishing certain goals plus the availability of funds. Dividends can also be restricted to a time when the IEJV has covered all previous losses or restricted as long as the IEJV has outstanding debts.

Restrictions on Dividend Payments

A typical dividend policy may take the following approach. All profits of the IEJV during its first three years must be reinvested in the company. In years four through six, one half of the profits may be distributed as dividends with the rest to be invested in the company. Beginning in the seventh year, profits will be distributed as the majority deems fit.

Information and Reporting

The parties must decide what type of information they would like to have from the joint venture and what rights they would have to audit the records of the organization. This is often an area of great dispute, especially when the partners to the venture have different methods of reporting. It is also often an area where cultural differences play a significant role.

Obviously, the nature and type of the business to be pursued will impact greatly on what information needs to be reported, and why. As a general rule, however, the parties should give at least some consideration to:

■ The scope of records needed to be maintained by the joint venture
■ The frequency and types of reports needed
■ Length of retention of records
■ Audit rights of all parties

Intellectual Property

Any and all types of intellectual property that will be contributed or licensed by the parties, should be subject to separate license agreements that will be attached to the joint venture agreement. The IEJVA should include a description of these attachments and perhaps make clear that in the case of intellectual property that is licensed, the license(s) granted shall only continue for the term of the agreement, or the dissolution of the joint venture, whichever comes first. If training and/or technical support is included with the licenses, the degree and extent of such training and technical support should be defined, along with any fees to be charged to the IEJV.

The IEJVA should also consider what might happen to intellectual property developed by the IEJV itself. The two key areas of concern are the right to the intellectual property by the shareholders and what happens to such intellectual property if the joint venture ceases operations.

Joint Venture Opportunities

As a separate legal organization, the equity joint venture is likely to develop *its own business opportunities*. The parties to the joint venture should consider:

- The criteria by which the joint venture can accept these opportunities (e.g., are high vote majorities necessary and, if so, at what level of commitment?).
- Which opportunities must be referred to the shareholders.

Admission of New Shareholders

The parties to the joint venture need to decide under what conditions, if any, they are willing to allow for new shareholders. At the very least, they should consider providing preemptive rights to the original shareholders. These rights would allow shareholders the opportunity to purchase the shares of shareholders withdrawing from the joint venture, and assure that if additional shares are issued, that each original party shall have the right to purchase those shares in proportion to their existing equity in the joint venture.

Disputes and Dispute Resolution

No matter how well planned and organized, there is a high potential for disputes among shareholders of the IEJV. Should conflicts and disputes reach a level in which one party decides to litigate, there is a strong likelihood that the IEJV is destined for failure. Therefore, it is incumbent upon the parties to build into the joint venture methods of dispute resolution that allow for meaningful solutions short of litigation.

One of the best methods created to resolve disputes short of litigation or arbitration is the Center for Public Resources "CPR Model Procedure for Settlement of Transnational Business Disputes."[6] The CPR Procedure consists of conciliation short of arbitration, which is normally fashioned by business executives and not judges or lawyers. As in all conciliation procedures, the results are non-binding. It is recommended that the CPR Procedures be included in the IEJVA under dispute resolution as the first form of dispute resolution to be sought when the parties have reached an impasse.

Under the CPR Procedure, the parties sign *initiating agreements*, which can be done after the dispute arises, which cover:

- The nature of the dispute and the relief sought.
- Names of the management representatives of each party.
- The time and place of a meeting.
- The language to be used at the meeting.
- What information will be exchanged.
- An agreement to suspend any legal proceedings until after the meeting takes place.

In the CPR Procedure, the parties may withdraw at any time. The parties also appoint a neutral advisor who is normally a businessperson in the same, or related, industry. The meeting is conducted in a formal manner in which all sides present their positions under the supervision of the neutral advisor. At the conclusion of the meeting, the management representatives meet with the neutral advisor and try to reach agreement. In absence of an agreement, the management representative may then agree to arbitrate or to litigate.

This procedure has tended to be very effective, especially in cases where the neutral advisor is culturally sensitive to the issues of all the parties. When successful, it is an inexpensive and sensible alternative to time-consuming and costly arbitration and/or litigation. Most importantly, it keeps lawyers out of the process until it can be determined that the businesspersons cannot resolve the issues on their own.

Should conciliation or mediation not be successful, the parties should seriously consider using some form of binding arbitration. *Arbitration* has the following advantages over litigation:

- It keeps disputes out of the national (local) courts that would tend to favor the local party over the foreign party.
- It allows the parties to select decision-makers (arbitrators) who are knowledgeable in the business aspects of the dispute instead on relying on local judges and court-appointed "experts."

■ It tends to take less time, and sometimes is less expensive than using the court systems.

■ Arbitration is recognized by most countries as an effective alternative to litigation, and most courts will enforce the judgment of internationally recognized arbitrators.

The IEJVA should include a description of the arbitration convention agency and forum to be used. Check with your attorney to determine which conventions apply to which countries. The two most popular arbitration rules used in international business are the International Chamber of Commerce (ICC) and United Nations Commission for International Trade Law (UNCITRAL). If the parties are unable to agree on arbitration in one of their countries, the favored international forums are Geneva, London, New York, Paris and Stockholm (which is favored by the PRC).

In preparing for arbitration in the IEJVA agreement, the arbitration clause should contain:

■ A provision for conciliation (CPR) before arbitration.

■ A determination of what types of issues can be arbitrated (e.g., broad—covering all items, or narrow, e.g., technical issues only, with other issues to be litigated).

■ Have a governing law.

■ Have a place of hearing—forum.

■ Designate the applicable set of rules (e.g., ICC or UNCITRAL).

■ Have rules for appointment and the number of arbitrators (normally an odd number, 1, 3, 5, etc.).

■ Try to set limits on self-settlement; contain a trigger clause, after so many days, which institutes the arbitration procedure.

■ Designate the language in which the arbitration will be conducted.

■ Determine, in advance, how arbitration costs will be borne (e.g., the loser or equally).

■ Determine the currency of payment.

■ Have a provision for enforcement of the award through a particular court or courts.

Dissolution and Buy-Out

If the IEJV is designed for a limited period, a provision for the dissolution and buy-out is absolutely essential. However, because many IEJVs will ultimately be purchased by one of the parties, it is probably wise to have such a provision even in the IEJVs of unlimited duration. The dissolution and buy-out provisions should consider:

- The price of purchase or sale that can be accomplished by tieing price to certain financial formulas (net book value; x times profits; x times revenues; agreed to value).
- The time at which the formula(s) would apply.
- The time necessary for sale completion.
- The terms of early dissolution for cause or by agreement.
- How assets and liabilities will be distributed upon dissolution (see discussion on intellectual property on pp. 194–195).
- Survival of obligations of the parties.

Miscellaneous Provisions

- The governing law and choice of forum.
- The controlling language to be used in the IEJV, particularly in communications.
- Notices—form and delivery method.
- Insurance.
- Publicity. To what extent should the IEJV be public and to what extent are the shareholders involved in making decisions about publicity.

SUMMARY AND CONCLUSION

Equity and non-equity joint ventures offer a viable method of entering and expanding activities in the global marketplace. Under the right circumstances, they can be a very effective way to avoid going it alone in new, or difficult, markets. With the right partners, and with appropriate attention to detail, particularly in the early years, they can be quite successful.

However, joint ventures—particularly equity joint ventures—are difficult to design and manage, and therefore should not be entered into without considerable research and commitment. For those companies who are willing to make such commitments, the rewards can be great.

REFERENCES

1. Business International Corporation, *201 Checklists: Decision-Making in International Operations*, New York: BIC, 1980, See Checklists 44 through 48.

2. An excellent brief article on the Bhopal case is Subrata, N. Chakravarty, "The Ghost Returns," *Forbes*, December 10, 1990, p. 7.

3. Bleeke, Joel and Ernst, David "The Way to Win in Cross-Border Alliances," *Harvard Business Review*, November–December, 1991, Vol. 69, No. 6. pp. 127–135.

4. An overview on equity joint venture agreements found in Goldsweig, David N., and Cummings, Roger H., *International Joint Ventures: A Practical Approach to Working With Foreign Investors in the U.S. and Abroad*, 2nd Edition, Chicago: American Bar Association, Section of International Law and Practice, 1990, p. 428.

5. Ibid., see pp. 13–29.

6. For further information on the CPR Procedure, contact the Center for Public Resources in New York, New York.

Chapter 12

METHOD 9: ESTABLISHING DIRECT OPERATIONS ABROAD

INTRODUCTION

The establishment of your company's own operations abroad is perhaps the most complicated and expensive of all of the international business transactions. For definitional purposes, we are describing the acquisition of, or the formation of, a wholly-owned direct operation outside the territorial boundaries of the home country.

The direct operation is more complicated for a number of reasons. First, everything associated with the direct operations will have to be performed by the company. Using agents, distributors, licensees, or joint venture partners gives you a local presence that now must be acquired through your own efforts. Second, you now must deal directly with the local government agencies including those associated with granting licenses and—with the exception of the creation of a representative office—the local tax authorities.

Third are the staffing problems associated with your own operations. These are particularly difficult in the initial years where you may wish to use a number of expatriates to get the business going, and to train their local replacements. Finally, is the issue of conforming your local operations to the overall goals and strategic objectives of the parent company. This becomes particularly complicated when the parent company begins to develop global tax strategies which may require the foreign direct operations to "minimize" their profits. This may require companies to develop incentive packages based on "company contributions" rather than "company profits," and becomes very difficult in countries where profit sharing is required among the local employees.[1]

Yet most major companies prefer, where the market dictates, to create their own direct operations abroad. For this, there are many reasons, the three most important are control, profit maximization and global image. The pros and cons of establishing direct operations abroad are discussed in detail in the next section.

While some companies prefer to start their foreign operations with the direct approach, most companies "graduate" to direct operations after experimenting with other forms of international business transactions. An agent or distributor's business may have grown in the market to the point where the economies of scale dictate the establishment of your own marketing subsidiary. Your company may desire, after an effective licensing arrangement, to manufacture and sell the product on a direct basis. Direct operations are also created often by the purchase of the entire equity in an existing equity joint venture. Finally, the foreign company may establish direct operations through the merger or acquisition of a local company.

As with other international strategies, establishing a network of direct operations may stand alone or it could be combined as part of a global strategy that uses a combination of direct operations in key countries, distributors and agents in others, and licensing in still other countries. Often, regional wholly-owned subsidiaries are established to service the needs of agents, distributors, and licensees.

Direct operations can take many forms. These include:

- *Representative Office,* where a small staff is located in a jurisdiction to explore possibilities and to fly the global corporate flag.
- *Financial Subsidiary,* which is established primarily to take advantage of the availability of financing and/or for tax reasons, including the use of tax treaties.
- *Regional Headquarters,* which are established to service marketing and manufacturing entities in a particular region (e.g., Europe, Latin America, or Asia).

- *Marketing subsidiary,* which is normally established to provide a direct sales force in a particular country or region.

- *Manufacturing subsidiary,* which is established to take advantage of the benefits of local manufacturing.

- *Full subsidiary,* which could perform finance, marketing and manufacturing functions.

ADVANTAGES OF DIRECT OPERATIONS

The major reasons why companies establish direct operations abroad are control, profit maximization, and global image. These and other advantages of direct operations are explored below:

CONTROL

The major reason why a company will establish direct operations is to achieve the control it cannot achieve with other forms of international business transactions. The more global a company is, the more it will attempt to *rationalize manufacturing, sales, services and R&D* to achieve its various global strategies of revenues, marketshare and profit maximization. This can best be achieved by obtaining, and maintaining, direct control over all of its operations. For example, in the area of marketing and sales, the company knows its customers, and their needs. It receives direct feedback from its direct sales force and can adjust to customer needs and market forces.

Direct control also allows a global-oriented company to be more *flexible*, which allows it to respond more rapidly and effectively to global changes in such areas as taxation, accounting standards and currency fluctuations. Production and sales can be moved to areas of more favorable tax regimes or weaker currencies, allowing for the rational policies previously mentioned.

Finally, direct control provides the greatest amount of *protection of a company's intellectual property*. Agents and distributors could negatively impact a company's trade names and trademarks. Licensees can do the same, but also may bring into question a company's patents, trade secrets, and know-how. The same problems could result from consortium and/or equity joint ventures.

PROFIT MAXIMIZATION

The truly global company will have, as one of its highest priorities, the maximization of its profits on a global basis. This can best be accomplished with direct control over all foreign operations. This is normally achieved through a combination of creative sourcing, tax incentives, transfer pricing, intercompany royalties, and global management and control of currency fluctuations. Central management can direct captive operations to achieve maximum results for the benefit of the entire company.

GLOBAL IMAGE

It is more difficult to create a positive global image if the company's international strategy is subject to the whims of "partners" who may see things differently than headquarters. Larger companies may be expected by their customers to have direct operations in the key countries, particularly if they are providers of goods and services to other global companies. Corporate image, goals and objectives can best be accomplished when the company directly controls the forces which assist in establishing those images, goals and objectives.

BARRIERS TO ENTRY

A company may wish to establish direct operations in order to overcome barriers to entry which are imposed by various countries or regions. Many companies have established direct operations in the European Economic Community in order to qualify as a European company, and thereby enhance their access into the EEC. Asian and European companies have established operations in North America to take advantage of the North American Free Trade Agreement (NAFTA).

GOVERNMENT INCENTIVES

Most governments now have some forms of financial and market incentives to companies willing to locate in their countries. Some of these incentives are on the state or provincial level. Various Canadian provinces offer incentives, as do countries like Belgium, Ireland, Luxembourg and Spain within the EEC. These incentives may include free manufacturing space, worker reimbursement, training and various tax incentives.

AVAILABILITY OF LOCAL FINANCING

The ability to develop a global financial strategy may be enhanced by having direct operations in numerous jurisdictions. The establishment of local operations normally enhances the ability to borrow in the local market. Sometimes the funds acquired in one country can be used in others. Therefore, a global company may be able to borrow in countries with lower interest rates and expand operations in countries with higher interest rates.

ATTRACTION OF THE BEST HUMAN RESOURCES

It is almost conventional wisdom to suggest that the best and the brightest people are more likely to be attracted by the global corporation than by their domestic counterparts. Global corporations may offer better financial packages and benefits, more global opportunities and more prestige.

LEGAL INSULATION

If a company has a direct local presence and contracts locally, it may have created a certain level of legal insulation for the parent company. This tends to lessen the number of lawsuits and decrease the amounts paid in settlements.

DISADVANTAGES OF DIRECT OPERATIONS

The complexity and expense of direct operations are their greatest disadvantages. Those, and other disadvantages, are explored below.

COMPLEXITY

The commitment to establish direct local operations is a complex one. The best way to characterize this is to describe the events of a small U.S. company that decided to establish its first overseas direct marketing operations in England. The company felt that England was the logical place to establish its first direct operations because of the size of the market plus what it felt were language and cultural similarities. In reality, it learned quickly that England was indeed a true foreign operation. In acquiring its property lease, the company was placed up against a property system that was totally different from anything it had experienced in the U.S. It had considerable difficulties in obtaining permission to send one of its employees to manage the operation. Recruiting local employees was a nightmare, as were obtaining local licenses. It had little idea of the costs of doing business in the London area, including such basics as telephones and office supplies. Finally, the company had considerable difficulty in importing its first product shipment. Nevertheless, all problems were eventually solved in England and the local operation has been a success. The corporate executive in charge told me: "If England is so difficult, I wonder what it would have been like in a developing country. It was worth it, but you must be committed and have the patience of Job."

TAKES MORE CAPITAL/ASSUMES ALL RISKS

Clearly the advantages of such transactions as licensing and equity joint ventures are the ability to share the costs with your technology or equity partners. Additionally, the start-up costs associated with a direct operation are normally much more than twice the value of a 50% ownership in an equity joint venture. This is because the cost of outside advice, initial travel and deposits are considerable. If establishing a direct operation requires the use of expatriates (people from the home, or other countries, in the country in which the direct operations are established), the cost soars. The cost of an employee, spouse, and two children, living abroad normally can be 2½ to 3 times that of New York if placed in London or Frankfurt, and 4 times the cost if placed in Tokyo.

With the increased costs comes increased risks. The company establishing the direct operations now must bear all risks associated with the local operations. Risks may also be increased during the learning curve when it is becoming more familiar with local customs, procedures and laws.

HIGHER TAX LIABILITIES

The foreign tax liabilities associated with agents and distributors, if handled correctly, should be negligible. With licensing, there may be some royalty withholding taxes but the foreign party is usually spared other taxes including corporate tax. With a consortium, tax liabilities are considerably lessened and in the equity joint venture, tax may be limited to the participant's percentage of ownership plus, perhaps, taxes on royalty withholding and some taxes on profit repatriation. With a direct operation, all taxes could apply, and it will be easier for the tax authorities to locate and collect taxes.

DISFAVOR OF LOCAL GOVERNMENTS

Although this has changed for the better in the past decade, some countries still look with disfavor on wholly-owned direct operations. They may be restricted in bidding government projects and, in some cases, wholly-owned operations have been under considerable pressure to bring in local partners.

The experience of the Control Data Corporation in Mexico is illustrative. Because it was created prior to 1973, Control Data de Mexico (CDM) was "grandfathered"—that is, it was able to remain 100% foreign-owned. In 1985, CDM desired to expand its space in Mexico City. It was told that it could not do so unless it sold some of its equity to Mexican nationals or companies. CDM was allowed to go ahead with its plans without "nationalizing" after a major earthquake in Mexico City lessened the amount of available commercial property. CDM agreed to lease some of its space to a Mexican government agency in exchange for being allowed to retain its total foreign ownership.[2]

STRUGGLE BETWEEN HEADQUARTERS AND SUBSIDIARIES

Later in this chapter, we will discuss parent/subsidiary relationships. Suffice it is to say at this point, problems are likely to surface between the parent and foreign subsidiary over such matters as:

- Assessment of subsidiary performance
- Where profits should be taken
- Accounting, ordering and billing procedures
- Motivation of local personnel
- Quality issues
- Ethical standards and company policies
- Role the company plays in the community
- Different conceptions of the corporation

TYPES OF DIRECT OPERATIONS

REPRESENTATIVE OFFICE

Sometimes also known as a liaison office, this type of direct operation is established when a company wishes to explore a market but is not yet willing to establish an operation that will subject the parent company to the general legal jurisdiction of a country, including taxation. It is also used in cases where a company is unable to sell in the local market, because of boycott and other restrictions, but wants to plant its flag so that it is able to operate quickly when the boycott is lifted. One example of this was the boycott on certain products imposed by President Carter after the Soviet Union invaded Afghanistan in the late 1970s. Representative offices were also popular for U.S. companies in Vietnam during 1994 and 1995, and are used frequently in Algeria because it is illegal to appoint agents and distributors in that country.

Once established, a representative office allows you to establish a few people in the country and to rent space for the purpose of conducting business on a limited basis. Marketing (not sales) personnel are free to call on prospective clients for the purpose of distributing sales brochures and, in some cases, product samples. The office can also rent, or lease, a hotel room or apartment for the purpose of serving company personnel and others who visit the territory. However, the office itself is not allowed to book orders or to receive payments from customers of any kind or it will lose its tax-free status. Orders can be passed back to the foreign parent for "acceptance" at home.

The cost of representative offices are often shared by a number of companies who wish to leverage the opportunity to serve markets in the future. This was common in the People's Republic of China in the 1970s and in the Soviet Union in the 1980s. Today, many consulting and law firms have opened representative offices in Hanoi or Ho Chi Minh City (Saigon), which can be used for marketing purposes and product promotion.

THE BRANCH OFFICE

Normally, a company would consider a branch office if it desires total home office control, secrecy, and simplicity of management. A branch office is exactly how it sounds. Rather than establishing a legally distinct subsidiary in another country, the branch is registered with the local authorities as another office (branch) of the parent company, or in some cases, a branch of a subsidiary of the parent company. The major disadvantage of the branch office is that it subjects the parent company itself to local taxation. Additionally, the assets of the parent or subsidiary company are also exposed in the country(ies) of registration.

Most international lawyers would generally advise against using branch offices because of the exposure of the parent company to local taxation, but in some cases they may be necessary or the favored form of direct operations. A branch may be necessary for U.S. companies who make a Subchapter S election for tax purposes. Subchapter S corporations are precluded by law from having foreign subsidiaries. While this election generally applies to smaller companies (although some have been known to reach more than U.S. $100 Million in revenues), some Subchapter S corporations do establish foreign operations.

If the operation to be started abroad is likely to have substantial losses in its initial years, the branch office may be a viable alternative. Just as all profits will be ascribed to the parent company, so will the losses of its foreign branches. Taking these losses against the profits of the parent company may then result in a significant tax savings to the parent company. Therefore, a company may desire to begin as a branch operation and shift to a subsidiary form when the branch office becomes profitable.

As mentioned previously, one of the major advantages of a branch office over a subsidiary is the simplicity of management, and secrecy. In most countries, branch offices are easier to set up and dismantle. Because the office is completely controlled by the parent company, the parent company can maintain full control and secrecy over company records and intellectual property. Although there are a few exceptions, the U.K. included, most countries to not require financial disclosures of the branch office, while such are required for subsidiary entities.

THE SUBSIDIARY

When a company creates a subsidiary, it creates a distinct company (in this case, foreign), which, although it might be entirely owned and "controlled" by the parent company, or a second-tier subsidiary, is distinct in terms of having its own stock, management team and physical and intangible assets and liabilities. Figure 12-1 illustrates the forms it might take.

Once you have decided to use a subsidiary, it is important to select the *type of subsidiary company* that is appropriate to the company's business. A "stock" company is the appropriate type of subsidiary if you are creating a large company, bid on large projects or plan to take the company public. A "limited liability" company is preferable for ease of administration, less reporting requirements, and fewer upfront and continuing costs. This type of company is most similar to the privately-held U.S. corporation. Almost every legal system provides for both stock and limited liability companies. Table 12-1 indicates some of the types of companies available.

The structures of German companies provide good examples of the types of subsidiaries that may be formed:

Figure 12-1

SUBSIDIARY FORMS

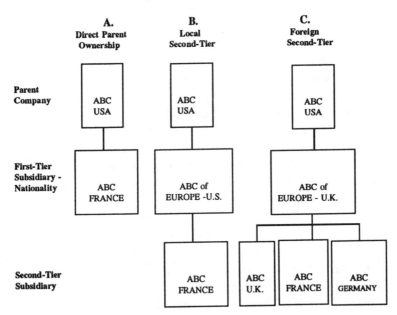

Table 12-1
Stock Corporation and Limited Liability Companies

	Stock Corporations	Limited Liability Companies
Brazil	Sociedade anónima (SA)	Limitada (Ltda.)
U.K.	Public or Private Company, Limited	Private Company, Ltd. (Pte. Co. Ltd.)
France	Société anonyme (SA)	Societe a responsabilite limitee (SARL)
Germany	Aktiengesellschaft (AG)	Gesellschaft mit beschränkter Haftung (GmbH)
Italy	Societa Per Azioni (SPA)	Societa a responsibilita limitata (SRL)
Japan	Kabushiki kaisha (KK)	Yugen kaisha (YK)
Republic of Korea	Chusik hoesa (CH)	Yuhan hoesa (YH)
Spain	Sociedad anónima (SA)	Sociedad de Responsibilidad Limitada (SL)
Turkey	Anonim Sirket (AS)	Turk Limited Sirket (TLS)

Aktiengesellschaft (AG) Is The Stock Company

This company is normally used for large operations, or for those companies that require a substantial registered capital in order to bid on large projects, particularly government projects. An AG can also be traded on local, and perhaps foreign, stock markets. To start an AG, a minimum of one hundred thousand DM are required as registered capital, of which 25% must be paid in. The AG requires a minimum of five shareholders (which can be natural or legal persons). This prevents, at least in a formal sense, 100% ownership by the parent, or first-tier, subsidiary. If 1,000 shares are issued, 996 might be held by the parent and one share each by four trusted individuals, normally company employees. This nominal ownership does increase paperwork and sometimes creates problems when one of the employees leaves the company, retires, or dies.

An AG must have both a supervisory board and a management board. The supervisory board must be composed of at least three (3) natural persons elected by stockholders or in some large companies, by stockholders and employees. The supervisory board controls and supervises the management board. The management board may be composed of one or more natural persons. They are appointed by the supervisory board and are responsible for day-to-day management of the company. Additionally, the AG has a greater responsibility of reporting its activities to government agencies.

Gesellschaft mit beschränkter Haftung (GmbH) Is the Limited Liability Company

It is the most frequently chosen by foreign investors because of its lower costs and simplicity of operation. It *cannot* be publically traded and may place the company at a disadvantage if it plans to bid large public projects. The GmbH requires a start-up capital of DM 50,000 (with at least DM 25,000 contributed when application for registration is made). It requires only one shareholder who can be a natural or legal person.

Management of a GmbH is much less complex. No supervisory board is required unless the GmbH regularly employs more than 2,000 people. A management board is also not required, but the company must have a managing director who is responsible for managing and representing the company. This must be a natural person, but there are no citizen, domicile, or residence requirements for the managing director. The company, however, must have a corporate office within Germany. In summary, with a

GmbH, a foreign investor can hold all of the shares and appoint someone to manage the company who does not have to be present in Germany.

ACQUIRING A LOCAL COMPANY

Some companies will chose to establish direct operations abroad through the acquisition of an existing local company. This is often accomplished through the acquisition of an existing distributor, licensee, or joint venture partner. In other cases, a company will try to acquire a totally unrelated party. In either case, acquiring a local operation is normally undertaken to capture or establish marketshare; to create a local presence and acquire local facilities; to acquire products and services that are unavailable to the foreign investor in order to complement existing product lines; and/or to enter into new or related markets.

The rules and techniques for acquiring companies are fairly standard throughout the world, but acquiring companies must also look for certain country-unique variables which are imposed by local governments. Examples of these local requirements are limitations on foreign ownership, and other requirements for employee retention, reporting and additional investment considerations.

RULES AND TECHNIQUES

The two general ways to acquire a foreign company are to acquire either part or all of its assets, or to acquire all or part of its stock. Because assets and stock purchases are very different, each will be discussed individually.

Asset Purchase

An asset purchase is one in which one party purchases all, or part, of the assets of an existing company. That is, Company F, the foreign company, purchases assets from Company L, the local company. Because the stock of Company L is not purchased, that company continues to exist—at least on paper. Company F will then need to place the assets within an existing local company, or establish a new company in the local jurisdiction, in which to place the acquired assets.

Foreign companies undertake asset purchases for a number of reasons. Asset purchases allow the company to acquire only those assets needed. This is particularly useful if the foreign company only wishes to acquire part of the business. This would also allow the remaining part of the acquired company to continue its operations. It is common for one company to purchase only a division or product line of another company. For example, this approach is useful if Company L has three divisions and/or product lines and desires to sell only one division and/or product line to acquire cash or other assets needed to invest in the other two divisions and/or product lines.

Another advantage of the asset purchase approach is that the acquiring company should not be responsible for any liability not assumed, although some contractual and labor obligations may have to be assumed. In a stock purchase, all liabilities associated with the shares will normally be assumed by the purchaser. Finally, it is sometimes a better approach for the seller to separate the assets from shares and sell each as separate transactions to different parties. For example, a transaction I was involved in in Brazil a number of years ago worked as follows:

- All of the operating assets except real estate of a foreign-held corporation were sold to a local Brazilian party. This party did not assume any liabilities, except those associated with the particular assets.

- The foreign-held corporation then sold the real estate in the local market and used the proceeds, in part, to pay off remaining liabilities.

- The foreign-held corporation then sold the shares to another foreign party. The additional foreign party desired the shares of the paper company because it had some tax losses and registered capital. The tax losses can be carried forward for up to five years and the purchaser desired to apply such losses to their current profits. The registered capital could be used to remit profits at a lower tax rate since the allowable amount of remittances at the lower tax level was dependent upon the total amount of registered capital. Registered capital is that amount registered with the Central Bank of Brazil, and parties were allowed to repatriate up to 12.5% of that amount at a lower tax level.

In both an asset and stock purchase, the buying company should perform very careful due diligence on the assets to be acquired. This due diligence would cover the following assets (and the liabilities, if any, tied to the assets):

- *Cash* on hand and in financial institutions.
- *Real and personal property.* In the case of real property, the buying company should make sure that a foreign company has the right to acquire it. Mexico, Switzerland, and certain parts of Australia, along with the United States, are examples where restrictions against foreign ownership of real estate may apply. It is also advisable to check states and provinces. In the state of Minnesota, for example, foreign individuals and companies cannot acquire certain agricultural properties. Additionally, in Eastern Europe and the former Soviet Union, land titles may not be clear and it may take years to establish ownership.
- *Accounts Receivable.* These should be reviewed carefully, and aged. In the case of government debt, be sure it is assignable.
- *Inventory.* This should be checked carefully. Boxes should be opened. One company found empty boxes after acquiring the inventory. The purchaser may wish to hold back on some of the payment until the useability of the inventory can be determined.
- *Contracts.* If acquiring contracts (e.g., purchase and sales, distributor, etc.), make sure they are assignable or have been assigned before closing.
- *Intellectual Property.* Check registration, ownership and assignability of the intellectual property. I stopped one transaction when we determined that so-called license rights were really only unassignable distribution rights.
- *Employment Agreements.* These can be both a benefit and/or a detriment depending on who is covered, and under what circumstances. In countries with tough labor laws (Western Europe and Latin America are regions which come to mind), the purchaser may wish to decide which employees it wants the seller to terminate before assuming ownership. In places like Germany, be very careful to determine all labor rights before acquiring any assets or stock.
- *Miscellaneous.* Insurance, telephone lines, etc. Be very careful to understand your acquired liabilities, and the cost of insurance. In certain countries such items as telephone lines and equipment may be very valuable. Up to a few years ago in Mexico you needed to purchase stock in the telephone company before you could acquire telephone lines. I know of one case in Brazil where a company acquired a whole business in order to acquire access to telephone lines. Be particularly careful in Eastern Europe and the former Soviet Union.

Stock Purchase

A stock purchase is one in which the foreign company (F) acquires some, or all, of the stock of the local company (L). In this case, Company F will be acquiring not only the assets but also the liabilities of the company through its acquisition of the company stock.

On the surface, this appears to be a much simpler transaction than the asset purchase. For starters, it is possible to avoid dealing with company management by going directly to the shareholders. Additionally, the purchaser should be able to avoid having to establish a new company by transferring all documents as part of the transaction. Corporate identity is also preserved as it should be easier to reserve the corporate name and logos. Finally, if the commercial contracts and intellectual property agreements have a "successor in interest" clause, it may not be necessary to assign them.

However, the stock purchase is not without its disadvantages. Some of these include:

- There may be disagreements among shareholders which could hold up or prevent the transaction.
- Because you are assuming all liabilities, more careful due diligence may be required.
- If the stock is publicly traded, the purchaser may be required to obtain the approval of a local securities and exchange agency.
- The purchaser is more likely to have to assume employee contracts and liabilities. In some countries—Germany, Austria, and Benelux—workers counsels or union approval may be required.
- The purchaser will also need to acquire all outstanding stock options and warrants.

GOVERNMENT REQUIREMENTS

Besides the considerations applied to asset and stock purchases, a company may need to consider additional requirements that might be imposed by governments (national and local). These may apply even if a new foreign investment is made, but governments are particularly concerned when local companies are acquired. In addition to the real estate ownership prohibitions, there may be other basic requirements, including balancing imports with exports, training of local personnel, restricted geographical access and the requirement to use state-of-the art technology.

In recent years, the trend has been to lessen these government-imposed requirements. Mexico, for example, in its Foreign Investment Law of 1993, considerably weakened, or ended, all of the above requirements that had existed for 20 years.

SUBSIDIARY/PARENT RELATIONSHIPS: MOTIVATING SUBSIDIARY SUCCESS

Now that you have created your direct operations, you need to examine how they will be managed and controlled. This final section of the chapter examines the general approach you can take to operations management, how to evaluate performance, and a discussion of motivation techniques used by successful companies for their foreign operations. This discussion centers around the foreign subsidiary, but it also can apply to representative offices and branch companies.

APPROACH TO SUBSIDIARY MANAGEMENT[3]

Historically, how companies managed and controlled their overseas operations was, in part, a result of home country culture and relative positions of their countries in world trade. After World War II, the United States was predominant in world trade, and the internationalization of U.S.-based companies tended to reflect this predominance. Beginning in the 1970s, and strengthening throughout the 1980s and early 1990s, Western Europe and Japan arose as significant challengers to the United States for a major portion of trade between, and among, nations. This was further complicated in the 1980s and 1990s by the creation of globally-oriented companies.

U.S. companies expanded abroad in the 1950s and 1960s as the result of post-war reconstruction, and the pent-up demand for products and services which the United States was best able to provide. Significant U.S. companies developed an *"international" strategy.* That is, one in which development of overseas subsidiaries was centered around products developed in the United States which were then "internationalized" for global use. Research and development tended to take place primarily, or totally, in the United States with overseas subsidiaries producing products and services to U.S. specifications and with only marketing and sales left to local control. This was a logical outgrowth of economic conditions, and the U.S. "can do" attitude.

European companies took a very different approach. For starters, more significant European companies were still family-owned, which allowed for more independence of action. Additionally, Europe was more oriented to smaller, more independent, markets. As a result, the Europeans tended to take more of a *"portfolio" approach* to international management, where each foreign subsidiary was allowed to operate independently in meeting the needs of its local market, subject primarily to overall financial bottom-lines.

The approach of Japanese companies was different than either that of the U.S. or European companies. The Japanese developed an *"export-based" strategy* in which the world was treated as a single market but tied to tight control from the home office in product creation, production and marketing and sales. This was the logical outgrowth of the lowered trade barriers brought about by the GATT, and the policies of the Japanese government which imposed limitations on overseas investment.

While all three strategies were somewhat effective in the 1980s, the world of today and of the 21st century calls for some creative approaches to subsidiary management which need to keep the following factors in mind:

- The need to create international opportunities for all key employees. Suffice it is to say that a German engineer has more in common with an American engineer than a German farmer.

- The need to take advantage of the creative skills found in all countries, rather than reliance on home-country talent only. This has required a shift in thinking of some U.S. and Japanese companies in particular. (See Chapter 4 on Sourcing.)

- Creation of global competitiveness to capture economies of scale. Knowing what products and services can be globalized, which products and services might respond to local considerations.

- The need to understand and react to the contradictory world forces of the one hand, the increasing globalization of communications, transportation, banking and finance, and data management; while on the other hand the increasing desire of humans to establish their own national and ethnic identity, which has resulted in the explosion of nation-states and inter-ethnic conflict. This is discussed in more detail in Chapter 13.

SUBSIDIARY PERFORMANCE EVALUATION

Evaluating the performance of domestic operations is difficult enough, but once you cross international borders, the process becomes considerably more difficult. This is especially true if the company has developed a global approach to its operations, products and profits. In this section we will discuss briefly some of the performance evaluation criteria which are unique to foreign subsidiaries.

Profitability

As a company develops a global, profit-maximization strategy, each subsidiary may be asked to sacrifice some, or all, of its individual profits for the sake of the entire company. In those cases, the company may wish to develop a performance criteria which is based more on "country contribution" than country, or subsidiary, profit.

Normally, the parent company, or one of its first or second tier subsidiaries, can attempt to reduce the taxable profits of the subsidiary through *transfer pricing*. Transfer pricing is the intercompany pricing practice which apply to goods, services, technical assistance, trademarks, or other assets that are transferred between related parties. This policy would also apply if the subsidiary was transferring the above items *to* the parent company, or the subsidiaries of the parent company. Companies wishing to maximize their global profits will attempt, to the extent possible, to take their profits in lower tax jurisdictions. As an example, if U.S. corporate income is taxed at 36%, while German corporate income is taxed at 50%, then a global company with U.S. operations may wish to charge the German subsidiary at a higher rate so that it maximizes its profits in the lower tax jurisdiction.

Transfer pricing is scrutinized very heavily by the respective governments. The standard applied by most countries is that sales between related parties must be priced on an *arm's length basis*. An arm's length price is the price that would exist if the related parties to the transaction were dealing with each other as independent parties. The United States has recently toughened its transfer pricing regulations, making transfer pricing one of the most difficult financial issues facing companies in that country. In addition to transfer pricing, governments also have developed other methods to assure that the local operations retain their profits. One such scheme is limiting the percentage of royalties which can be charged to related companies.

Nevertheless, companies with sophisticated tax and treasury departments have been successful in making global profits through transfer pricing. This creates a dilemma in subsidiary management, especially if a subsidiary's performance is to be judged on a financial basis. The following example is illustrative:

A marginally profitable U.S. parent company desires to increase the intercompany royalty amounts and transfer prices from goods and services provided to its very profitable Mexican subsidiary. While the effective corporate tax rates in the two countries are similar, the U.S. company has sufficient losses in previous years for which it has substantial tax loss carry forward. The company was able to obtain approval from the Mexican tax authorities to increase the intercompany royalty and transfer prices to the local subsidiary.

This created an additional problem for the Mexican subsidiary because local law requires that 10% of adjusted taxable income must be given to the subsidiary employees as part of a nationally mandated profit sharing plan. Therefore, the parent company's policy of profit maximization impacted, in a very real sense, almost every employee of the Mexican subsidiary.

The problem was solved in two ways. First, the company developed a policy of country contribution, which valued the financial contribution of the subsidiary based on many factors including what its arm's length profits would have been, and in this particular year, ascribing a "contribution" to the subsidiary for its assistance in obtaining the Mexican government's approval to increase transfer pricing. Second, the parent company allowed the Mexican subsidiary to pay bonuses to employees which were similar to what was lost through profit reduction.

Market Penetration, Productivity, and Product Performance

In addition to financial considerations, a subsidary's performance can be evaluated on the basis of *market penetration*. The parent and subsidiary can agree on each year's marketing plan to a percentage of the market that the subsidiary will achieve in the coming year. This performance evaluation criteria is particularly important in the early years while the subsidiary is trying to achieve the economy of scale which would justify its costs. Additionally, even if the subsidiary is not profitable, if its market penetration is able to increase the economies of scale and reduce production costs in the home country, that factor should be given consideration.

Productivity is another measure of performance evaluation. If the subsidiary is assembling and/or manufacturing products, various techniques in the areas of quality, quantity, production time and amount of scrap can be applied. If the subsidiary is marketing finished products and services, techniques such as sales per employee and customer retention can be applied.

Finally, *subsidiary performance evaluation* should take into consideration product performance. Since the subsidiary will often serve as the "local" home office for customers in its territory, the evaluation process should consider whether the subsidiary is installing and maintaining the products up to global standards. This, along with other measures of customer satisfaction, should be considered.

Personnel Development and Labor Relations

Because locally-developed and trained employees will almost always be less expensive than expatriates, a subsidiary should be evaluated on its ability and willingness to develop a highly-motivated and efficient local workforce. Sufficient career opportunities must be created, and an understanding of the company's global vision should be instilled in the employees of the subsidiary. Additionally, local management should be able to respond to, and limit, any potential labor problems.

Public and Government Relations

Success or failure is often dependent upon the subsidiary's ability to create a positive image of the company and its products and services in the local market. This is especially true in creating good relationships with the local government agencies. The transfer pricing illustration used previously is a good example of how the subsidiary's relationship with the Mexican government was effective in assisting the company meet its global objectives.

Contributions to Global Planning

Many companies have, historically, developed their global plans without sufficient input from their foreign subsidiaries. A truly global company will solicit ideas from subsidiary management on how the plan will impact that country or region, as well as solicit ideas on the entire global plan. As will be discussed below, this is not only a useful way to acquire information, but it also allows the company to select individuals in the subsidiaries who could be promoted to positions in global management and operations.

SUBSIDIARY MOTIVATION TECHNIQUES

We will now conclude this chapter with a brief overview of some of the best methods for motivating subsidiary success. The approach taken here will be from a macro perspective as it is difficult to mention specific techniques without knowing the individual circumstances of each company.

Establish a Global Plan and Let Each Subsidiary Know Its Role or Mandate Within That Plan

Once you cross international boundaries, the levels of perceived, and real, misunderstandings are bound to increase. It is very important that the subsidiary not be allowed to operate in a vacuum. Subsidiary leadership must be told and, if necessary, be made to understand the global vision and plans. The given role of the subsidiary within that plan must also be understood, and advice and counsel should be sought from subsidiary management before the plans are finalized and put in place.

If subsidiary management understands and feels that they have been made part of the global vision and plans, they will logically work harder to see that it is implemented. However, be prepared to make changes on the advice of local management. Encourage constructive criticism, and act on it when the criticism is valid.

Establish a Fair Assessment of Subsidiary Performance

Consider the use of a "country," or "subsidiary," contribution to replace a bottom-line financial assessment. Develop criteria based on market penetration, productivity, product and personnel development and performance, public and government relations, and contribution to global planning.

Consider the Creation of a Career-Oriented International Division and Company Foreign Service

Many international companies view foreign assignments for home office personnel, to be given either to people on the "fast track," to season them for greater opportunities, or to technical types for the purpose of addressing individual assignments or problems. Foreign employees are seen as staying in their own subsidiaries with only occasional placement in other operations.

With the growth of international business, and the increasing need for people with international orientation, companies should consider offering long-term opportunities within an international division. As discussed in Chapter 3, international (read global) work requires a somewhat different skill set. Internationalists will tend to be generalists, with an entrepreneurial bent, who function well in diverse and ever changing environments.

Graduate schools of business are beginning to understand this, and many have developed individual Master of International Management programs which reflect the above-mentioned characteristics. Graduates of these schools, and others, are looking for international careers which normally include a mixture of expatriate assignments and home office positions with international responsibility. Require people interested in doing international business to learn a second (or third) language. The language itself is not as important as the learning process, which requires the individual to learn and absorb cultural differences.

With this in mind, consider rotating country managers and other key individuals. Knowledge of the company and its products, and experience in international assignments, are the key variables to consider even over nationality. One of the most successful international managers I have known is a person of Greek origin who has been successful in such diverse assignments as India, Japan, Singapore and Mexico. If people in the subsidiaries know there are true opportunities in the international (global) division, they are then more likely to advocate company goals over local considerations.

Allow All Significant Employees to Visit the Corporate Headquarters on a Regular Basis

The clearest way to increase understanding is to have all key individuals know the persons on the other side of the international phone call, or facsimile. Consider providing this opportunity to all loyal and effective employees, no matter what their level. For some lower-level employees, the company-sponsored international trip may be the opportunity of a lifetime and would insure their loyalty for some time to come.

We have now completed nine methods. The last method for building a global business involves perceptions and reactions to key international trends as we approach the 21th century and how they may impact business in the future.

REFERENCES

1. One such example of required profit sharing is Mexico, where 10% of the after-tax profit must be shared with most employees. See Section IX of Article 12.3 of the Political Constitution of Mexico, and Article 120 of the Federal Labor Law.
2. Control Data Systems (a successor to the Control Data Corporation) sold the Mexican Subsidiary in late 1995.
3. An excellent article on this subject is Bartlett, Christopher and Ghoshal, Sumantra "Transactional Tactics," *Report on Business Magazine,* January, 1990, pp. 138–139.

Chapter 13

METHOD 10: CAPITALIZING ON INTERNATIONAL TRENDS

INTRODUCTION

The world around us is changing more rapidly than any time in the history of humankind. While the 1990s seems to be more peaceful and prosperous than other periods in recent times, it is clear that we are undergoing a significant transition in the political and military arenas, with the end of the Cold War, and breakup of the Soviet Union, and certain Eastern European nations. This, coupled with the continued knowledge explosion and the exponential growth in international trade, makes it more and more difficult to determine what the world will look like in the not too distant future.

This book has been devoted to providing a practical, straightforward means by which to analyze entry into the international marketplace, and to examine the type(s) of business transactions which are most suitable to each individual company environment and products. While the concepts provided in this book should stand the test of time, we must devote at least some attention to the global environment in which these business decisions will be made. As stated in Chapter 3, a good international businessperson is both flexible and adaptable. It can also be said that being "international" means that the person is a globalist who has a sense of the great changes taking place in the world. All internationalists should have some understanding of technology, and must be at least an amateur political economist.

This final chapter begins by exploring six of the major trends taking place today. These are:

- The end of the Cold War.
- The explosive growth of global finance, trade and commerce, and the continued strengthening of global companies.
- The continued population growth, with its positive and negative implications.
- The explosion of knowledge.
- The development of a global culture.
- The growth of the number of national units, coupled with the increasing inability of nations to control their own destinies.

This chapter and book concludes with an analysis of how and why these international trends may impact your business, both today and in the future, and how you may wish to plan for future growth in terms of the type of international transactions that are suitable to your company.

THE SIX MAJOR INTERNATIONAL TRENDS

TREND NO. 1: THE END OF THE COLD WAR

Anwar Sadat and Mikhail Gorbachev will be remembered as two of the most important people of the last quarter of the 20th century. Anwar Sadat, because he promoted, in fact, gave his life for, the creation of a diplomatic and trade relationships between Egypt and Israel, thereby ending an over thirty-year period of extreme hostilities, which included four significant wars that had bankrupted Egypt. This set off a process which ultimately resulted in the creation of a Palestinian nation and the development of commercial ties between Israel and its neighbors, thereby likely defusing one of the key powderkegs of international violence. When late 20th century history is written, Mikhail Gorbachev will be remembered as the primary reason behind the end of the Cold War between the so-called "capitalist" and "communist" worlds. When reality sets in, our grandchildren will learn that the Cold War did not end because of U.S. geopolitical containment, or the Reagan military buildup of the 1980s, it ended instead because a new generation of Soviet politicians realized the need for a political awakening.

Throughout the late 1970s and 1980s, the Soviet Union's economy was growing at a respectable overall rate. While income and product distribution remained key issues, that alone would not have brought down the Soviet Union in 1991, if it were not for the political chaos brought about by Gorbachev's policies of *perestroika* and *glasnost.* These policies started a political force that could not be stopped. Former President Salinas of Mexico visited the Soviet Union shortly after taking office in late 1988. Upon his return, he criticized Mikhail Gorbachev for undertaking political reform before economic reform, and announced what became known as *Salinastroika,* or the emphasis, for Mexico, on economic reform before political reform.

The emphasis, at least in the first half of the 1990s, on political change, may be the short-term legacy of the end of the Cold War. What we have seen since the late 1980s is the increasing growth of political and ethnic nationalism brought about by the fall of the "Soviet Empire." This is not only true in the former Soviet Union and its socialist siblings like Czechoslovakia and Yugoslavia, but it has also exacerbated the sense of national identity in North America (Quebec), Africa (South Africa, Burundi, and Rwanda), and Asia (India and Pakistan).

The end of the Cold War may also result in the changing nature of warfare. Major military conflicts will be all but unthinkable, because the concern over nuclear destruction has been replaced with the mutual interest of nations that are interdependent on the global economy. But wars will not disappear, in fact, they may be likely to increase in number. However, they should be smaller and more regional in nature. These wars will be encouraged, not only by the new sense of nationalism, but also because of the decrease in defense expenditures, coupled with a massive surplus of weapons, particularly advanced weaponry. Former weapons producers, particularly Russia, will be looking to export. Other countries, such as Brazil and Israel, will be looking to develop products for niche military markets.

With the nuclear threat effectively gone, the former superpowers, or the existing superpower (the United States), will not be as likely to be able to restrain their more aggressive junior allies should they desire to attempt to grab a valuable prize as Iraq tried to do with Kuwait in 1990–1991. Finally, the 21st century may witness an increase of religious wars, particularly with the growth rate in the number of Moslems and the threat of Islamic fundamentalism. This is discussed in more detail later in this chapter. While these elements will create a certain level of political instability, they also should be understood within the context of international business. This is discussed in the conclusion of this chapter.

TREND NO. 2: THE EXPLOSIVE GROWTH OF GLOBAL FINANCE, TRADE AND COMMERCE, AND THE CONTINUED STRENGTHENING OF GLOBAL COMPANIES

There has been substantial international trade and global corporations (Hudson Bay Company) for hundreds of years, but it has only been for the past fifty years that we have seen the explosive growth of international finance and trade, and the massive expansion in numbers and powers of businesses engaged in global business. This explosion has been the result of many reasons, a few of which are presented here:

- Exponential growth of communications and production technologies.
- Rapid increases in the methods and speed of international transportation.
- Development of international monetary and trade mechanisms, including the GATT and the World Trade Organization (WTO).
- The relative freedom and power of the United States of America who, in the 1950s and 1960s, controlled over 40% of the world's trade, and in the 1970s and 1980s, developed the marketing and cultural tools to dominate significant aspects of popular global culture.[1]
- The rise of Western Europe, Japan and the Asian "Tigers" as significant global economic actors, which have challenged the U.S.'s economic position with the ability to compete with U.S.-headquartered companies on a global basis.
- The privatization of public companies which began in Britain in the 1970s and has continued to the present in most parts of the world.

The growth of global finance has been occasioned by a combination of government actions and the adaptation of technology. Throughout the 1970s and 1980s, government after government went through periods of deregulation followed by regulation and followed again by deregulation. In response to this, emerged a number of internationally-coordinated efforts by the major banks and financial institutions which set global rules of engagement. This movement towards globalization was encouraged by the widespread use of computers and artificial intelligence to create new products and services.

One major result of this movement was the process of disintermediation—or the removal of banks as intermediaries in the accessing of capital markets, usually accomplished by the issuance of commercial paper. This process, which began in North America, is now pretty well complete among the major Western European states, except Germany, where a close relationship still exists between the local banks and companies.

While the volume of global financial transactions increased dramatically, the number of banks will continue to decrease, and the remaining banks involved in international transactions will have to become more and more specialized to meet the needs of their increasingly sophisticated customers. The decline of the traditional bank is further exacerbated by the increasing abundance of money coupled with the decline of the banknote as a vehicle of business. Being more plastic, or electronic as the case may be, money will be less subject to definition and control, by banks or by governments.

These trends will continue into the 21st century as financial services reach the home computer. Investors of all sizes will have global portfolios designed to match their demographics. Corporate and commercial borrowers will use the services of the financial industry to place their securities with these "global" investors. As information becomes cheaper and artificial intelligence is used to analyze the information and suggest investment alternatives, the power once employed only by big investors will become available even to small investors.

The expansion and strength of global corporations is another phenomenon of the second half of the 20th century. Global corporations can be defined as a cluster of business entities with different nationalities that are joined by a common parent through bonds of ownership and/or control, that respond to a common global strategy and share a common pool of human, financial and physical assets. Some global corporations have become so large that their annual revenues could compare favorably with the gross domestic product of many middle-sized nations (e.g., General Motors, AT&T, and Mitsubishi as compared with Norway or Chile).

Global corporations have become successful because of six distinct advantages they have over their domestic counterparts and/or government agencies:

Labor and Component Savings. The ability to source products and labor from those nations or parts of nations where overall efficiency prevails. (Efficiency consists of many factors, and a company may seek a relatively expensive, but productive, workforce as the most efficient.)

The point here is not so much where a company chooses to source its labor and components, but the fact that it has the ability to negotiate with any number of national and/or provincial units to meet its needs.

Global Tax Planning. Responding to a common strategy means that a global corporation will seek, whenever possible, to minimize its global tax obligations. This can be done by structuring operations so that profits are taken in tax-free or low tax jurisdictions by taking advantage of favorable tax treaties or by structuring intercompany prices to move profits to lower tax jurisdictions.

International Financial Power. As stated previously, it is now possible for companies to seek their financial needs from an increasingly greater number of global sources. Additionally, global companies are better posed to take advantage of numerous local government financial schemes in areas where they choose to operate, and particularly in jurisdictions from which they will export. Finally, some very sophisticated companies have created elaborate internal treasury departments which allow them to take advantage of fluctuations in currency exchange.

Ease of Technology Transfer. Global corporations not only have the financial power to create, or acquire, valuable intellectual properties and technologies, but they also have acquired an advantage over domestic companies and governments in terms of their ability to transfer technology among their global units. This ability to transfer technology normally avoids the scrutiny of government approvals (or even registration), and the complexity and risks associated with the transfer of valuable technologies to third parties. Additionally, technology transfer, in certain cases, can assist the global corporation in its global tax planning, by allowing the technology to be transferred from a low tax jurisdiction to an intercompany licensee in a high tax jurisdiction which pays a royalty or other fees for the right to use that technology. What results is a tax write-off in the high tax jurisdiction and the transfer of revenues/profits to a low tax jurisdiction.

Globalization of Products. Whenever possible, the best of all possible worlds is to create a single product, or product line, which can be sold without major adjustments throughout the entire world. The globalization of a product allows for substantial economies of scale, and the standardization of manufacturing facilities. Marketing replaces local adaptation as the way to differentiate the product to local cultures. The classic example of this was the marketing of the Honda 50 motorcycle in the 1960s. Introduced in the U.S. as a recreational vehicle, with the slogan "You meet the nicest people on a Honda," the same exact product was sold in Brazil as affordable basic transportation.

Greater Autonomy. This advantage of global corporations is perhaps the culmination of the other five mentioned advantages. The mere size of many of the global corporations, coupled with their ability to manipulate raw material and financial suppliers, labor, and governments, give the global corporation a somewhat unique sense of autonomy. There is no question that the global corporations have contributed significantly to economic growth and the financial well-being of large parts of the world, but the traditional institutions, which might normally check their powers and autonomy, seem to be continually too late with too little.

While global trends continue to show that most jobs and a substantial part of new technologies are being created by smaller non-global companies, there is no question that the large global corporations are now a significant actor on the world scene and likely to remain so for some time to come. This has, in turn, weakened the nation-state, which is discussed later in this chapter.

Before leaving this second trend, it is also useful to mention another variable which is similar to the cluster mentality and global strategic vision which are common to global corporations. In a controversial book called *Tribes*,[2] Joel Kotkin suggested the existence of five dispersed ethnic groups—the British, Chinese, Indians, Japanese, and Jews—that influence global business as distinct groups because of:

■ Strong ethnic identities, mutual dependence, and family structures
■ Global network, based on tribal trust
■ Passion for technology, and belief in scientific progress

Kotkin suggests these groups may also intermingle (e.g., Chinese and Jewish), and identifies a number of "Future Tribes," which, among them, include Lebanese, Palestinians, Russians, Armenians, Vietnamese, and Mormons, and have the characteristics to function as more than regional actors.

TREND NO. 3: POPULATION GROWTH

Baring any major global catastrophes, it seems clear that the world's population will continue to grow well into the 21st century. While this will probably not be at the rate of the past 50 years, the 1990 world population of 5.3 billion should grow to 6.3 billion by 2000, and to between 7.6 to 9.4 billion by 2025, with 8.5 billion being the most likely. This growth will have a number of positive and negative implications, although it will, overall, be favorable to the growth of international business.

One observation which now seems safe to make is that our planet has the resources to provide for the projected population growth in the next four decades. The dire predictions of *The Population Bomb*,[3] and other like publications of the late 1960s and early 1970s, have simply not come to pass, and many of the former "third world" nations have made significant progress at population management. There is, however, still a number of significant demographic problems to be considered, which fall under the general description of the "rich get richer and the poor get poorer," or "the rich get richer and the poor have children."[4] Additionally, almost all studies of the future point out that water will replace oil as the most important liquid of the 21st century.

This section addresses three demographic trends:

■ If one looks at demographics from a regional perspective, North America, with its slow growth rate, will be better off than Europe and Japan with their no-growth rate, and Asia, Latin America, and Africa with their higher growth rates.

■ The majority of population growth in the "third world" will be felt in the urban areas, creating considerable infrastructure problems and substantial business opportunities. In general, the expanding countries of Latin America and Asia will create massive markets for consumer goods.

■ The rapid growth of the Islamic population is the most significant wildcard in demographic projections.

The North American region is probably in the best demographic position of any country in the world. Table 13-1, illustrates the moderate growth of that region in relation to the remainder of the world.

Most economists and demographers will tell you that moderate population growth (given adequate space and resources), is better than either no-growth or rapid-growth scenarios. No-growth scenarios lead to older population with ratios of idle people dependent upon working people far too high to support viable public services. No-growth scenarios increases labor costs and limit market growth only to increasing living standards. Today, most of Europe and Japan find themselves in this predicament.

Table 13-1
Population Growth: 1990–2025[5]

	1990		2000		2025	
United States	251*		276		336	
Canada	27		29		32	
Mexico	89		107		150	
NAFTA (Total)	367	6.9%**	412	6.5%	518	6.1%
Japan	124	2.3%	129	2.0%	128	1.5%
W. Europe	361		360		350	
E. Europe	140		148		160	
Europe (Total)	501	9.5%	509	8.1%	510	6.0%
Rest of the World	4,380	82.6%	5,250	83.3%	7,344	86.4%
TOTAL	5,300		6,300		8,500	

*Millions
**Percentage of world total   *Most-likely projections.*

Rapid population growth creates incredible burdens on all levels of infrastructure, and other problems which will be discussed below. Moderate growth, however, leads to a situation where idle to working ratios remain reasonable, and where logical market expansion is viable. The United States of America and Canada are particularly lucky in that regard. While their national growth rates are closer to Europe's than Asia's, both countries are seen as immigration heavens, and both have adopted (all things considered), reasonable immigration policies which result, for the most part, in "designer" immigration, that is, immigrants with education, skills, ambition and, in many cases, considerable resources. Added to that is the young and dynamic Mexican market with opportunities to provide low cost production and a rapidly growing market for all types of goods and services.

Growth in the developing world (Asia, Africa, and Latin America), will remain rapid, although it will decline as the years progress. Africa's population growth rate is scheduled at 3% for the 1990s. While China's (PRC's) growth rate is slower, it is projected to level off at 1.5 billion by 2025 (1.15 in 1990). India could approach the same number and overtake China as the world's most populous nation during the 2020s. In addition to the problems created by rapid growth, another phenomenon of the late 20th century and early 21st century will be the urbanization of the developing world. Mexico City (23 million) and Sao Paulo (16 million) have already replaced New York, London, and Tokyo as the world's largest cities. Shanghai, Calcutta, Bombay, and Jakarta will soon be among the biggest cities in the world. This urbanization extracts a significant toll on limited resources. Mexico City now has "rush hour" from 7:00 to 22:00, and was forced to close down certain refineries and factories because air pollution had reached dangerous levels. Even NAFTA will have its negative impact as removal of government support on Mexico's traditional corn agriculture will push thousands of undereducated and impoverished farmers into its cities, while U.S. farmers in the Red River Valley will enjoy the fruits of increased sales. Along with urbanization will come the need for pure drinking water.

However difficult this growth is to manage, it does have its positve side. Parts of Asia and Latin America are expected to have GDP growth rates far in excess of population growth. Table 13-2 below illustrates, only in the area of communications, the pent-up needs of the existing population, much less the population growth, which will increase the need for radios, televisions, telephones and newspapers.

Table 13-2
Communications per 1,000 People—1993[6]

	North America	Western Europe	Eastern Europe	Africa	Middle East	Latin America
Radios	2,017	817	592	150	318	292
TVs	798	444	308	23	250	150
Telephones	788	522	108	18	97	74
Newspaper Circulation	247	253	428	11	40	87

The greatest wild card in the near-term demographic future is the growth of the numbers of people who are Islamic. In 1990, Muslims numbered approximately 1 billion, or about 19% of the world's population. By 2025, this number is expected to be in excess of 2 billion, or nearly 25% of the world's population. The Muslim population has expanded dramatically in the 20th century, primarily because of high population growth rates in the Arab world and in other Muslim countries like Russia, Pakistan, and Indonesia. While the Islam religion has many disparate points of view and belief systems, it is interesting to at least speculate on what the impact of 1 billion new Muslims might mean in the next three decades.

The pessimists suggest that the Muslim population growth rate could be the cause of continuing wars and civil strife. They point to the current chaotic conditions in many parts of the Middle East and the potential difficulties that may result from population shifts in the Indian subcontinent, and Indonesia. Additionally, considerable attention is paid to the activities of the fundamentalist Shiite minority with its attempts to destabilize societies by bombing the World Trade Center in New York, the destruction of the Israeli Embassy and Jewish organizations in Buenos Aires, and a series of bombings in London. Two of the most unstable political leaders are said to reside in Iraq and Libya.

An optimistic viewpoint would lead to other results with the resources available in the Middle East and other Muslim areas, coupled with the pent-up needs of the people, the Muslim world would appear to be an area of great business potential. The work to reconstruct Kuwait continues. Smart businesspersons see Palestine as an incredible business opportunity, with its tremendous need for infrastructure, its educated overseas population, and financial assistance from its wealthier Muslim neighbors. While Iraq and Libya seem unstable, Indonesia, Pakistan and Egypt are seen as large markets with considerable growth potential.

TREND NO. 4: THE KNOWLEDGE EXPLOSION

Between the time I finished high school in the early 1960s, to the time I attended my 30th reunion, the amount of knowledge available to humankind had increased by 10 times, yet all the technical knowledge we work with today will, according to experts, represent only 1% of the knowledge that will be available in 2050.[4]

While the accumulated knowledge has to be considered positive, too much knowledge, too soon, may lead to individual and/or societal overload. The knowledge explosion is upon us. The question is whether our institutions can evolve and survive to deal with the paradoxes which are sure to result.

In the 1960s, American television brought us the in-person deaths of a President and two other of its greatest leaders. Americans watched people die in Vietnam, and it changed the course of U.S. foreign relations. Today, in the world of CNN, and computer news access, the average American annually receives 100 newspapers, 3,000 notices or forms to complete, 2,460 hours of television, and 730 hours of radio. Over one-third of their time is spent watching or listening to television and radio.[7]

In 1986, my family purchased for approximately U.S. $3,000, a Macintosh 512K computer system. At the time, it was nicknamed the "Fat Mac" because it had 4 times the capacity of the 128K model. By 1989, we had to upgrade to run most of the software available. In 1993, we finally replaced it with an IBM compatible machine with ten times its capacity, color, CD ROM, and laser-like printer for less than U.S. $2,000. It is clear that we now have, at our fingertips, an incredible ability to organize knowledge. However, the attempt now is to move beyond mere organization to automating information, to obtain knowledge (artificial intelligence). AI is the future, and the future is here. The language translation business has been revolutionized by programs that now can effectively translate, with accuracy, up to 90% of the text provided. The financial industry has now developed pension plan checking software which takes into account different tax withholding rates, and programs that help prevent credit card fraud.

Medical knowledge is now growing at an exponential rate. The science of genetics has now unlocked 8–10% of the human genetic code versus less than 1% known 20 years ago.[8] While this can end suffering, and extend life, it can also lead to ethical considerations which did not exist in the past. My friends and colleagues in genetics tell me that law, government, and religion have simply not kept up with the growth in their profession, and they are correct.

Also needed to be addressed is the tremendous impact the field of robotics may have on our conception of, and ability to, "work." While the Industrial Revolution of two centuries past replaced hand work with machines, the post-Industrial Revolution of today is replacing factory workers with robots, thereby lessening the necessity of bringing human beings together at a place of work. Facsimile machines, modems, and other communication devices are doing the same to the white collar office environment.

The world of the future may best be described by Charles Handy,[9] who describes nine paradoxes that result from the knowledge explosion. Three such paradoxes are mentioned here:

■ *The Paradox of Intelligence.* Intelligence is a new form of property, but it does not behave like other forms of property. You can not distribute it, and you can not leave it to your children when you die.

■ *The Paradox of Time.* We have never had so much time available to us, yet the most successful of us have turned this commodity into a

competitive weapon, where we are willing to pay good money to purchase time.
- *The Paradox of the Individual.* We are encouraged to be ourselves, to be entrepreneurial. The knowledge explosion allows us the freedom to pursue our own course as long as we respect the rights of others. Yet, it is difficult to make a phone call without being asked "Whom to do represent?" or "What organization are you from?"

Therein may be the business advice for the early 21st century. Gear products for individuals, for leisure time activities and for planned obsolescence. However, remember that the bulk of technological innovations will continue to spring from corporate laboratories, or be acquired from individuals or smaller companies, by corporate giants. These giants will have a great interest in keeping these developments proprietary. Coupled with the growth of global corporate structure, the bulk of technology will be passed between the segments of related corporations, and while knowledge will expand, much will be kept in private hands.

TREND NO. 5: DEVELOPMENT OF A GLOBAL CULTURE

As communications, finance and business techniques become more global, it seems logical to address whether this will result in the development of a global culture. The answer, depending on how you ultimately define the question, is probably "Yes." In my view we are entering an era where there will be three types of global cultures. The intellectual culture, which will be, as it always has been, a mixture of the perceived "best" from all cultures; the professional culture, which will be most heavily influenced by the culture, or cultures, which most impact each profession; and the mass, or popular culture, in which the American culture will predominate.

The world anticipated by Marshall McLuhan, who coined the term "Global Village,"[10] is already here. A billion telephones are in place, all interconnected, and capable of reaching each other, and the phones are used across borders. In the United States alone, the number of international calls originating from that country increased from 23 million in 1970 to 580 million in 1987.

The growth in telecommunications is being accompanied by growth in the various forms of video communications, especially through the use of television. Today, nearly 75% of U.S. homes are cable connected, and specialized cable information services are an increasingly cost-effective way for business to communicate with niche markets. A recent conference of U.S. cable companies and suppliers estimated the global market for cable services between 1994 and 2004 to be more than U.S. $3 trillion.

While the manner of "delivering" culture may change from the printed word to the visual image, and perhaps from more live performances to more videotape and cable television, intellectual-oriented culture will remain much the same. Intellectuals throughout the world will continue to opt for the perceived "best" of what is being offered in the arts, literature and the stage. Availability will increase, and a greater number of cultures will be represented, but people considering themselves to be intellectuals will still orient themselves to the global great masters.

As a practicing attorney and businessperson from the United States, I realize that other than popular culture, I have more in common with a German attorney than I do with an American farmer. Clearly, as those people who provide "symbolic analyst services," (Robert Reich's term), or members of the professions as they are more commonly known, will continue to adapt to their own professional's language and techniques.[11] Marketeers will most likely be influenced by America, while technical-oriented professionals will take their cues from a combination of Japanese, European and American professional developments. Law, on the other hand, seems to be undergoing a merger between the common law system used in most of the English-speaking countries and the civil law system found in Continental Europe and Latin America. The best example of this merger is the development of the United Nations Convention on Contracts for the International Sale of Goods, which was finally passed in 1980, went into effect in 1988, and is now in use in nearly forty countries.

Popular, or mass culture, is, and continues to be, overwhelmingly dominated by American culture. In fact, it is probably safe to say that as global communications accelerate, and American marketing techniques and institutions grow, that popular global culture will be an extension of American popular culture. The explanation for this phenomenon is explained by different people in somewhat similar manner. Ben J. Wattenberg[12] explains the popularity of American culture because of the popularity of the American values of political freedom and personal independence. David Rieff, in an insightful article in *World Policy*, explains the popularity of American culture because of its ability to change rapidly, based on the fact that America is a new society and ". . . that there was always less of a firebreak made up of traditions and institutions of high culture to hold it back."[13]

While it seems clear that American films, music, and fast food will dominate popular culture, and indeed create a global culture, we should not leave this discussion without mentioning the manner in which the United States has begun to dominate university education. While the United States is soundly criticized for its pre-university education, few question the quality of its top universities and the solid quantity available through its thousands of institutions of higher learning.

Today, while less than 100,000 Americans may be studying abroad at any time, six times their numbers are currently foreigners studying at American universities. While American schools have become of particular interest to Asians in recent years, it is fair to say that the United States enjoys large numbers of foreign students from all regions. This has become big business, and has played a major role in keeping some economically marginal colleges and universities afloat.

The *Wall Street Journal*[14] published a front page story that said much about the influence of America's top universities on the world. The story tells of the meeting of three Latin Americans at universities in Cambridge, Massachusetts, (Harvard and MIT) in the 1970s, who developed life-long friendships and ultimately became, at the same time, the finance ministers of Argentina, Chile, and Mexico. Whether referring to Pedro Aspe (of Mexico), Domingo Cavallo (of Argentina), or Alejandro Foxley (of Chile), all have developed and applied similar free-market techniques to open up the economies of their respective countries. This has, in part, resulted from their exposure to the "cutting-edge" economic theory taught at the universities at that time, and the advise and counsel shared with their student colleagues and professors over the years.

TREND NO. 6: THE INCREASE OF NATION-STATES, COUPLED WITH THE INCREASING INABILITY OF NATIONS TO CONTROL THEIR OWN DESTINIES

For the past four centuries, the nation-state has served as the chief organizing unit for human activity. In fact, the number of nation-states has grown throughout that period, and now numbers nearly 200. (More than 3,500 groups exist that call themselves nations.) If one considers the number of nationalities that would like to achieve nation-state status, that number could easily be doubled.

A nation-state can best be defined as a national unit, or units, which has achieved sovereignty (the ability to make and enforce independent decisions). Few nation-states consist primarily of one nationality (Japan and Iceland come to mind). Most consist of a multitude of nations and nationalities. Some nation-states have done a relatively good job of integrating nationalities (Brazil, the United States and France), while others have had considerable problems (Canada with Quebec, Nigeria with Biafra). The recent trend has been for the expansion of the number of nation-states. The United Nations was founded in 1945, with 51 members. There were, at that time, another 20 nation-states. By the end of the colonial period in the 1970s, the numbers had doubled, and continued to grow throughout the 1970s and 1980s.

With the end of the Cold War came another proliferation of nation-states, with the breakup of the Soviet Union and Yugoslavia, and the separation of the Czech Republic and Slovakia. Palestine is soon to join the community of nation-states, and many other national units continue to seek such status.

Nation-states as organizing units reached the height of their economic power in the middle 20th century, and have been in economic decline since that point. The nation-state is now in the middle of a profound transformation. Economic forces seem to be moving in a direction that implies that in the future there will be no national products, no national technology, and probably no national industry in the sense that we use these concepts today. The concept of national economy is becoming obsolete as capital, technologies, and products become more global. The process of privatization of state-run industries in places as disparate as Great Britain and Bolivia further exacerbate the process. The nation-state, while desired and admired for its nationalism, common history and symbols, is a probable casualty of the first five trends discussed in this chapter.

Yet, the nation-state has not gone away, nor is it likely to do so for some time to come. The nation-state is likely to remain as the political organizing unit and primary source of identity well into the 21st century. Nothing as of yet has been developed to replace it. While the United Nations and other global organizations have strengthened, and while economic regionalization is certainly the trend, humankind has not developed a viable option for the nation-state.[15]

Earlier in this chapter, I mentioned that as part of the knowledge explosion, law or religion was unable to keep up with advances in genetics. In a similar vein, the advances in economics and technology in the past 50 years have overwhelmed the advances in politics. The nation-state, today, is a political unit that has lost, to a certain extent, its ability to make independent economic decisions. Herein lies one of the most interesting and challenging problems that must be dealt with in the years to come, and the one with the biggest potential impact on the growth of international business.

The degree to which international business will continue to grow will be dependent upon whether nation-states will attempt to reassert their control over the economy or whether nation-states will move away from economic nationalism to evolve to an approach that Robert R. Reich (the secretary of labor under U.S. President Clinton) calls "Positive Nationalism."[16] Economic nationalism (which is another name for protectionism), is the recognition of the rights of nation-states to control their economic destinies within the framework of the international economic systems, but, if necessary, move within their own borders to change the rules of the game by which global business is transacted.

Economic nationalism was popular during the 1960s and 1970s, but began to decline in the 1980s as more nation-states moved towards free market economies. Examples of economic nationalism are:

- Nationalization, expropriation, and confiscation.
- Restrictive foreign investment laws—which limited foreign ownership and reserved certain industries to locals.
- Artistic or cultural restrictions.
- Domestic content requirements.
- Technology transfer restrictions (as to royalties permitted), and requirements (e.g., quality guarantees).
- Restrictions on foreign workers.
- Foreign exchange requirements.
- High tariff and non-tariff barriers.

These types of restrictions are more likely to succeed in countries with larger markets, or as countries attempt to form economic unions. The North American Free Trade Agreement (NAFTA), although presented as opening up a free market union amongst its members, has elements of nearly all the above-mentioned examples as European and Japanese manufacturers are now virtually "required" to manufacture products in North America to remain competitive with local manufacturers in the region. Additionally, all three countries retain strict restrictions on certain artistic and cultural artifacts.

The other scenario for nation-states in the coming decade is to recognize the loss of control in the economic sector and concentrate instead in developing a "positive nationalism." This approach is based on a number factors. These are:

- A certain sector of the population will benefit from the global economy.
- While these people will be influenced by the global economy, they will still be oriented to the nation-state as their source of nationalism and politics.
- They will realize that the future of the nation-state will not be in national control of the economy but will be in preparing their populations to be part of, and compete in, the global economy.
- The government will play some role in assisting the nation-state to compete in the new realities by assisting in the preparation of citizens with global awareness and purchasing power. This will require the rich to share with the poor.[16]

I suspect that the next few decades will bring a mixture of these approaches with the poorer nations attempting a return to economic nationalism, while the richer nations will, at least, try to develop some aspects of positive nationalism. Nation-states still possess a number of weapons to be used to reestablish the economic side of their sovereignty and the battle for control of the global economy is far from over. The clash between the rapidly expanding economy and the traditional means of politics should be interesting to watch.

HOW INTERNATIONAL TRENDS WILL IMPACT YOUR FUTURE

In my concluding remarks, I will address how the six trends discussed in this chapter may impact business planning in the medium to long-term future. While it is impossible to be completely specific, it is possible to identify some significant changes, and to comment on how these changes might impact international business decisions. I will concentrate on three areas: Politics and the nation-state; economics and business; and changes to business structures.

POLITICS AND THE NATION-STATE

The following seems likely in the coming years:

- The number of nation-states will continue to proliferate.
- Developing states will attempt to bring about economic growth and stability before undergoing democratization and other political development.

■ Nation-states will attempt new techniques to reassert their economic independence.

■ Urbanization and infrastructure development will be the biggest challenges to the nation-state in the early 21st century. They will also offer the greatest business opportunities.

■ Tremendous business opportunities will exist in much of the developing world, Eastern Europe, and Russia; they will be especially interesting in China, Indonesia, Palestine/Jordan, Vietnam, South Africa, and a unified Korea.

In the next three to four decades, another 30 to 40 nation-states will join the community of nations. While obvious new players may be Quebec and Palestine, it is also probable that large parts of Africa will be redrawn to reflect traditional ethnic, tribal and language groups. The former Soviet Union will also continue to splinter with the creation of the possible Armenian and Georgian nation-states. Additional changes are possible in the area stretching from the Middle East to South-East Asia. This proliferation of nation-states will result from continued ethnic uprisings and racial/ethnic conflict. This will be true even in the multi-ethnic states that survive, and will result in the need to maintain armed forces, and the continued need for substantial defense budgets.

Defense needs will also be enhanced by the continuance of the acceptance by national leaders of the process of economic development before political development. The success of South Korea, Chile, and Mexico of putting their economic house in order before moving to democratize their political systems will continue to be used as models for other "developing" nations. Additionally, the selection of this approach is likely to sit well with the existing power structure, who can use it as a means to continue in power for some time to come. The economic before political strategy, however, will put considerable pressure on nation-states from those groups of persons that do not benefit immediately from the economic progress. The 1994 uprising in Chiapas, Mexico, and the continued pressure on the South Korean government by middle class elements and student groups, are recent examples of this pressure.

While the actual ownership of the economy is not as likely to be in nation-state hands, governments have not lost the ability to tax and regulate those who do business in their country. As countries have moved away from economic nationalism, governments have shifted the focus of regulating behavior to concern themselves with quality, safety, environment, anti-trust and consumer protection. The clearest example of this is

Mexico, which liberalized its foreign investment and transfer of technology laws, but has increased its scrutiny over brand labeling, qualifying products to certain safety and usage norms, and enforcing its rigorous environmental protection laws. This will provide work for a wide variety of professional consultants.

The process of urbanization is unending (with minor reverse trends in certain developed nations). With urbanization, comes the need for infrastructure. Companies providing infrastructure products and services will have ample business opportunities in the years to come. Even developed countries such as the United States will need to rebuild much of the national highway system built in the 1950s, and the infrastructure of its great cities. Additionally, as privatization continues into the 21st century, global companies will have infrastructure opportunities which never existed in the past. PT&T's (Post Telephone & Telegraph) will be privatized, and private toll roads will be common. Municipal services will go to private providers (e.g., trash and street cleaning), and education institutions will be run by private management firms. There are even some who predict that police, fire and military will eventually be privatized.

While we now look to China (whose GDP is expected to exceed that of the U.S. sometime between 2005–2010), Mexico, Brazil, and India as major areas of expansion, there are a number of other countries we should look at as potential growth areas. These are:

- *Indonesia.* 200 million people with substantial physical resources. A middle class the size of many of the larger European countries.
- *Palestine/Jordan.* The advantage for Palestine is that it has a number of wealthy Arab neighbors who recognize the value of preserving and enhancing its existence. Look for a number of infrastructure opportunities in the projects financed by Saudi Arabia, Kuwait, and the U.A.E.
- *Vietnam.* Nearly 80 million people with a long tradition as traders, with one of the lowest standards of living in the world. Excellent natural resources and substantial infrastructure opportunities. An especially good opportunity for United States products.
- *South Africa.* A potential economic powerhouse in its own right. South Africa has now begun to attract human talent from the North, and expand its business into such places as Tanzania and Kenya, as the racial barriers fall. South Africa is likely to be to Southern Africa what the United States is to NAFTA.

■ *Unified Korea.* This will only be a matter of time. When it happens, bringing the North up to the standards of the South will rival German unification, and the Unified Korea will receive substantial world assistance for having helped to defuse a major global hotspot.

ECONOMICS AND BUSINESS

The explosion of knowledge (described earlier in Trend No. 4), must lead one to conclude that the world economy is indeed shifting from a command model to a knowledge model. While it is still necessary to be well connected, who you know is becoming less important than what you know. The amount of knowledge available is, and will be, so large and diverse that the future will be bright for those who know how to organize knowledge into niches and distill it into components which are more easily absorbed. We live in a world where books went to condensed books, then to audio tapes, and then to condensed audio tapes. A niche industry has developed to allow an individual to get the "gist" of two or three new business books by audio tape during the 90-minute round trip commute from the home to the office, and books that summarize useful information in frameworks or paradigms stay on the best seller lists for years.

Knowledge and complexity of knowledge, will define hierarchial structure and rewards. A corporate treasurer, with a staff of five, may be more responsible for corporate success than a large Human Resources or MIS department. Because of the resources available, all employees at all levels will be given more responsibility for their actions. Finally, as employment is more and more removed from the physical office, knowledge, and knowledge access, will be even more critical to performance.

Any company that provides products and/or services related to knowledge, and filling knowledge gaps, should be well positioned for the future. This is going to be especially true in a world in which a small percentage of the population will grow all of our food, and another small group will be able, with the assistance of robots and other high technology tools, to manufacture every product that we will need. Services, particularly communications services, will provide the bulk of our interest and employment. Additionally, people will be free to travel, and will do so often.

One would think that the existence of facsimiles, electronic mail, and video conferencing, would lessen the need for business travel, but it is likely that the opposite will be true. People, despite any amount of electronic gadgets, will believe in face-to-face contact and interaction. Additional means of communication will only increase the number of people who come in contact and ultimately increase travel among those people. Travel will also be increased as more smaller and mid-sized companies enter into the global marketplace.

STRUCTURING INTERNATIONAL BUSINESS RELATIONSHIPS

Look for the following changes in ways global business will be structured:

- Large global companies will continue to dominate significant parts of world business. However, local autonomy and decision-making will increase.
- Smaller and mid-sized companies will "go global," and U.S., European and Japanese multinationals will begin to see significant competition from companies headquartered in the "developing" nations.
- The traditional forms of international business (agents, distributors, franchising, licensing and equity joint ventures) will remain, but unique types of strategic alliances will develop in response to changing conditions and government deregulation.
- The time from making the decision to "go international" to the creation of a true global company will be shortened.

The 21st century will still belong to the large global corporation, but it will evolve in a manner that reflects global trends. Headquarters will still define global strategy, business relationships, global profit maximization and tax minimization. Global products will still be sought, as will networks of distribution and service. However, some level of decentralization will occur on the regional, national and sub-national levels. Local subsidiaries and offices will be given more authority over marketing and sales, and in dealing with local suppliers. Additionally, local employees will be able to offer suggestions to headquarters and global careers (where employees move between numerous countries), will become the norm rather than the exception.

One advantage of the exploding technology in communications and transportation is that it will let smaller and middle-sized companies operate as true global companies. In some cases, these middle-sized companies, with their unique technologies, more manageable product lines and limited bureaucracies, will actually have an advantage over the global giants. IBM found this out when EMC, a storage disk drive manufacturer out of Massachusetts, took a good part of its European market. EMC's international sales went from zero in 1989 to over U.S. $400 million in 1994.[17]

As middle-sized companies begin to assume a larger share of international markets, the nationality of these companies will become more diverse. Strong local players in national economies in developing nations, now faced with open borders within a free market economy, will strike out for international markets. Mexico, with its new contingent of billionaires created by privatization, has been particularly aggressive. In the past few years, Mexican companies have acquired U.S. competitors in the areas of ceramics/glass, food products and motorbus manufacturing. This trend will continue, not only with Latin American companies, but will become a major vehicle for businesses in such countries as Hungary, Poland, and South Africa.

Whether large or small, more and more global players will look for different ways of operating in the international marketplace. While the traditional forms of operation (direct sales, agents, distributors, licensing and equity joint ventures) will continue, companies will look for different ways of conducting business. The following lists some of the possibilities:

■ Joint R&D and product development. This has been encouraged by the weakening of some anti-trust laws, which now allows competitors to cooperate.
■ Outsourcing of all but critical components or technologies. Global products produced in a number of locations by a number of suppliers and/or competitors.
■ Sharing of distribution networks between companies with complementary products and/or customer bases.
■ Strategic alliances (consortiums) between suppliers of related products and services to respond to project-type business.

In this book we have examined the various ways in which you can take your company into the global marketplace. Different forms will appeal to different types of businesses, but one can look at a logical progression that many businesses make from direct sales to distribution, to licensing. to equity joint venture, to wholly-owned operations. While all of these are time-tested mechanisms to expand businesses, two critical factors you may want to keep in mind are that (1) the speed by which your company may go through this progression is likely to increase, and (2) many new forms of structuring international business relationships will arise to challenge your methods of operations.

Global business is necessary for many companies to survive and for nearly all to flourish. The process of going global will energize any company no matter what it produces or sells. With opportunities so great, and with so many untapped markets, most of you will join with me in the pursuit of international business. I look forward to meeting you sometime at one of the London airports, or in a restaurant in Hanoi.

REFERENCES

1. Kennedy, Paul, *The Rise and Fall of the Great Powers,* New York: Random House, 1987.
2. Kotkin, Joel, *Tribes: How Race, Religion, and Identity Determine Success in the New Global Economy,* New York: Random House, 1993.
3. Ehrlich, Paul and Anne, *The Population Bomb,* New York: Ballantine Books, 1968.
4. Cetron, Merton, and Davies, Owen, "50 Trends Shaping the World," *The Futurist,* September–October, 1991, pp. 11–21.
5. U.S. Bureau of Census, "World Population Profile, 1989," in *Statistical Abstract of the United States,* 1990.
6. "The New Global Consumer," *Fortune,* Autumn/Winter, 1993, pp. 68–77.
7. Kennedy, Paul, *Preparing for the Twenty-First Century,* Chapter 3, New York: Random House, 1993.
8. Interview, Dr. Richard King, University of Minnesota Medical School.
9. Handy, Charles, *The Age of Paradox,* Boston: Harvard Business School Press, 1994.
10. McLuhan, Marshall, *The Global Village,* New York: Oxford University Press, 1989.
11. Reich, Robert B., *The Work of Nations,* New York: Vintage Books, 1991.
12. Wattenberg, Ben J., *The First Universal Nation,* New York: Free Press, 1991.
13. Rieff, David, "A Global Culture," *World Policy,* Winter, 1993/4, p. 78.
14. Moffett, Matt, "Seeds of Reform: Key Finance Ministers in Latin America Are Old Harvard-MIT Pals," *Wall Street Journal,* August 1, 1994, p. A1.
15. See "The Myth of the Powerless State," *The Economist,* October 7, 1995, pp. 15–16.
16. Reich, op. cit., pp. 311–314.
17. Miles, Gregory L., "Managing Explosive Foreign Growth," *International Business,* June, 1994, pp. 49–60.

INDEX